GURPS Traveller

STAR MERCS

Military and Mercenary Campaigning

GMG '98

By
Martin J. Dougherty
and Neil A. Frier
Based on the award-winning Traveller science fiction universe by **Marc Miller**
Edited by **Loren K. Wiseman and Gene Seabolt**

GURPS System Design ■ STEVE JACKSON
Chief Operations Officer ■ GENE SEABOLT
GURPS Line Editor ■ SEAN PUNCH
Design and Typography ■ JACK ELMY
Production ■ ALAIN H. DAWSON, S. JOHN ROSS and GENE SEABOLT
Print Buying ■ MONICA STEPHENS
Art Director ■ ALAIN H. DAWSON
GURPS Errata Coordinator ■ HUNTER JOHNSON

Vehicles, Additional Weapons Design and Fact Checking:
Aerron Winsor, Anthony Jackson, David Pulver and Christopher Thrash

Cover by **Doug Chaffee**

Illustrated by **Rob Caswell, Glenn Grant, John Grigni, John Lucas and Tom Peters**

Additional Illustrations by **Kent Burles, Jose Corpuz, C. Bradford Gorby, David Monette, Joey Robinson, Jason Waltrip, John Waltrip and Mike Worley**

Playtesters: John Macpherson, Bryan Borich, David Smart, Steven Anderson, Shawn Fisher, Peter V. Dell'Orto, Christian Friberg, David Summers, Hans Rancke . . . and our thanks to the dozens of great folk who helped out on the *Pyramid* playtest.

ISBN 1-55634-364-7   1 2 3 4 5 6 7 8 9 10

STEVE JACKSON GAMES

Contents

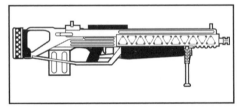

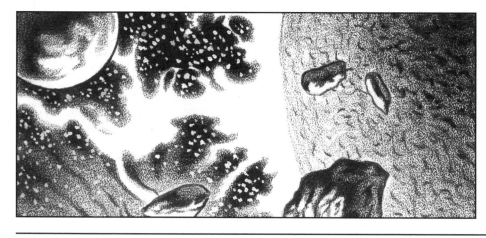

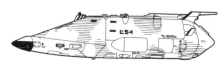

INTRODUCTION

Mercenary was the first major rules addition to *Classic Traveller*. It contained rules for advanced character generation, weaponry by TL, and most important, it provided us with big guns. Suddenly player-characters were all ex-Marines running around with gauss rifles at high port. Everybody wanted to be a mercenary. *Mercenary* expanded the *Traveller* universe and allowed players to break parts of it.

It was an exciting book.

Star Mercs was equally exciting for us, a chance to explore mercenary action in the *GURPS Traveller* universe, to clarify and codify and, well, to shoot at people. The aim behind the book was to let players become a single mercenary or the leader of a merc unit, playing out the missions and dealing with the issues of taking a contract to fight for "the wrong side" or dealing with the machinations of an unscrupulous employer. And of course to deal out some really Grade-A violence to all comers!

To this end we have tried to present all aspects of the merc trade, not just the ground-pounders and the shipboard teams. We wanted to address the legal and day-to-day aspects of the merc trade as well as the ripsnorting gun battles (but mainly those). We wanted to look at who becomes a mercenary, and why. We wanted to produce a resource that would enable us to play out classic scenarios in the style of *Starship Troopers, Hammer's Slammers* or the *Janissaries* series.

The life of a mercenary soldier isn't easy, but we've made playing one a bit simpler. So: Come on, you apes! You want to live forever?

– *Martin J. Dougherty & Neil A. Frier*

ABOUT THE AUTHORS

Martin J. Dougherty has been involved with *Traveller* since 1983. An electronic engineer by training, he now teaches science, and blames the game's influence for his career choice. Other occupations have included computer-games design and freelance writing. He has written several fiction and non-fiction books, and many articles for gaming magazines. Martin's writing partnership with Neil began in 1994, and has not been confined to *Traveller.* Current projects include a new SF novel, more *Traveller* and other games material, and an attempt to get *Traveller* on TV. He is married with two cats. Ambitions include paying off the credit-card bill and getting-his-act-together. Interests include fencing, firearms, gaming and annoying Neil.

Neil Andrew Frier lives with his wife and son in South Shields, England, where as a graduate of Loughborough University he pursues a career as a transport engineer for the local authority. A keen cyclist, Neil splits his free time between this, being a dad and roleplaying. Neil's love of the roleplaying concept began back in 1980 when he bought the original *Traveller* black box set. Since then he has played all of *Traveller's* many versions as well as *RuneQuest, Pendragon* and *Vampire.*

Both Neil and Martin are members of the British Isles Traveller Support group and have been involved in *Traveller* for Imperium Games and *GURPS Traveller.*

ABOUT THE EDITOR

Loren Wiseman was one of the founding partners of GDW, Inc., original publisher of *Traveller,* and spent over 20 years there as a game designer, developer, typesetter and editor. After GDW closed, Loren free-lanced, then came to SJ Games, where he is the art director and *Traveller* line editor and expert-in-residence.

THE TRAVELLER NEWS SERVICE

For many years a feature of the *Journal of the Travellers' Aid Society*, *TNS* chronicled the ongoing life and times of the Imperium. Loren Wiseman is once again writing *TNS* as the alternate history of the Third Imperium develops. It is updated regularly; read it online at **www.sjgames.com/gurps/traveller/news.html**. "Back issues" of *TNS* are also online. The SJ Games *Traveller* page has links to the *Traveller* Web Ring, and thus links to most of the major *Traveller*-oriented web sites that exist. For information on subscribing to the *Traveller* Mailing List, contact rwm@mpgn.com.

CHAPTER ONE

Combat in the 57th Century

GURPS Traveller allows players to travel between the stars and experience the dangers and rewards of many different styles of adventuring. This book assumes that military-oriented campaigns will be heavily slanted toward mercenaries. This is because, over the years, these have proven more popular than campaigns where the PCs are members of a planetary (or Imperial) military force. In either case, the Game Master's job is almost identical.

THE NATURE OF WARFARE

Armed force is the ultimate political statement, the best defense against aggression, and the final arbiter of disputes. The Imperium is not immune to conflict: the enormous campaigns of the Frontier Wars or the Solomani Rim War affected hundreds of worlds and devastated a few, though fortunately this kind of external conflict is rare. Smaller-scale open wars between nations or factions are more common. Most of the armed confrontations taking place within the Imperium are low-intensity, short-duration conflicts, rarely involving more than one or two worlds. The vast majority of these conflicts take place in frontier regions or areas where other means of settling disputes are less effective.

For the most part, military actions in the Imperium consist of small-scale actions involving local forces and a few outside mercenary troops hired by one or more parties in the conflict. The Imperium considers short wars to be less damaging than long non-military disputes. This "safety valve" allows limited conflicts to be fought within the Imperial borders without triggering intervention, though observers may be sent to ensure that the rules of war are observed and the conflict does not spread.

Outside the Imperium, of course, things are different, but Imperial forces may still intervene where Imperial interests are involved (usually at the invitation of one of the parties in the conflict).

CATEGORIES OF WARFARE

Several kinds of warfare exist, but most conflicts fall into one of the following categories: Insurgency, Brushfire War, Corporate Disputes and Open Warfare.

Insurgency

There are many groups with axes to grind. The usual reasons are, as they have always been, politics and religion. Ranging from a few youths chanting slogans and throwing rocks to vast organized paramilitaries, insurgents are a common opponent for local planetary forces and their mercenary adjuncts. Counterinsurgency operations may take the form of troops patrolling a city's streets in support of the local security forces, or troops may sweep the countryside, seeking terrorist bases and field units. Counterinsurgency is a long, drawn-out and bitter process characterized by snipers, suicide bombers and ambuscades. The enemy and the civilian population often overlap. Today's non-combatant may be tomorrow's terrorist. The 9-year-old orphan who attaches herself to the platoon may prove to be a spy (or worse). Soldiers are universal in their distaste for this kind of conflict: it represents the worst aspects of all warfare.

Resources

The *GURPS Basic Set, GURPS Compendium I,* and *GURPS Traveller* are required for any *GURPS Traveller* campaign.

The following are strongly recommended: *GURPS Vehicles* contains a detailed vehicle combat system as well as detailed rules for building just about anything that moves. *GURPS Ultra-Tech I* and *GURPS Ultra-Tech II* cover higher tech level equipment (but not all of it fits within the *GURPS Traveller* milieu).

GMs may find the following books useful: *GURPS Compendium II* for the mass combat system. *GURPS High Tech* discusses a wide variety of weapons and equipment from TLs 4 through 7, for those running campaigns involving lower tech level equipment and weapons.

As for fiction, the list of military-oriented SF is long, and some of it fits into the *Traveller* universe better than other works, but here are a few starting points (enthusiasts will forgive us if their favorite is omitted):

Starship Troopers, Robert Heinlein
The Forever War, Joe W. Haldeman
The Uplift War, David Brin
Ender's Game, Orson Scott Card
Armor, John Steakley
The Bug Wars, by Robert Asprin
Battlefield: Earth, Ron Hubbard
The Man Who Pulled Down the Sky, John Barnes
The Reality Dysfunction, The Neutronium Alchemist, The Naked God, Peter Hamilton
The Forlorn Hope, David Drake
Gamma LAW, Brian Dailey
and a few series:
Hammer's Slammers series, David Drake
Falkenberg series, Jerry Pournelle, et al
Janissaries series, Jerry Pournelle, et al
Miles Vorkosigan series, Lois McMaster Bujold
Honor Harrington series, David Weber
Mutineer's Moon series, David Weber
Dorsai series, Gordon R. Dickson
Greg Mandel series, Peter Hamilton
Starcruiser Shenandoah series, Roland J. Green

Send the Marines!

It can be taken as a sign that the player characters have messed up big time if they end up facing the Imperial Marines in combat. The Marines are the "Big Stick," the "First Team," the "Pros from Dover," and their primary job is to kill people and blow things up in the name of the Imperium. They are only committed when there is a serious threat to the peace and stability of the Imperium, and they never leave a job half-done.

Because the Imperial Marines are the top of the military food chain, players tend to want to demonstrate their own superiority by engaging and defeating Imperial Marines. Some players will spend a lot of time organizing the "perfect" force and equipping it with "perfect" weapons (of their own design, of course) and they want the additional ego boost that comes from seeing their creations defeat the best of the best. In the short term, this can be satisfying for the players, but ultimately will probably be destructive to the campaign.

The best use of the Imperial Marines in mercenary-oriented campaigns is as the "or else" factor, for use when the PCs' machinations threaten to do something the GM does not want to happen. If you have to use them, don't go with half-measures. Marines come in full throttle, with full naval support, orbital bombardment if needed, lots of advance preparation and in numbers sufficient to handle the situation.

Fighting Imperial Marines should be a sobering experience. If the characters manage to get out alive and reasonably intact, they should count themselves among the happy few.

A Band of Brothers

If the PC's unit has been heavily recruited from former Imperial Marines, another factor arises: Marines (even ex-marines) don't like to fight brother Marines. Such things have happened in the past, during the Civil War, and it was traumatic for the units involved. A mercenary unit consisting largely of Marine veterans is likely to refuse to fight another unit of veterans, *if they know ahead of time*. Marine veterans will most likely refuse to fight (and may mutiny) if called upon to attack serving Imperial Marines. The reverse is not necessarily true: Marines can and will attack mercenary units of ex-Marines if ordered to do so (but they still won't like it much).

Another aspect of "every Marine is a brother" is the rule to never abandon wounded to the enemy. Marines take extreme risks to recover their wounded, and expend great energy to destroy any enemy who willfully mistreats them.

Brushfire War

Small groups may go to war over some local issue. Territory, resources or ethnic differences are common reasons. Sometimes it is no more than a tradition of hatred. Such conflicts are minor in scope, usually fought with outdated or low-tech weapons. Many such "little wars" are nothing more than oversized insurgencies, degenerating into sporadic sniping and small-arms exchanges, but they cause untold misery and destruction.

Mercenaries are frequently hired to train local troops or to participate in these local attempts at mutual destruction. Conflicts often drag on far longer than either side's capacity to actually win, dying down and flaring up at intervals. Imperial or mercenary forces, intervening to end the conflict, often find themselves targets for both sides.

Corporate Dispute

The vast Imperial megacorporations are known to intervene in local affairs through the use of mercenary forces. A dispute between corporations may sometimes become a full-blown trade war. This is quite legal, and is preferred by the Imperium to a long period of cutthroat business competition that may actually be worse for the economy than a short war. Corporate wars are characterized by surgical strikes carried out by expensive, highly professional mercenary forces.

Open Warfare

Nations – whole planets even – may go to war with one another. So long as the Imperial rules of war are observed and the fighting does not spread, the Imperium accepts this situation as a useful "safety valve," releasing tensions and resolving conflicts that might otherwise have dragged on for years. The war and subsequent rearmament might even be good for the economy.

Open warfare is an intense situation, characterized by enormous rates of ammunition and equipment expenditure. Most combat is fluid in three dimensions, with close orbit and airspace control being vital to operational success. Grav vehicles are capable of reaching orbit, but generally stay very low, using ground cover. In the 3D aerospace battlefield, there are no "battle lines" as found at lower tech levels.

Instead there are *secure zones* (which are considered more or less impregnable to the enemy) *defended zones* (held but not invulnerable), *disputed zones* (both sides have forces that can influence the region) and *hostile zones* (controlled by the enemy).

A defended zone will be set up around any important installation or feature (supply facilities, headquarters and so on) by siting appropriate defensive units there. All such defense is active – anything coming into the defended zone is attacked and destroyed – rather than relying on distance "behind the lines." Defended zones must be three-dimensional, reaching up to orbital distances, to be effective.

TYPES OF COMBAT

All conflicts will involve one or more of the following modes of combat.

Urban Combat

Population centers, industrial facilities and starports are the scene for this most bitter of combats. Built-up areas are not only the prizes to be fought over, they are also the best of defensive terrain.

This close-quarters fighting, with every street, every building, every room contested, is a punishing and exhausting business. The battle is one of constant ambush and counter-ambush, plagued by snipers and booby-traps. The weapons of choice are light, handy automatic rifles and SMGs, with flamethrowers, shotguns, grenades, pistols and even the bayonet seeing use.

Vehicles are vulnerable to close-range anti-armor weapons. Artillery and sophisticated support munitions are useless if the combatants mean to do anything more than simply flatten the area into a sea of rubble. Someone has to go in and take the cities away from the enemy, then hold them.

This is the domain of the infantryman. It is simultaneously his hell and his killing ground. This is why the infantry still exist in an age of grav tanks, meson accelerators and tac missiles. This is why they call them PBIs ("poor bloody infantry").

Boarding Actions and Zero-G Combat

Many of the comments applicable to urban combat are also relevant here. Zero-G combat, however, presents its own unique challenges to combatants, with the recoil of firing a weapon enough to send a combatant spinning out of control. Specialized low-gravity weapons are issued where possible. If not, the combatants must simply use their training and experience to cope.

With the threat of a stray round causing explosive decompression or damage to a ship's systems, many combatants favor low-penetration weapons and blades. A suit tear is enough to kill or at least put a combatant out of a fight while he frantically slaps on a patch. A starship boarding action is perhaps the most lethal of all combat environments. Those who make it their specialty are universally respected.

Meteoric Assault

"Strike From Space," says the shoulder patch of the Archduke of Regina's Own Huscarles, representing the unit's training in meteoric assault techniques. In a meteoric assault, troops and equipment are dropped from orbit in individual re-entry cap-

Close Combat

Our orders were simple: pro-Eco Faction terrorists had taken over the Social Sciences building at the university. There were no hostages. We were to go in at midnight and clear the place. Prisoners were optional, but we were to avoid unnecessary damage to the building.

We got as close as we could through the grounds. My section blew an entry through the blind-side wall while the lieutenant's section went in through the doors. We heard them firing as we cleared the dust and fanned out by fire teams, moving fast through the dark corridors.

I led my team toward the main staircase. A terrorist guard leaped out ahead of us, rifle raised. I dropped the would-be hero with a short burst without breaking stride. McKenner put a round into him as we passed, just in case. We reached the stairs. Francessi and I sprinted up. Another terrorist appeared at the top of the stairs. I ignored him, trusting McKenner and Suliina. Just as the terrorist's pistol was lined up on me his chest exploded with two simultaneous bursts.

Francessi turned left at the top, stopped and crouched. I went right, covering the corridor as the others caught up. I heard Francessi open up behind me, but I kept watching my section of the corridor. Two more goons came piling out of a side door, waving handguns. My SMG jerked and they both went down. One of them managed to pop one off as he went down; I heard the round ricochet off something.

As the others reached the top, I rose and ran forward. Francessi was a few paces back, covering me. I heard automatic fire somewhere below.

The dark corridor lit up with a long tongue of flame from the muzzle of a heavy caliber revolver. I returned fire in the general direction as I hit the wall. My helmet display showed two hotspots in a doorway further down, one more behind a steel cabinet.

Three targets, in cover, between me and the three-minute objective.

I smiled wryly as I pulled the grenade from my webbing . . .

– Corporal Styli Oporto,
Kaski's Infantry

R & R

We were at one side of the room, making a point of staying clear of the Scout S-3 guys in the corner. We thought we might get into a rumble with them. You know how these things happen. They'd just taken down an Ine Givar active service unit and got the hostages out unscathed, so they were understandably whooping it up a little. Good luck to them, we said, and kept out of their way.

Then the doors opened, and in came Trouble. There were six, five humans and an Aslan. They wore black, except for a silver death's head on the collar. They all wore cavalry sabers, knee-high boots and – Buddha preserve me – silver spurs.

They looked around, noted the unit insignia. One of them snorted dismissively. They walked, no, they strutted, over to the crowded bar, where a space had opened for them. They owned the place and they knew it.

It was too much. Too damned much to take from a bunch of grav-pansies. Who do these guys think they are? They go into battle sitting down in their nice comfy air-conditioned vehicles while we crawl about in the mud, and they call themselves "soldiers." They hide behind a wall of armor plate, and pose like heroes. They drink wine and live like dandies and they're proud of it.

We strolled over to the bar, all nine of us. They looked us up and down. One of them said, "Infantry" like he was saying "Scum."

The owner was already calling the MPs when the punches started flying.

– Private K. J. Ingarnii, Maogan's Company

sules, which maneuver violently all the way down. A shower of decoys, orbital fire and electronic countermeasures attempts to shield the troops during their descent.

Once the drop troops (as they are popularly known) are on their way, there is no turning back. The only way to extract them is by interface craft, and such craft need a secure landing zone. The drop troops must capture such a zone and hold it until their ride arrives. Otherwise, death and surrender are their only options.

GMG '98

THE NATURE OF MERCENARIES

To many people, the word *mercenary* conjures up the image of soldiers loyal only to the highest bidder, and preferring maneuver to actual combat. While this may be true of some mercenaries, it is by no means true of all of them. A unit with a reputation for switching sides or one that regularly shows a lack of fighting spirit will soon find itself unemployed. Soldiers fight for many reasons: duty, honor, loyalty, money or defense of home, family, a way of life or a fervently held ideal. At the bottom of it all, however, is this: good soldiers fight because their fellow soldiers expect it of them. Whole books have been written on the subject of small-group loyalty and the military, and this is not the place to go into the topic in detail, but this is as true for a mercenary as for the most devoted, selfless member of the Imperial Guard.

The typical mercenary soldier is no pushover. He spends much of his life surrounded by people who pay him to fight but mistrust him as a hired gun. He is sometimes called upon to fight against enemies who will mistreat "offworlder scum" who surrender, whatever the rules of war might say on the matter. The individual mercenary's livelihood and his life depend upon his personal weapon. It is his best and most reliable friend, and he will take good care of it. Many mercenaries take this attitude to extremes, purchasing every gimmick and gadget their credits can buy, while others simply find a reliable tool they are happy with, and look after it.

Most mercenary commanders dictate what weapons their unit will carry for the sake of standardizing ammunition, but there will always be some variations around a standard theme within a unit. Most mercs like to have a personal sidearm as a last-ditch weapon, and this is not subject to any policy. The individual purchases whatever he likes and provides his own ammunition for it.

Mercenaries value clear communications. Units almost always have the very best commo gear they can buy. On a hostile world you need to be sure that your friends (especially those in the artillery or medevac units) know exactly where you are.

Units tend to have very distinctive names, usually taken from the commander's name (SB Rangers, Jamison's Death Commandos or the Inikaani Rifles). This identity is taken very seriously. Since a mercenary can only truly trust his fellows in the unit and has no ideological, nationalistic or religious bond with them, the feeling of belonging to a unit with a strong identity has a profound effect upon morale.

Unit identities are proudly displayed on arms, uniforms and equipment, tattooed on bodies and shouted about in bars. When the mercs run across one another, those who have moved on to other units are sometimes reviled and sometimes greeted as long-lost cousins.

The mercenary soldier is set apart from local soldiers, whom he will often view with condescension or outright contempt. He lives by his own code of loyalty to his unit, care of his personal kit and professionalism first. Everything else comes a long way behind.

Mercenaries (and soldiers in general) fall into several basic types, sometimes called *branches* or *arms of service*. These will be discussed from a mercenary perspective.

GROUND FORCES

Except for flying or aquatic races, the oldest form of combat is on land. Most races live, travel and feed on the ground, and warfare tends to take place there also. This does not preclude the formation of units of aerial or aquatic soldiers.

Infantry

War usually involves taking ground from an enemy and holding it against counterattacks – this is what infantry does best. Though tactics and equipment may change, the role and function of the infantry have remained unchanged for thousands of years. The infantryman carries and operates a personal weapon – from pike to plasma gun – and (occasionally) some specialist equipment for dealing with circumstances such as close combat, fortifications or armored vehicles.

Infantry forms the backbone of most nations' military forces. A poor state, faced with invasion, will often simply arm the population with a cheap mass-produced rifle, spear or whatever else is available, and thus create a large, if badly trained, "army."

The pure infantry soldier has neither the mobility of a combat vehicle nor the firepower of artillery. What makes him indispensable is his flexibility. It is the ability to fight anywhere, any time that has kept the infantry in business.

The typical mercenary infantry unit is generally equipped to a moderate to high tech level. It is this technological advantage that gives the mercenaries an edge over most local forces. Mercenary units are often hired by poor states without highly trained forces of their own, to form a cadre around which the local forces can be mustered. Richer states may hire mercenaries to act as shock troops.

Artillery

In most of the cultures of the Imperium the advent of civilization created a need to protect the cities and brought about the advent of fortifications. Not long after-

Anti-Tank

I was crouched in a gully on Aramanx, hefting my missile launcher and awaiting the armored assault we'd been warned was coming. It was taking a while arriving, and frankly I was getting jittery. Finally I heard the rumble and clatter of tracks. I listened . . . four, no, six tanks. The sound was familiar, yet strange. I slowly raised the missile launcher to a firing position, then blinked in disbelief.

*We knew these guys were using tanks, and we knew their tech was low. But when recon had reported an armored assault we'd not quite expected **this**.*

They were tanks all right, great armored behemoths massing about 70 tons, with 60mm guns in sponsons on the sides, a heavy machine-gun on the front and what seemed at first glance to be a great huge mortar sticking up on top with smoke pouring out of it. They were big and rectangular, high slab sides making a wonderful target if I could control the laughter long enough to fire.

Those weren't mortars on top, they were funnels! They'd built themselves a bunch of armored land-battleships. I sniggered. Then the MGs started spraying, and I saw the horsed cavalry moving up behind, sabers bright in the sunlight. Their tech was low but they meant business.

It didn't mean they had a chance, though. The laughter went away.

"Sorry, guys," I whispered, taking aim. "I guess you just don't know any better."

We mowed them down in about 90 seconds. I think one of them made it into our position on foot before he collapsed.

– Gunner Mik Polishio,
Spinward Heavy Weapons
Services, LIC

Sniper

Most sniping is done in binom teams, spotter and sniper, but I like to work alone.

I was out in the backwoods on Lakou, working for Lord Urlaain if it matters. He had nearly a hundred household grunts and three offworld mercs, but in his infinite wisdom Urlaain was trying to take on six other local nobles in some petty feud.

I was scout and advance guard for a platoon-strength advance into the Jul Mine area, assigned both recon and defense-suppression duties.

The opposition had deployed a couple of platoons to secure the area. They were armed peasants, just guys with guns, except for an officer and the crew of a HMG who seemed to be professionals. They set up the HMG covering the road and were making a half-hearted attempt to dig in. Apparently they were expecting us to move that way.

I let them search and secure their position, then get complacent and settle down for a brew. I selected armor piercing, took aim, and smashed the breech of their MG to scrap. Heads turned as they looked to see what the noise had been, the poor amateur fools. I switched to conventional antipersonnel ammo and shot the officer dead center in the forehead (I know, some people think that's showboating, but it scares the yellow porridge out of everybody who is standing next to the mark). Most of them dived into their scanty trenches, and I encouraged the rest to do likewise. They left six dead in the open.

I kept them cowering in their holes for over twelve hours. If anyone showed himself I shot him in the leg or abdomen, then killed the three or four guys who came out to the rescue.

Once it got dark some of them tried to slip out, maybe to escape or maybe to hunt me. Like hunting snipers in the dark is a good idea or something. I killed them all, except the one I kneecapped to draw the others out. By then they weren't willing to play any more, so I put him out of his misery.

At dawn our attack force came up and the survivors fell over themselves to surrender. The platoon commander got a medal for taking an enemy position without loss. I got a good breakfast and another mission. But I'd rather be me than him.

I'm the hunter, and he's just a target.

– Lance-Corporal Marie Kellermann, Freelance Sniper

ward, the need arose to smash them. Big walls worked well enough until explosives were developed and the first artillery piece was turned against stone walls.

Early guns were very large, and not very accurate. They were ideal for blasting large unmoving stone walls to pieces and could (if the operators were very lucky) actually hit a large body of infantry. From Terra to Sylea, guns that were developed to destroy defenses gradually evolved into lighter pieces that could be deployed on the battlefield for the real business of warfare – killing people. Guns evolved from fort-busters to support weapons capable of shattering infantry formations and breaking up cavalry attacks. As range, accuracy and speed of loading increased with technological advances, artillery became and remains a cost-effective way of delivering huge amounts of firepower over ranges an infantry unit could not hope to achieve.

Mercenary artillery is often hired by poorer states, which can muster a large number of militia but cannot train nor equip the specialist artillery units. Mercenary artillery units are often seen as a deterrent to aggression, covering vulnerable border crossings with the threat of pinpoint bombardment. Richer nations see the employment of mercenary artillery as a cost-effective way to acquire high-technology weaponry without having to develop the expensive infrastructure and manufacturing capabilities required to build it, nor bear the cost of training and refining procedures.

Mercenary artillery units are generally part of larger infantry formations, but can be found as elite units in their own right. The high-tech equipment employed by these units ensures that they are always expensive to hire.

The mercenary gunner is very like his colleagues in the infantry. He is a member of a close-knit team of highly trained experts whose identity is defined by their weapon. Beyond this small world there is the rest of the unit and fellow gunners from other outfits, and "everyone else," with whom the artillery gunner has little in common.

The artillery piece he serves is the focus for the mercenary gunner's existence. A great deal of time and effort goes into ensuring that it is in top-notch condition, monitoring its performance for the slightest flaw or aberration.

Although artillery is not a close-combat arm, all mercenary gunners carry a personal weapon. This is usually a pistol or small SMG – something that will not get in the way while carrying out normal tasks – but might be just about anything: sawed-off shotguns, special combat knives, fully automatic pistols, and so on. Gunners occasionally have to fight off close-quarters attacks or defend themselves while engaged in tasks away from the gun.

Mercenary artillery units sometimes seem to be a single entity comprising a weapon and its flesh-and-blood servants. The artillery piece is the object of pride and affection, and often bears a name given to it by its crew. This is often quite fanciful, such as "Aslan Woe," a multiple-fire rocket launcher forming part of "Longshot," a merc artillery outfit operating in the Reavers' Deep. Weapon names are prominently displayed on uniforms, support vehicles and on the weapon itself.

All mercenary artillery units deploy *forward observers* (FOs). FOs use their experience and the best technology available to get close to the enemy and direct their unit's firepower to where it will do the most damage. It is a lonely job, as the FO has to spend hours or days alone in hostile territory, only communicating with his unit in short coded bursts. Apart from the communications gear, the FO is equipped more like an infantryman than a gunner. A favorite weapon is the laser rifle or carbine, which can often double as a laser rangefinder/designator.

Cavalry and Armor

Once a culture learns to domesticate an animal, military use follows soon after. The mounted soldier has advantages of mobility and shock action, and these remain the characteristics of cavalry through the ages, whether mounted on a pony or kian or in an Intrepid grav tank. Most forms of cavalry emphasize either the mobility (light cavalry) or the shock (heavy cavalry) aspect.

As technology advances, riding animals are replaced with vehicles. The role of the cavalry remains the same, with fast recon vehicles performing scouting and screening operations and heavy armored vehicles (tanks) punching holes in enemy lines and exploiting breakthroughs. Fairly soon after mechanization, the heavier *armored fighting vehicles* (AFVs) split off into a separate branch, called armor.

Around TL6, some aspects of infantry and cavalry are merged to create armored infantry or mechanized infantry units, being a balanced force of foot troops and vehicles. While combined-arms practice requires that infantry are supported by heavy AFVs, and armored units have a small infantry contingent, the mechanized force is a genuinely combined unit, with vehicles and infantry fully integrated.

With the advent of mechanized forces, the "pure" cavalry or armored unit does not disappear, though it usually gains an infantry contingent riding lightly armored vehicles.

The mercenary cavalry unit is typically equipped at a moderate to high TL (9-10) with some higher TL gear seeing occasional use. Mercenary cavalry units tend to be recon outfits using lightly armored fast vehicles that mount heavy firepower but cannot sustain main-caliber hits. Armored (tank) units are usually equipped with powerful but outdated Imperial vehicles or foreign models such as the Sword World Gram heavy grav tank, due to the complications inherent in obtaining more advanced vehicles. For those with the resources, there are ways around the red tape, and a select few units are equipped with state-of-the art vehicles.

Poor states often hire mercenary cavalry units as rapid-response troops, hoping the mobility conferred by the mercenaries' vehicles will allow fast and effective counterattacks, and gain time for the state to marshal its local forces.

Richer states use mercenaries as specialist recon units, making contact with the enemy and relaying information back to local commanders, or as heavy shock troops to lead an assault on enemy positions.

A cavalry or armored unit (with or without supporting infantry) can give its employer a battlefield advantage out of all proportion to the unit's size.

The cavalry or armored soldier has much in common with his artillery cousins, in that he identifies strongly with his vehicle and fellow crewmembers. Likewise, cavalry and armored soldiers see themselves as an elite, heirs to the ancient romantic traditions of noble mounted warriors. Many view infantry as common peasant cannon fodder, who in turn view them as a bunch of snobs.

Vehicle crews wear little body armor and carry only a small amount of personal equipment. Most possess a sidearm or carry a carbine or SMG in the vehicle, and on some worlds they will work in protective suits. Away from his vehicle, the cavalry

Ambush

Hunter and I were herding our newly reconstituted platoon down a road when the machine gun opened up on us. We maneuvered around them and took some more hits, and as I was closing in on them, a white cloth on a stick came up out of their position. It took me a few seconds to decide. They had killed three of us and wounded two more with the first burst. That was their job – they were supposed to stop our advance, and we should have expected an ambush. They shot at first squad when they opened fire on them, and they shot at me as I led second squad around the flank. They did not shoot at Murphy when she crawled forward to drag back the wounded. They did not shoot at anyone who did not make an offensive move toward them – they did their job and fought fair, and I decided to accept their surrender.

– Sgt. Oskar Levrenti, Jink's Jaguars

Fighter Jocks

In any fighter outfit there are 50% adequate pilots, some of whom might become good pilots if they live long enough. There are 45% body-bag candidates, and there are one or two really talented, really cool experts. The ones who know all the old tricks and make up the new ones.

I was over the Plains of Ever-Changing Sand (Combat Zone 2 to off-worlders), flying top cover for the ground forces, when one of those really talented guys came out to play. My wingman was Jak Tersilli, a body-bag filler without the sense to quit. We were flying Instellarms FS-003 Banshees. Nice aircraft, very maneuverable, but nothing special. The bogey came up a wadi at zero feet while we were watching the sky. Radar never even spotted him. He stood his Banshee – identical to ours – on its tail and rippled a pair of missiles off at us. He watched us break to evade, and I swear, he made his plan then and there.

He ignored Jak, came after me with cannon. We got into a rolling scissors – both of us turning hard and getting nowhere. I prayed Jak would have the sense to climb out for a fast gun pass, but no. In he came, making three identical planes rolling and turning across the desert, trying for an advantage that nobody was going to get. That's why the scissors is so deadly. You're an equal threat to one another. First one to lose his nerve and try to roll out dies.

Continued on next page . . .

That guy played us for fools. He knew that Jak was a nugget, so he let him stay on his tail. There was no chance of Jak actually making a shot unless he got clear and came in again, so that pilot gave him several fleeting chances, kept him interested and in the scissors. He kept track of both of us in a seven-G corkscrew, set us up. And nailed us.

Gradually the scissors unraveled. We all lost so much airspeed that I had to make a desperate right break through his gunsights to avoid stalling. I got away with it but for exactly six seconds I was no threat.

By the time I'd come round, he'd turned inside Jak, fired by instinct at where he'd be in a split second – that guy had the most incredible feeling for where other planes were – and was already turning to engage me as Jak's Banshee fireballed.

I was really alive, totally focused. My life depended upon what I did next. I knew, as I have never known before or since, that I had all the cards. I had height and airspeed. Jak was dead, but he'd bought me a kill.

I nosed over into a diving gun pass, saw the enemy Banshee's nose come up, and I knew that he didn't have enough airspeed. I knew he was bluffing to the point of a stall, trying to make me break. I licked my lips as he rolled inverted, took up the slack on the trigger and forced the nose down to meet where he'd be as he stalled.

Both his remaining missiles flared, inside the minimum arming distance. They roared from his pylons, straight at my cockpit. I yanked back on the stick by instinct, trying to evade. One of them crashed into my port wing with its warhead still inert, and shattered. He stalled into a loop as I ripped by about nine feet away, my cannon burst going wild.

He came out of the loop on my tail. I was already breaking right, but he knew I'd do that. I'd gone that way twice before. His twin 30mms made confetti out of my fuselage as I ejected.

And then the cocky swine followed my chute to the deck, and circled until the rescue chopper arrived. I learned later he had radioed my position to our side. He even strafed some desert nomads who were closing in on me. They had a bad record for robbing and killing downed pilots, and apparently this guy believed that only us knights of the air are fit to kill one another.

That's fighter pilots for you.

– Pilot Officer Vicky Trantor, Carthin's Banshees

or armored soldier is poorly armed compared to an infantryman and can be considered relatively harmless.

Support

From the moment that armies ceased to be simple raiding parties and warbands, support units were a necessity. Engineers, transport, logistical and medical specialists support the combat troops in their tasks. As warfare became more technological, these support units ceased to be simply groups of soldiers detailed to the task for a time and became permanent units in their own right.

A mercenary support unit is a rare commodity. Engineering, medical and logistics units do exist, as there is a market among nations too poor or unwilling to spare the cost of adequate supports for the fighting troops. Such support units tend to be small and extremely professional, as it is the reputation for excellence that sells the unit to its employers.

Both rich and poor states tend to hire the services of mercenary support units for the same reason: to solve a problem that cannot be solved by local forces. While a mercenary engineering unit may at first seem a peculiar idea, many smaller states cannot afford to equip a corps of engineers, or may never have needed one before. Excellence can be bought for the duration of the project.

The support soldier is not a combat trooper. He can expect to be protected by combat troops while he fulfills his role as engineer, medic or whatever. Many carry a sidearm for personal protection, but do not expect to use it. The exceptions are combat engineers, whose personnel look remarkably like infantry, carrying an assortment of weapons and heavy armor.

Support units differ widely, and the actual equipment of a support soldier will vary depending upon his task and the level of perceived threat. In the Imperium there are numerous specialist support units. Some of the most important include:

Engineers: These soldiers have varied tasks and often specialize within the general heading of "engineers." Combat engineers build field fortifications and bridges. They also specialize in the destruction of same. Assault engineers (sometimes called "pioneers") prepare the way for infantry attacks by cutting wire and removing mines and other obstacles. Technical engineers construct and maintain electronic systems and communications links.

Logistics: An old saying has it that "amateurs study tactics. Professionals study logistics." Trite though it is, this is true. Soldiers and their equipment need to be transported to the battlefield, and this requires animals or vehicles to convey them. Any force (whether fighting or otherwise) requires supplies. Without air, food and water, the soldiers will cease to exist. Without ammunition and fuel, they cease to be an effective fighting unit.

Medical: Soldiers fight better with the knowledge that good medical care awaits the unlucky ones. Wounded also are more likely to return to duty if adequately cared for, saving the expense of training a new recruit to replace the discharged veteran. Thus a good medical service is not only a humanitarian option, it is a means of safeguarding the investment made in training good soldiers. In most cultures medical units are unarmed and bound by the ethics of the medical profession – they will treat both sides' wounded equally well, and are generally considered non-combatants.

Military Police/Provost: These units serve several functions: they maintain discipline in areas under military control, perform police functions near the front (such as traffic control), handle prisoners and collect deserters. Mercenary MP units are rare, but not unknown.

Other types of support units exist in a well-run military, but mercenary units of personnel clerks or judge-advocates are seldom needed.

DEEP SPACE

The term "star merc" is often applied to all mercenaries, since they normally come from off-planet. A second, more correct definition is a special type of mercenary: the merc equivalent of the Imperial Marines, a force trained and equipped to fight off of a world's surface, or in an environment so hostile it can be deadly in and of itself. Star mercs under this second definition include the crews of spaceships, soldiers equipped to fight in hostile environments.

Ship's Crew

Even in the 57th century, space is a dangerous environment with many unknown mysteries and hazards. Starship personnel, whether on the humblest free trader or the largest Imperial battleship, are highly trained experts. Not everyone has the resources to train such skilled personnel, especially in the numbers that a war can require.

Not everyone subscribes to a universal starfarers' code of mutual assistance, a "brotherhood of the void," or any such ideal. Indeed, many individuals and organizations work to make space hazardous for others. War, piracy and even business clashes can make the void a very dangerous place.

Starships need fuel and must travel to starport gas giants or seas to obtain this, which can mean hours if not days of travel in standard space and it is here that space warfare takes place. System defense boats (SDBs) can protect vessels near the starport, but star systems are huge and the SDBs cannot be everywhere at once. When worlds have problems with raiders or pirates or their own political problems have spread to encompass all the worlds in a system, then a star merc unit may be hired.

A star merc unit is generally equipped with obsolete equipment and older ships; the price of starships is truly astronomical, and the Imperial administration makes sure that the latest weapons, sensors and ships are kept for the fleet's own use. Even the mercenary cruiser and commerce raiders are kept at a high price to ensure only very successful and well-known units can afford to buy one.

Poor states, which cannot afford adequate system defenses, may be considered easy targets for raiders or pirates, especially those outside the Imperium. Even inside the Imperium, some states hire small star merc units to act as system defenses. Rich states and corporations purchase star mercs for convoy support, raids and many other uses, at times buying in very large star merc units as a cost-effective way of creating a small fleet.

A star merc crewman is an old hand at his particular duties, whether they are piloting, astrogation, boat crew or technical. Mercenaries almost never train new

Tactics

When you boil it all down, here's what you need to know as an officer: divide your command into three elements. When you contact the enemy, pin him with one element while you use the second to try to maneuver around a flank. Hold the third element in reserve to exploit any successes the first or second elements may achieve, or to cover their retreat in case of disaster.

It works for platoons, it works for companies, it works for divisions. There are a few refinements, which we'll cover in the rest of this course, but if you can remember that one basic tactic, you'll do fine.

– Major Ushuumgii Devereau,
Imperial Marine Academy

When Minister Rainey hired me to protect him, I insisted he also hire two hyper-muscled goons. Go look at the newspics of the assassination attempt and you'll see why. Those two gorillas with bulging armpits might as well be wearing big signs that say "bodyguard." But what about the short-haired woman in the business suit, the one with the attache case? That's me. Bet you didn't even notice me.

Neither did the assassins.

We visited a children's hospital as part of the election campaign, shook hands, kissed babies, you know the sort of thing. On the way out we pushed through the crowd of reporters toward the grav-limo. The two goons were doing the reporter-shoving act, clearing the way and completely forgetting their duties, when the assassins struck. Three of them, posing as a news crew. They came in from behind where the goons couldn't see them. One of them shoved me aside as he drew a pistol. I used his shoving arm to throw him against one of his friends, then rammed the attache case against the third's ribs as he got his handgun clear of his jacket. I triggered the automatic shotgun concealed in the case. He spun to the ground, arms flailing. In a close crowd, you want something like a shotgun that's not going to blow through the other side of your target and maybe damage an innocent bystander, but can be counted on to shred the target's innards, or bust a couple of ribs even if it doesn't punch through the body armor.

The other two had disentangled themselves. One made to shoot me. I swung the case around and pumped a round into him before his buddy kicked the case away.

Buddy then lunged at me, trying to bowl me aside and get to the minister (I'm a mere slip of a girl, remember?). I took a long step into him, left hand extended to shove him back. It's not much of a move, not even a blow at all, but it gives you time to draw the pistol from the small of your back (which is the best place for a hide-out piece if you don't want unsightly bulges to ruin the cut of your jacket). He started to throw a punch as my gun came around, and I shot him in the head.

One of the no-necks had finally realized what was going on and reacted. He had pushed the minister to the ground and was shielding him with his own body, which indicated a certain level of experience. I made a mental note to consider him for more complicated tasks than stalking horse in the future.

About this time no-neck No. 2 came rushing back, gun drawn. Too late to achieve anything, but he'd served his purpose, which was to draw attention away from me. Sometimes that's all it takes.

– Tala Kerfreise,
Freelance Bodyguard

crew. Instead they recruit ex-navy, scout or even merchant personnel who know what to do and who won't panic in a firefight.

Due to his obsolete equipment and older ships, the mercenary crewman must often use tactics and experience to outmaneuver superior forces. This leaves its mark on the mercenary. Star mercs are seen by others to be cold, obsessive individuals. Star mercs simply point out that they are still alive.

Crew members tend to be very loyal to their ship; it is wise never to voice any concern over the condition or performance of a star merc vessel within earshot of her crew. The ships are often given very bold names such as *Vengeance* or *Ravager*, which is attached to an equally bold badge usually showing a weapon or armor of some kind. This name and badge is present on the star mercs' flight uniforms, and is often the only common uniform among a particular group of star mercs. Standard practice is to wear the uniform of whatever previous service the merc was in.

The crewman tends to carry any weapons, armor or equipment that he can afford. Any scout would feel at home with the hodgepodge of equipment found on a star merc crew. In short, you can't describe the standard equipment for a crewman, as there is no standardization.

Profors Soldiers

Soldiers equipped to fight in very hostile environments such as vacuum or corrosive atmospheres are referred to as *protected forces* (abbreviated to *profors*). Profors training is necessary to fight aboard starships, as most ships decompress before combat. Security personnel require special weapons and protective equipment to operate in this environment, and this in turn leads to a style of combat requiring its own set of skills.

The profors soldier spends most of his professional life in such an environment. He is the mercenary equivalent of the Imperial Marine, who all receive profors training and are the masters of the art.

Most mercenary starships are quite small, and the number of troops they can carry is very limited. As a result, star merc personnel tend to be very effective as individuals and small-team members. They are equipped with high-technology gear. Units are very small and closely integrated, with troopers requiring complete trust in their squad-mates in order to survive.

A profors soldier tends to be highly motivated and individualistic in combat situations, with good technical skills for the maintenance of his equipment. Much of his gear is individually chosen or adapted to his personal preferences. At the very least, the trooper will have an armored vacc suit, and most wear combat armor. Weapons carried depend upon circumstances – specifically the amount of gravity, or its absence. Some troopers have a low-g weapon and another for the "normal" combat environment, while others just pick a single weapon system and use it for all situations.

Profors soldiers are not much concerned with the parade-ground trappings of the military. Each merc keeps his gear in perfect condition because to do less is to die. While armor and combat fatigues carry identification insignia, there is little in the way of uniform policy among profors outfits. When not on combat alert, troopers dress as they like. For most this is a simple set of fatigues.

The display of kill tallies is a common practice in some units. These can be as simple as a notch on a buttstock or a skull-and-crossbones inlay in a helmet. Tattoos are considered a "rookie" thing in some units, acceptable in others.

AEROSPACE WARRIORS

For most non-flying species, air forces are first formed as part of the land armies, soon afterward being acquired by nautical forces for the same purposes – scouting and artillery spotting.

As technology advances, aircraft roles become more varied, with reconnaissance being supplemented but by no means supplanted with bombing, ground support and airspace control. By this point the air force has become a separate service in most cultures. At high tech levels, advanced grav craft make possible combined forces incorporating the nautical, ground and air branches as a single service.

By late TL6 most cultures would define the mission of aerospace forces as:
- Gaining air superiority over rival aerospace forces.
- Reconnoitering enemy dispositions and gaining intelligence.
- Attacking enemy ground and nautical forces.
- Attacking enemy industrial and transport assets.
- Conducting air transport.

Ground or nautical operations carried out in areas where enemy aircraft can operate unopposed are subject to grave risk from air attack. For this reason the establishment of air superiority is often seen as the first priority in time of war. The early stages of any major conflict see a great deal of air-to-air combat, strikes on airfields and similar attempts to drive enemy units from the skies. When the assets to do this are not available, a policy of disputing airspace is employed, in an attempt to gain temporary control of the skies for a specific offensive or in a specific area. At the very least it is necessary to oppose enemy incursions – whether on offense or reconnaissance – into friendly air space, and to challenge enemy aircraft over the battle zone.

Mercenary Aerospace Units

Battalion-sized and larger mercenary ground units often incorporate a small air reconnaissance or ground-attack unit. Separate mercenary aerospace units are also available for hire, though they are extremely expensive. Many individual veteran

Surrender

There are plenty of reasons for respecting mercs' rights. Not just the rules of war, or the fact that you may want to hire some yourself someday, but a more basic common-sense reason. If you shoot surrendered mercs, they stop surrendering.

You do not want this to happen.

There was this one time on Pannet, where the Trads and the Progs were killing one another much as usual. The SB Rangers, the Free Troopers and Jinsin's Infantry were serving with the Progs. The Trads, being the hidebound sons of lungfishes that they are, wouldn't hire mercs. Despised them, in fact.

A recon squad from the Rangers found some Trad scouts poking about an unmarked river crossing. They dug in and reported back, but before backup arrived a whole Trad battalion turned up and began crossing. The flank was wide open, so Colonel Bond told his troopers to resist as long as they could while he organized some kind of defense. Anyone could see that it'd take about an hour at most to overrun the single squad.

Sure enough, the Trads got a couple of companies across, though they took more than a few casualties along the way. The squad found themselves surrounded, with two personnel wounded. They reckoned there was no further point in resisting, and asked for permission to surrender. Bond gave it and they marched out, expecting the honors of war, a couple of days in custody and passage off-planet.

The Trads disarmed them, then shot them out of hand.

Now that changed everything. Up to that point the Trads were winning the war. This operation should have clinched it, as they flung a fair-sized force around the open Prog flank. The only obstacle was the merc units.

But the mercs were real angry, and they knew that if they surrendered or got beat they were for the firing squad. So they stood their ground and fought to the last trooper. Jinsin's platoon was wiped out. The Rangers and the Troopers took heavy casualties, but they held on. The Trads took so many losses that their sweeping flank movement began to look like the Somme. The offensive failed.

And when the Imperials got wind of it, they sentenced the Trad commander to be handed over to the mercs for "justice."

The moral is: Mercs will surrender when there's nothing to be gained by fighting.

If you make it so there's nothing to be gained by surrender, they'll fight to the last.

And like I say, you do not want this to happen.

– Anders Breine, Amateur Historian

Combat Drop

A meteoric assault is such jolly fun. They chuck you out of a perfectly good starship in what amounts to an ablative-shielded coffin. You scream through the atmosphere while the drop capsule tries to rattle you to pieces with evasive maneuvers, all the while shedding pieces of itself as it partially melts away. Finally there's the series of tooth-loosening jerks as the capsule splits and falls away and the various chutes open, first the ribbon to slow you down enough so that the main chute won't get torn to shreds when it deploys, then the main itself. Then you feel your spine concertina as you hit dirt.

Quite frankly, at that point you're ready to kill anything out of spite.

It was my fifth combat drop, a minor affair by all accounts. Just a single squad deployed by capsule while the others came in by shuttle. Our job was to take down the HQ of a rebel column operating on Trane, attacking by surprise from orbit. The others would mop up after we'd made the initial attack.

For thin-atmosphere worlds like Trane we use a modified capsule, with rockets for braking. This was the first time I'd ridden one. It was very nearly the last.

Continued on next page . . .

fliers (a common title for aerospace personnel) are available with or (usually) without their own aircraft.

Poor states usually hire a few expert pilots to provide a nucleus of elite squadrons. They fly the state's own aircraft, and as a secondary function they train local forces up to a high standard.

For rich states, the expertise of individuals is in demand – often to make up crack "enemy" units for training purposes or as instructors. Entire units are also hired to provide immediate air supremacy.

When aerospace warriors are mentioned, most people think of aircrew: pilots, navigators and gunners. Depending on the size of an aircraft, its crew may range from one or two for fighters, interceptors and light strike aircraft to seven, 10 or even 12 aboard a detection and tracking aircraft (DATA) or a mid-tech heavy bomber. The more sensors, electronic warfare equipment and defensive weapons an aircraft has, the larger its crew complement.

Aircrews at any tech level tend to be very highly trained, seeing themselves as an elite and viewed by ground forces as pampered flyboys. To some extent this is true, as the crews' training represents a huge investment. They must be skilled enough to complete their mission and bring their "borrowed" aircraft home.

Mercenary aircrews realize that they are an elite and are very expensive to hire. They expect to be taken care of by the employer, freed from menial or security tasks and to have the support they require to carry out their assigned missions. If a merc flier has no aircraft of his own then he will expect to be assigned a well-maintained aircraft belonging to the hiring state.

Greater numbers of local forces almost always oppose mercenary fliers, so they have to be very good at their jobs. Their arrogance is partially the result of their status as an elite and partly a necessity of their duties. Self-confidence is vital to a fighter pilot, who wages war more or less alone. Loss of nerve is fatal. Consciously or otherwise, merc fliers build up their confidence by developing an inflated ego. There is a saying at the Imperial COACC advisory group's fighter school: "If you know who the best fighter pilot in the galaxy is, and it isn't you, you shouldn't be a fighter pilot."

Aircrew attitude is reflected in their mode of dress. Apparel often prominently displays the crewmember's tag or nickname. This tag is usually a reflection of the flier's personality, favored style of flying or some memorable exploit, and – most importantly – it is assigned by his peers.

There is no standard equipment for aircrews. Fliers tend to wear the best flight suits and carry the best survival gear they can obtain.

Ground Crew

Mercenary air squadrons rely upon a base of operations, as unlike other armed forces aircraft must return to a prepared base to refuel and re-arm. At higher TLs, this may be a mobile base, a ground craft or a seagoing vessel.

At the base, aircraft are maintained and re-equipped by a ground crew who need to be experts in their field if a speedy turnaround of aircraft is to be achieved. Grounded aircraft are nothing more than expensive targets, and it is the skills of the ground crew that keep them flying. Ground crew are specialists. Some are mechanics; some are electronics, weapons or communications technicians. Most ground crews also include a security contingent to protect the base and its aircraft from ground attack.

A wealthy mercenary squadron relies on its expert ground crew to get it to the area of operations and there create a secure base of operations.

Ground crew tend to be good team players, as their duties require everyone to correctly complete his task in the most efficient fashion. This team image is reflected in common uniforms with prominently displayed squadron markings. Different technical teams are often identified by their uniform color. While a little garish, this aids identification and thus efficiency.

Air Defense

Ground-to-air combat is a major part of modern warfare, and ground fire is a significant obstacle to the completion of many combat missions. Effective air defense is vital to all ground units, especially air bases.

Air defense methods change with TL, but can be considered to fall into one of two categories. Active methods attempt to destroy enemy aircraft with guns, beam wea-pons or missiles. Passive meth-ods include electronic countermeasures (ECM) and obstacles such as bar-rage balloons.

At low TLs, active air defense is a function of the artillery, with specially adapted guns being used to shoot at enemy aircraft. As TL increases air defense becomes more the province of special air defense units (though most ground units have some means of short-range air defense). These air defense units may be a part of a given world's aerospace forces (under the assumption that fliers know best how to deal with other fliers) or may be a part of the ground forces (the units most likely to need defending).

Specially designed guns and surface-to-air missiles (SAMs), some with very long ranges, are used to knock aircraft out of the skies. Electronic countermeasures become more than passive jamming at higher TLs, as it becomes possible to fool enemy sensors and weapons systems with false emissions.

Passive defenses usually begin with lighter-than-air obstacles such as barrage balloons, tethered to the ground by a steel cable above important locations to make overflights hazardous. With improved technology passive defenses become mainly electronic.

Mercenary air defense crew fall into two types: weapon crews and technical wizards. Active-weapon mercs are similar to artillery crews of a similar TL, while the technicians seem to many to be very unmilitary. They operate from secure areas, using the electromagnetic spectrum to spoof, jam or even destroy enemy weapons and sensors. Never coming anywhere near the enemy, techs are recruited for their skills, not for military prowess. Important defensive sites are sometimes the targets of enemy air attack, so are defended by their own batteries of active defense systems.

Mercenary air defense units are always high-tech, with a mixture of mobile active and passive weapons systems. Most air defense outfits are part of a larger ground or air unit, but independent units ranging in size from a single weapon and its crew to a battalion-equivalent can be hired. Their sophistication makes them expensive to employ, but cheaper than being bombed into eternity.

IMPERIAL INTERVENTION

The nature of the Imperium is such that individual worlds have a great deal of latitude in their internal affairs. Local governments are given broad guidelines to fol-low – and occasionally some specific instructions – but for the most part are left to deal with their own problems, reminded of their duties and responsibilities by the occasional visit from the Imperial Navy.

Mission

The battery had moved into position under cover of darkness, just a few miles from the Loyalist positions. Six self-propelled guns in light armored housings, waiting for the request to rain high-explosive death on the opposing ground troops.

In the fire direction APC, Captain Mike Berezhinho sipped at a cup of strong black coffee. Out there, the foot soldiers were moving into position for their assault. Any minute now.

His headset spoke quiet words in his ear, and the captain put down his cup. He pressed a key on the comm unit.

"Razor One. Smoke on following coordinates," the captain said softly, and repeated the forward observer's request. Seconds later the gun code-named Razor One slammed a round into the sky. The captain picked up his cup, mentally counting seconds.

"Battery, prepare to move. Alternate Zulu Four," he signaled to the commanders of all six guns, the ammunition carriers, and his own driver. The intelligence report said the Loyalist counterbattery radar was inferior, but there was no point in tempting fate.

The headset spoke again, and so did the captain. "Razor One. Up three hundred."

Again Razor One slammed back on its recoil dampers. Berezhinho waited.

The headset spoke softly, and he smiled.

"Razor One, on target. Battery, link to Razor One," he waited while the central fire control computer adjusted the aim of all six tubes. The ready light came on an instant later.

"Battery: Six rounds Hotel-Echo-Delta-Peter, fire for effect."

A second's delay while six crew chiefs verified the proper rounds were in the tubes, and that the trajectory had been adjusted slightly to allow for the different weight of the HEDP rounds. Then six guns fired as one.

Berezhinho keyed the connection to the FO and spoke softly: "On the way."

Autoloaders whined, the guns fired again. Again. The position lit up with fire and thunder, but it was as nothing to what the Loyalists were getting. Soon the counter-battery fire would be coming, but by then the battery would be long gone. Berezhinho smiled again as the sixth salvo crashed out and the command APC started to move. He'd bet good money the Loyalists were regretting their words now. Fee too high, indeed!

It is occasionally in the best interests of the Imperium as a whole to intervene in a local crisis. In these situations, it is usually the Navy that is first on the scene, deploying armed naval personnel and whatever Marines may be available to hold things together. Marine task forces are next, followed by deployment of major Imperial Army units if necessary. Planned interventions may be the province of the Army or the Marines, depending upon scale and force availability.

The goals of any intervention are:
• The safety of Imperial officials.
• The safety of loyal citizens and innocent bystanders.
• The security of vital installations.
• The restoration of order.
• The restoration of legitimate local government and resumption of home rule.
• Capture of guilty parties.
• Orderly withdrawal of Imperial forces.

These goals are open to local interpretation. For example, there is some debate as to what constitutes a vital installation, or exactly when local governments are ready to resume control of their affairs. But the ultimate goal is usually to restore a legitimate local government to power and then withdraw.

The decision to intervene in a world's affairs is a weighty one. There have been many cases in history when peace was given "one more chance," until bloody war broke out with the diplomats still at the table, millions dead in a conflict that could have been headed off by a timely airstrike or commando team. But once the troops go in, people die. At what point does the benefit of intervention outweigh the danger? This is the decision faced by Imperial politicians, and it is never an easy one.

Certain conditions require intervention; the use of nuclear weapons in ground combat, defiance of Imperial treaty obligations or interference with free trade.

Intervention may also be requested. For example, if rioting mobs have overwhelmed local security forces and are attempting to enter the government buildings in order to lynch the president, the captain of an orbiting Imperial Navy destroyer may be asked for help. The captain has the right to refuse such help under certain conditions, but had better have a good explanation ready.

The actual nature of the intervention depends upon the local commander's initiative and judgment. In the example above, a shore party would probably be sent, consisting of armed Naval personnel and whatever Marine complement the ship might have, to secure the palace and evacuate the endangered personnel. If matters were not quickly resolved then the ship would send to the nearest Naval base for instructions while attempting whatever measures the captain thought best to contain the situation. Once the situation reached this point, a crisis team would be placed in charge and this team would decide upon appropriate action.

Measures taken by the crisis team depend upon circumstances. Interventions may take the form of a fine or sanctions against the perpetrators, the dispatch of a few diplomats and mediators to find a compromise, or a Marine task force dropping from orbit to smash the agitators. In rare cases Army troops are deployed to the troubled world for a protracted campaign to restore Imperial rule.

THE IMPERIAL MODE OF WARFARE

Imperial strategies and tactics draw upon centuries of experience. In the end, any world can be reduced to a molten ball by orbital bombardment. Actual capture of a usable world is more difficult.

First, orbital craft and starships gain control of the upper atmosphere and close orbit, allowing orbital bombardment of ground targets. Almost any ground force can be eliminated from orbit, given sufficient attacking assets.

If ground combat is necessary (and it almost always is, if you want to do anything with a world other than convert its surface to molten rock), it is characterized by short strikes of unbelievable ferocity, with all-arms co-operation at a premium. Advance parties of grav-belt equipped forward observers, drop troops and commandos are employed to distract and confuse the enemy while guiding the main thrust. Breakthrough and deep penetration is achieved by grav armor with APCs and other vehicles in close support. Infantry dismount only to make the final assault under heavy covering fire.

Lighter mobile units are used for slashing diversionary raids and rapid exploitation/pursuit, the aim being to daze the enemy into paralysis, envelop and annihilate enemy formations by overwhelming firepower. The "battle zone" is generally some hundreds of miles deep, with some strategic point as the final objective. The aim is not usually to capture this objective, but to force the enemy to stand and defend it, thus enabling the Imperial forces to destroy the opposing army. Territory can be taken for free later, once the enemy's ability to resist is shattered.

On the defensive, perhaps during resupply or logistics buildup, a network of heavily defended strongpoints are set up as a base for constant spoiling attacks to keep the enemy off balance. Each strongpoint requires a considerable concentration of force to knock out, gaining time while Imperial forces gather for a massed counterattack to throw back the enemy. Standard imperial doctrine states that passive defense invites defeat.

Rapid maneuver, concentration of force and overwhelming firepower are the keys to victory.

THE BIG PLAYERS

One of the risks a successful mercenary group runs is becoming too successful. Eventually, someone will hire you for a mission that opposes the Imperium in some way, and that will bring in one of the groups the Imperium uses to make its military

A Choice of Mercs

There weren't many applicants for the Yres ticket. Only one outfit wanted it. I had a feeling I knew what the Admiral would say when I gave him the flimsy, but I still had to present it. That's what being an aide is all about.

Admiral Vadid Ligl took care that his waterproof gloves were in place before he took the flimsy from me. Being a Bwap, he's a truly great administrator, exactly what you need in a sector admiral's position. His damp skin is a bit hard on the flimsies, though.

The Admiral glanced once at the flimsy, then fixed me with that unsettling, unblinking stare of his.

"Wawa-trekaa-pecc waaka-wawa-watia karwu-waapa-pecc Yres 1802 wawawakaa-Vargr-wawa-scum-pecc wawa-wawa-karra-wad!"

He threw the flimsy back at me before continuing, "Wawa-Imperial-paapa-Navy-kaawa Mercenary-good-wawawa wabia kerwa-waqpa Bond-no-Vargr friend!"

I picked the flimsy up and saluted. "Yes sir! I'll inform the recruiting office to find someone else at once," I said and scuttled out the door as fast as I could.

I'd had a feeling he might say something like that.

Boarding Party

The body was in a bad way. Exposure to vacuum had ruptured all its blood vessels. Jones avoided looking at the eyes.

The free trader Cecilia *had been drifting at the edge of the Feneteman system for several days, her hull ripped open by a volley of missile strikes in a random pattern that only a Vargr gunner could have conceived.*

Jones had space-walked across with his team from the mercenary cruiser Scimitar *to survey the wreck and search for clues as to which Vargr band had sunk the* Cecilia. *They'd found nothing but the dead. The ship had been stripped of everything that wasn't nailed down, and a good many things that had been.*

The steward had evidently died when the compartment he was in had taken a direct hit, and had decompressed. He remained conscious long enough to get halfway into a vacc suit. It was a painful way to go.

"Mark, Mark!" Jones' helmet barked. "Get your butt up to the bridge! The doggies left us a calling card!"

Jones swore silently, then bellowed into his comm, "For Cleon's sake! Just tell me what you found, Akis!"

"Found a data pack. It's marked with the Kforuzeng badge!"

Jones' grin was predatory as he headed for the bridge.

COMBAT IN THE 57TH CENTURY

19

Overhead the stars shone with harsh, icy brightness. Some of them were moving.

Militia private Ericsanan pulled his government-issue cloak tighter around his shoulders and tried to rub a little warmth back into his frozen hands. He shivered and paced out his assigned sentry-path once more. Sarge would have him flogged if he found him stargazing instead of doing his duty.

As Ericsanan hunched deeper into his cloak the falling stars vanished behind the rolling hills to his north. A scattering of drop capsules, bringing the Sylean Rangers to Joyeuse. Silently, and almost unnoticed, the invasion had begun.

Security

Working security could be boring, generally involving standing around in body armor and looking mean. But this ticket wasn't boring.

In fact it was downright dangerous. It's not a good idea to sign on as a bodyguard when the client is an adult-holovid star and the world you're on is full of militant-prudish religious types.

To make matters worse, the liner was late and the client's only way of filling in the time was go to nightspots packed with the aforementioned religious types.

Once again the client emerged from his expensive suite, wearing his usual garish clothing.

"Where to, Mr. Costos?" the bodyguard asked nervously.

Costos smiled broadly, and the bodyguard shuddered.

It was going to be a long night.

The Imperial Rules of War

Imperial authorities tacitly acknowledge that warfare is sometimes the only option, although other resolutions are preferred. So long as the war is conducted "properly," i.e., in accordance with the rules as accepted and interpreted by the Imperium, there is normally no Imperial intervention.

Those who break the rules of war are punished in a variety of ways. Often it is sufficient to negate any gains made by the war, making the whole affair pointless. Sometimes the rules must be enforced by Imperial troops.

There is no "official text" of the Rules of War, thus preserving Imperial flexibility in all but the most blatant situations. Nevertheless, the general Imperial policy toward combatants' behavior is quite clear:

Continued on next page . . .

problems go away. These are the Imperial Marines or one of the various special forces groups, depending upon the individual situation (for hints on their use in a campaign, see p. 6).

IMPERIAL MARINES

The Imperial Marines are sent in when something or someone presents a serious threat to the well-being of the Imperium and its member worlds. They are never used lightly, and once committed, they never leave a job half done.

History

The Imperial Marines were founded by Cleon Zhunastu, who transformed the landing forces of the Sylean Navy into the imperial Marines over 1,100 years ago. Weapons and tactics have changed, but the Marines' basic function remains the same: move fast, strike hard, and enforce the Emperor's will.

Role

Imperial Marines serve a twin function: they act as security forces for the vessels and installations of the Imperial Navy, and are a hard-hitting mobile strike force, the Imperium's "big stick." They come in, hit hard, turn things over to the Imperial Army or local planetary forces and move on. Mercenaries may encounter the Imperial Marines in one of both of these functions.

Organization

The largest standard unit of Imperial Marines is the division, but these are fairly rare except in times of war. In peacetime, most Marine units serve on board vessels of the Imperial navy as *Fleet Marines* or in the various units of the *Rapid-Reaction Force.*

Fleet Marines: Fleet Marines are deployed to various units of the Imperial Navy as ship's troops, landing forces or to guard bases and other important installations. Units normally range from the shipboard security detachment of 10 Marines (see p. 116) up to company-sized contingents deployed as landing forces.

Rapid-Reaction Force: Rapid-Reaction Marines are deployed in units as small as a single independent company, but the battalion-sized Task Force, individually tailored for a specific mission, is the most common unit. Task Forces are assembled from the component units available to a Marine regiment (see pp. 116-118), and vary in composition, but normally include all assets necessary to complete the mission, including transport, escort and combat-support craft, and administrative and logistical personnel.

Equipment

Marines are equipped according to their specific assignment. This can range from maroon full dress uniforms and ceremonial weapons up to drop capsules, grav tanks, battledress and FGMPs.

SPECIAL FORCES – THE ELITE

Local planetary forces often see mercenary troops as an elite: supermen with unbelievable skills, fantastic equipment and terrifying weaponry. If you ask a typical mercenary who the real elite are, he will either mention one of a very select group of merc outfits, or one of the Imperial special-forces units.

These units are famous throughout the Imperium and beyond. While most branches of service have elite units, the most famous and instantly recognizable special forces units of the Imperium are the Imperial Marine Commandos, the Sylean Rangers and the Scout Service's S-3 operatives.

These units represent a small but very potent elite of Imperial military might.

THE IMPERIAL MARINE COMMANDOS

History

The word *commando* comes from Afrikaner, an ancient Terran language. It was originally used to describe the lightly armed but highly motivated bands of irregulars who fought against Terra's then largest empire, the British. The commandos specialized in hit-and-run tactics and avoided set-piece battles where possible. The term was later used to describe highly trained raiding forces used for special operations in many theaters of Terran warfare. In one particular period the commando forces operated from ships, hitting enemy targets on the coastline and a connection with the Marines was formed.

With the Terran victory of -2219, the idea of "commando" elite forces was introduced to the Vilani and other cultures throughout the old Imperium. When the Third Imperium's Marines formed its special operations units the name "commando" was a logical one. Today the commandos are the special strike arm of the Imperial Marines.

Imperial Marine Commandos are recruited from Marine and Navy personnel, with 90% of recruits being Marines. Selection is rigorous, but troopers fight for a chance to wear the famous green beret embossed with a golden starburst badge and the legend "All means to Victory."

Role

The Imperial Marine commando has the same role as his distant ancestors on Terra. He is employed in hit-and-run raids, gaining intelligence or inflicting damage on the enemy by destroying key installations or killing command staff.

Organization

The largest standard unit of Imperial commandos is the commando company (see p. 118). One company is assigned to each fleet headquarters of the Imperial Navy, and one to each Marine regiment.

Equipment

The Imperial commando has access to an awesome variety of equipment to allow him to operate in any environment and to enhance his already considerable abilities.

The primary item of equipment is commando battle dress, which is composed of a powered, strength-enhanced exoskeletal suit covered in a carapace of environmentally sealed armor. The suit has IR masking, chameleon surface, smoke and

The Imperial Rules of War (Continued)

The War Shall Be Just

This rule is often cynically restated as "have a good excuse, don't upset anyone important or rock the boat, and nobody will take any notice."

In practice this means that there must be a reason for the conflict that can be defended in an Imperial Court. Response (even preemptive response) to perceived threat is the usual reason given, and as long as a reasonable threat can be shown this is quite acceptable.

There are many gray areas in this rule, though. The overthrow of a world government is usually seen as a legitimate statement of the will of the populace. Economic or territorial gain (much the same thing in most cases) is accepted by the Imperium as legitimate on a moderate scale.

The War Shall Not Interrupt Free Trade

The Imperium is built on trade and commerce, and many of its most powerful institutions are commercial in nature. Once a war starts to cost the Imperium money, perhaps by closing a world's ports or making life dangerous for traders, intervention is sure to follow. The trade wars between megacorporations have been known to disrupt commerce in an entire sector, and the Imperium will not tolerate this situation for long.

Continued on next page . . .

The Use of Weapons of Mass Destruction Against Civilian Targets Is Forbidden

The normal interpretation of this rule is "no nukes in ground combat," but in fact the situation is more complicated. The use of any weapon of mass destruction (nuclear and certain large conventional explosives, biological and lethal chemical agents) in areas where there is a civilian population is completely forbidden. Certain other techniques, such as carpet-bombing of cities, are forbidden no matter what military targets are within the city.

The use of lethal biotoxins and large strategic nuclear weapons is always a capital offense. Small nuclear explosives are legal in some circumstances: aerospace defense and space combat primarily. Nonpersistent lethal chemical agents may be used away from civilian populations. Nonlethal chemical agents are acceptable in most situations.

Most commanders try to err on the safe side, as no one can predict exactly what the result of the Imperial intervention will be.

The War Shall Not Cause Unnecessary Suffering to Non-Combatants

The rule is both humane and a cynical preservation of interests. The citizens of the Imperium are more productive as happy workers than they are as desperate refugees. Wars are prohibited from causing the destruction of civilian amenities (reservoirs, hospitals, housing, power grids, etc.), mass exodus of populations, famine or plague.

The Imperium acknowledges that much fighting takes place in built-up areas. Indeed, many command bunkers and defense installations are situated in cities for the very reason that they cannot be bombarded from orbit. It is thus necessary to enter the city and fight there, and this will cause civilian casualties in come cases. Combat must be conducted as "cleanly" as possible, not involving civilians unless they take up arms and thus become combatants. Combat techniques must take account of the need to avoid collateral damage and casualties.

Continued on next page . . .

anti-laser aerosol dispensers, scrambled continental-range commo unit, tactical battle computer, advanced sensors package, IR and LI telescopic visor and heads-up targeting/information display. A grav flight pack is attached to the suit when necessary.

Commandos use drop capsules during meteoric assault or scouting missions. Each capsule weighs approximately 2 tons and carries one commando trooper. The capsule is capable of limited maneuver as it descends from an orbiting starship, shedding pieces of its ablative heat shield as it descends to prevent the occupant from melting. During the descent, the capsule loses speed by various means and finally opens to release the commando to complete the descent by parachute or gravitic means. Drop capsules contain a large variety of electronic countermeasures and have stealth characteristics making radar detection quite difficult.

Commandos have many different weapons, but the standard firearm is the FGMP-12 when in battledress, and the 4mm gauss rifle otherwise. Officers are armed with 4mm gauss pistols or rifles as the situation and their individual preferences warrant. Other weapons are issued as the individual mission may require. Commando knives are carried by all personnel, and see use more often than most outsiders imagine.

SYLEAN RANGERS

History

The Imperial Army was formed from the Sylean Federation forces in the Year 0. Unlike the Imperial Navy, it quickly became heavily decentralized, with each member world maintaining its own forces. In the early years of the Imperium,

Imperial forces supplied to member worlds a cadre of officers and NCOs who trained the local forces to a common standard.

For the most part the Imperium, with its "rule of space" policy, relies on the Imperial Marines to bear the brunt of the ground combat. During the wars with the Zhodani and the Pacification Campaigns, large ground forces were needed to occupy and hold worlds, a job the Army has always done well. The Imperium keeps a small standing army available at all times, with extra forces "on call" at need from member worlds. These standing forces are drawn from a multiplicity of high-tech, high-population worlds, and it is from these units that the members of the Sylean Rangers are chosen.

The name Sylean Rangers comes down from the cadre of Sylean forces who trained the Imperial forces of early years. The members of the Rangers are now drawn from all across Imperial space, with less than 1% of the personnel coming from Core sector.

The rangers mark their unit identity with crimson berets bearing a golden badge with the legend "First to the Fight, Last from the Field."

Role

The military role of the rangers can be broken into two core functions: *recon* and *assault*.

In the recon role the rangers are sent ahead of an attacking force, often inserted by drop capsule to scout out an objective and report back on enemy forces and dispositions, possible landing sites and hard targets for planetary bombardment. The Imperial fleet arriving in-system will send a coded message and await the rangers' report in the form of a squirt transmission, The recon mission is extremely dangerous, since the rangers are heavily outnumbered and cut off from friendly forces for as long as 5-10 days. Their main defense is to avoid detection for as long as possible.

In the assault role, their objective is to take and hold a bridgehead to allow the main Imperial force to land and deploy as safely as possible. Again the rangers are often heavily outnumbered, but in this role they are heavily armed and need only hold on for a few hours. Losses are usually high, as the enemy normally makes a maximum effort to eliminate the bridgehead and prevent the landing.

Organization

Rangers, like all special forces, are quite rare. Usually one battalion is maintained per sector, though the sectors of the Domain of Deneb and the Domain of Sol each have two due to the threat of invasion. The battalions are organized as standard Imperial forces and are commanded by a full colonel who answers directly to the Domain commanding general (the senior army officer in the entire Domain).

Recon teams of rangers are very small, usually no more than a squad led by a sergeant. These personnel are trained to work very closely together and to live off the land to such an extent that soldiers often say that a recon ranger is "more native than the natives."

Equipment

A ranger's armor depends upon his assigned role. In a recon force, gear will be limited to a combat environment suit or sometimes commando battle dress (see p. 61). In the assault role the rangers use enhanced battle dress as noted on p. GT118.

Rangers (especially recon teams) use drop capsules for insertion. The standard small arm for recon units is the 4mm gauss rifle and pistol. In the assault role the troops hit the ground carrying FGMPs, PGMPs, auto-grenade launchers and (sometimes) tac nuke launchers. Recon units are more lavishly equipped with communications equipment, for obvious reasons.

The Imperial Rules of War (Continued)

The War Shall Be Conducted With Respect to Sophonts' Rights

The basic sophonts' rights of all enemy personnel must be respected. This is primarily concerned with the proper treatment of prisoners of war (POWs). Surrendered personnel become non-combatants, and must be escorted to a rear area and held in suitable accommodations. They may not be forced to perform work that directly benefits the war effort (munitions manufacture, fortification construction, etc.), or to perform any task not acceptable to a civilian member of the combatant nation; i.e., any task that is unduly dangerous or injurious to health.

Repatriation bonds of surrendered mercenaries must be respected. Repatriation or exchange is to take place at the earliest opportunity.

Personal property of surrendered personnel must be returned upon release.

The name and ID code of all surrendered personnel must be reported as soon as is practical to the proper authorities (which vary depending on location and circumstances).

Imperial Observers Shall Be Granted Unlimited Access to the Conflict

Assuming an official observer team can get there in time, all member nations are legally bound to allow them to investigate any and all aspects of the conflict. This process has once or twice been hijacked for intelligence-gathering purposes, but this is dealt with harshly by the authorities and is very rarely even attempted.

Continued on next page . . .

S-3 Scouts

The Scout Service has a variety of missions, some of them extremely hazardous. The Scouts explore uncharted areas, make first contact with new races, control dissemination of technical or social data to prevent culture shock on backward worlds, and operate the express boat network and the Imperial courier service.

Scout personnel often operate in small teams, far from support. They can easily find themselves taken captive by unfriendly aliens during first contact, criminals introducing technology to an interdicted world or cutthroats after the valuable mail. When things go badly awry, the IISS Security Branch sends "S-3" to the rescue.

History

S-3 was established shortly after the IISS was formed, in the earliest days of the Third Imperium. The name arises from the unit's official designation of "Special Security Service" (SSS).

Role

The primary mission of S-3 is to recover Scout personnel who have fallen into unfriendly hands. S-3 operatives are also sometimes sent onto interdicted worlds to locate, recover or destroy prohibited technology.

Strictly speaking, the IISS is not a military organization. S-3 teams are not on a par with Imperial Commandos or Sylean Rangers. Even so, the military services give the Scout commandos grudging respect. Although S-3 training emphasizes getting the job done quietly and with a minimum of bloodshed, its members are widely known for their resourcefulness and courage.

Organization

Unlike most of the Scout Service, the Security Branch is organized along military lines, with ranks and a formal chain of command. S-3 members are recruited as the elite of Security Branch. They are top-notch soldiers, trained in commando and covert operations. They also receive training from Contact & Liaison Branch on the sociology of low-tech cultures.

S-3 is organized around teams of roughly squad size, with 5-8 personnel per team depending on the local situation. Teams practice together until they can operate smoothly as a unit. In most sectors, there are four teams formally organized as a platoon. In troubled regions such as the Spinward Marches, more than one platoon may be present.

S-3 headquarters for a given sector is usually located at an IISS way station, staffed by members of the other branches of the Scout bureaucracy. The S-3 squads actually spend very little time at headquarters, and are constantly out on training assignments or actual operations.

Equipment

S-3 teams are equipped according to the requirements of a specific mission. Personal weapons are a matter of individual choice and specialty. Vehicles, spacecraft and other items are issued as needed.

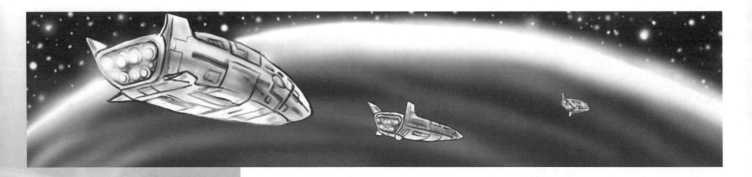

CHAPTER TWO

Running a Mercenary Campaign

The first problems facing a prospective mercenary leader are recruitment, training and organization of troops. This will be followed rapidly by the problems of upkeep and payment of mercenary units and the resolution of missions carried out by those units.

RECRUITING

"Name any naval base, marine camp or army garrison behind the claw and I will tell you the name of the local **Bwapaalapawd** *("face that sees all"), the one you humans call a "Jim." He may not wear a sign, but he knows everyone and everyone knows him. The day you muster out the Bwapaalapawd will find you in a bar or a lobby. He will do you a little favor – buy a drink or get a cab for you – and he will mention that if you are ever stuck for work, he can find you a job. The job, of course, is as a mercenary."*

– Sector Admiral Baron Vadid Ligl

OBTAINING RECRUITS

Mercenaries are often recruited from among personnel leaving conventional military services, by local freelance recruiters known as "Jims." The name comes from the legendary James Bradshaw, who assisted Empress Arabellatra by forming a fleet of mercenaries for the pivotal Second Battle of Zhimaway in 622.

Some mercenary units do maintain permanent bases or depot units, which serve as recruitment and training centers. Most cannot afford this luxury and depend upon free-lance recruiters.

Recruiters

Recruiters operate around Imperial bases and are also found near the garrison towns of planetary armed forces. The recruiter charges a fee for each recruit he finds. This is usually agreed upon before he begins recruiting, though special arrangements are always possible.

One such special arrangement is the "commissioning rate," where the recruiter is paid a salary or retainer by the mercenary unit to look out for exceptional recruits even if the unit is not actively seeking personnel at that time – mercenary units can usually find room for a specialist or expert, even if the unit is ostensibly full.

A recruiter's fee does not include any consideration for expenses, but at a standard rate of Cr500 per recruit, the business can keep a competent Jim very comfortable.

Only the largest and most profitable units pay salaries to "cherry-pick" the best recruits, but such a retainer will bring in Cr1,000-2,000 a month in addition to normal fees. To remain on retainer, a Jim must provide the unit with a steady stream of high-quality personnel.

Recruits put forward by the recruiter are usually then tested by a mercenary unit. This includes a medical check, psychological test and a 6-8 week training period. Part or all of this process is waived in the case of recruits coming in with a solid reputation gained elsewhere.

Vilani Military Traditions

The vast majority of military organizations within the Imperium are based on Solomani traditions. However, the Vilani have their own set of traditions stretching back millennia. The most striking difference between the two is that the Vilani are truly a "nation under arms." In traditional Vilani military thinking there is no such thing as a non-combatant; every member of a society contributes to the war effort and therefore all are equally legitimate targets. Vilani warfare has been characterized as being ruthless, with any means acceptable to conclude a war successfully. The Vilani military thinking is also very concerned with cost-effectiveness. To the Vilani mind, war is exclusively a means to an end, and the cost must be weighed against the gains. Traditionally, the Vilani have regarded nuclear weapons as being highly cost effective. Consequently, the Imperium tends to take a very close look at mercenary units claiming to recreate the military glories of Vland.

The Vilani also place great emphasis on teamwork and their military structures tend to follow a "square" pattern (combat units tend to be in fours). This square organization tends to be less flexible than the more familiar Solomani "triangular" pattern (combat units tend to be in threes) and this is probably the greatest reason for the rarity of Vilani units. However, Vilani patterned units may occasionally be encountered, and these units often retain their own distinctive names and designations. A list of the most common, with their Galanglic equivalent, is given below:

Soldier*	Dagashii
Infantry	Nikha
Cavalry	Iladuka
Artillery	Amlekim
Squad	Kadigar
Section	Dikadigar
Platoon	Igkadigar
Company	Shuguus
Battalion	Khasliim
Regiment	Erka
Brigade	Gikamarga
Division	Lurkugi
Corp	Arkhe
Army	Gisadi

*Both officer and enlisted.

The Icetina Conflict
1: Hiring-On

The skipper had been on-planet for two days. He called us in for a briefing as soon as he got back aboard. We all knew what that meant.

We assembled in the lounge to hear what he had to say. He glanced around at us; the exec, gunnery master, surgeon, and finally me, commander of ground troops.

"We have a deal," the skipper said without preamble. "The Technocrats of Ivendo have agreed to all our terms."

He passed a pile of contract flimsies out. We skimmed them, each of us looking to see what the contract meant for our own department.

The job looked simple enough from our end. Ivendo had maintained an outpost in the Icetina system for centuries. Just a little mining village on some outsystem rock, settled long ago and all but played out. It'd changed hands a few times over the years, and both Icetina and Ivendo had a claim to it. But the folks were Ivendo citizens and they'd recently held a referendum to stay that way. About a week later the Icetinans had annexed the place by force. The Imperials shrugged and said something about internal affairs. Icetina issued a declaration that the place was theirs and they'd defend it. Besides, it's infinitely closer to Icetina than Ivendo. They'd just accept it, wouldn't they?

Normally, maybe. But there must have been some sort of political stink going on, because the Technocrats were assembling mercs and a ramshackle navy to take back their bit of rock, presumably hoping to distract everyone's attention from internal affairs. Neither side has much in the way of starfaring ships of their own, so we were going to be a naval asset as well as transport for my team. Lucky us.

The skipper let us read the contracts through, then spoke up, "You have the usual six hours to protest any details or the whole deal. We'll be working with **Lystander Rampant;** *you all know they're a good outfit. The Technocrats have another escort of their own, a couple of patrol ships and a bulk freighter they're converting to carry troops, shuttles and a few fighters. There are a couple of merchants along as rescue and hospital ships. They're deploying in reinforced company strength, and we're the spearhead. They don't have much PROFORS experience. Questions?"*

Continued on next page . . .

The testing and training process is detailed later in this chapter. Those who fail will receive expenses and a small fee for their time. Highly prestigious units sometimes also offer a recommendation to lesser outfits, reasoning that even a rejection from the Death's Head Hussars is worth entry into a less well regarded unit. Such recommendations are usually respected if they come from a reputable outfit.

Recruiting Procedure

Personnel recently mustered-out of the armed forces automatically know the name and location of a Jim. The big recruiting centers operated by Instellarms and the major mercenary outfits are easily found in local library data. Success in finding one is automatic, though the center may be several parsecs away.

To find a mercenary recruiter at the character's present location, the character must make a Streetwise or Carousing check at a penalty equal to the world's Control Rating.

To be recruited, the would-be mercenary needs to convince the recruiter that he is a worthy soldier. This should be roleplayed out. Generally anyone who has completed military training (especially Imperial military training) will be acceptable for infantry units, and good potential (but untrained) recruits will be spotted by Jims with an eye for physique and attitude.

The GM should decide what sort of personnel the Jim is looking out for. The character has the chance to impress the Jim by showing his knowledge or skill. Test the character's highest military skill while roleplaying the encounter. The Jim will talk to the character and will be able to spot a bluffer easily. If the potential recruit passes the skill test (or straight HT in the case of raw recruits), he will be referred to an appropriate unit. If he is particularly impressed, the Jim may recommend a recruit to a high-prestige unit, or write a personal recommendation. This occurs if the recruit rolls 7 or more better than the required score.

The recruiting process offers great roleplaying opportunities, and attempts by PCs to influence the Jim should be appropriately rewarded.

Finding Recruits: Should the PCs be in search of recruits, rather than being recruited themselves, use these rules:

One attempt to recruit can be made each day in a high-population area (cities with 1 million or more inhabitants) or somewhere a lot of people pass through, such as a large city or busy starport. One attempt per week can be made in moderate population areas (between 25,000 and 1 million inhabitants), and one per two weeks in low-population regions (anywhere with a population under 25,000). In a garrison town the number of recruits gained is doubled.

A successful check of Fast-Talk or Carousing skill will attract 1d recruits, of indiscriminate quality.

A successful check of Leadership skill will attract 1d recruits of high quality or 2d of basic quality (GM's option). These totals should be adjusted up or down at the GM's discretion, depending on factors such as the presence or absence of a military base, or the conclusion of a local conflict (large numbers of soldiers leave service at the end of a war).

Mercenary Recruiting Centers

Larger mercenary units almost always have a base of operations where troops are barracked between operations. The base also carries out other duties such as medical rehabilitation, training and assessment of potential recruits.

Such bases are a focal point for would-be mercenaries, so a recruiting station is attached, manned by loyal ex-combatants who have grown too old for field duty or have retired due to injuries. The recruiting station consists of an interview office, test facilities and a training barracks.

Any would-be recruit will be interviewed by an ex-trooper, usually an NCO, who will talk to the candidate and explain the standard mercenary contract. The NCO will also ask for and then check the candidate's papers, weapon permits and so forth.

At this stage the recruit will be rejected, offered a contract immediately or placed on a waiting list if his skills are not immediately required.

A contracted candidate will then undergo a series of medical and psychological tests. Failure will cause the contract to be withdrawn. Assuming the candidate passes, he embarks on a 6-8 week basic training period, tailored to his military specialization and the type of unit he has joined.

Most mercenary training facilities are situated on low law-level worlds, and the instructors are sometimes very brutal during training and in their treatment of rejected recruits.

Once the candidate has completed the training period, the contract is formalized with the unit's commanding officer. The new mercenary takes his place with the unit, often receiving a welcome in the form of a "purse" (enlistment bonus) containing Cr300-1,000. Much of this money is traditionally spent in bars with the help of the new recruit's squad mates.

To convince the recruiting-sergeant at the initial appraisal: make a check against the character's choice of appropriate skill (weapon skill or an outdoor skill for infantry, a technical skill for specialist units). Defaults are:

HT for infantry or security units, or deep space ground troop contingents.

DX for cavalry.

IQ for artillery, technical or aircraft ground crew.

Note that mercenary units do not train raw recruits for complex jobs such as pilots or starship engineers. If the applicant does not already have appropriate training, he becomes a ground-pounder or finds another career.

Modifiers

+2 if the applicant was recommended by a Jim
+5 if highly recommended by a Jim
+3 if previous military experience
+ (rank) if military rank held.
-2 If unit has high standards
-5 If an elite or deep space unit
-3 if artillery or armor unit
-5 if ship crew or aerospace flight crew
Use all the modifiers that apply.

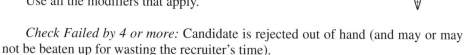

Check Failed by 4 or more: Candidate is rejected out of hand (and may or may not be beaten up for wasting the recruiter's time).

Check Failed: Candidate is placed on waiting list. Can retake the test after four weeks.

The Icetina Conflict 1: Hiring-On (Continued)

*I asked, "We're the only **Broadsword** class?"*

*The skipper nodded. "**Lystander** will be our close escort. We're the command ship."*

"Hope that's worth a bonus," I muttered.

"Lieutenant Milles, your faith is touching. Of course I demanded extra for the honor of carrying their glorious leaders into battle. Now, I want you on liaison duty for the next couple of days. Go mingle with their officers and find out what you can. Be nice to them. They're only amateurs."

"Sir!" I replied crisply. We both smiled faintly.

*– Lieutenant John Milles, Mercenary Cruiser **Javelin***

The Icetina Conflict 2: Going to War

I sat in the officers' bar and listened to the conversations going on around me. Two captains by the bar were lamenting how they'd been passed over for the ground force command slots. Most of the room buzzed with war talk. Across the table from me sat two local lieutenants and a captain, who had been lucky enough to be picked for this fight. The captain was more worried about missing a shooting trip he'd planned, and one of the lieutenants – of similarly insufferable upper-class background – was holding forth about the Chirper problem and how a pogrom might be the answer. I tried to shut them out and not feed anyone a glass. The other lieutenant was smart enough to be scared. She'd downed a fair amount of Vatabell liquor already, but said little. I'd tried to prompt her but I'd got nothing out of her. This whole liaison malarkey was a waste of time.

There was a big display unit over the bar. The planetary news came on, another bulletin repeating the same stuff we'd seen 30 minutes ago. Pictures of Icetina troopers shooting their way through the corridors of Pebble Station, a skirmish in deep space between a recce vessel and Icetina's SDB force, and endless firm declarations of intent from the Technocrats. I sighed and looked away from the screen and its mass-market jingoism.

Straight into the scared brown eyes of the lieutenant.

"Dear God," she said softly. "We're going to war."

– Lieutenant John Milles, Ivendo Ground Forces HQ

Check Passed: Offered training to join the unit.

Check Passed by 5 or more **and** *the candidate has previous military or mercenary experience:* Candidate joins the unit immediately and begins orientation.

Initial Rank: Default rank upon joining the unit is private or equivalent. Check Tactics *and* Leadership skills. If either is failed, rank is private. Average the amount the character passed both checks by, and add military rank if held. Apply the final number to the *Starting Rank Table.* The GM may add modifiers for special reputation or recommendations. Nobody joins a mercenary unit as more than a captain.

Starting Rank Table

Total:	Starting Rank:
1-3	Lance Corporal
6-8	Corporal
9-11	Lance Sergeant
12-14	Sergeant
15-18	First Sergeant
19-21	Second Lieutenant
22-25	First Lieutenant
25+	Captain

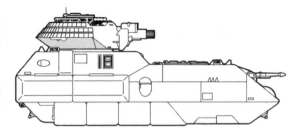

THE MERCENARY CONTRACT

No matter how a mercenary was recruited, he will be presented with a contract which formalizes the obligations and duties required between the individual and his commanding officer.

Contracts vary considerably, but most contain at least the following clauses:

• The mercenary will obey without exception the Imperial rules of war.

• The unit will respect the individual mercenary's rights as a sophont, and provide sufficient food, light, water, heat and shelter except where prevented from doing so by hostile action.

• The unit will pay the contracted salary every 30 days. Absence of payment for 60 days or more will render void the individual mercenary's contract unless the mercenary agrees to an extension. Individual shares allocated to the mercenary shall be paid in full from a ticket's profits after the unit's owner has deducted no more than 50%.

• The unit will pay the salaries of deceased mercenaries to next of kin for the duration of the contract. No shares will be paid to next of kin. Contracts of deceased mercenaries expire automatically at the end of a *ticket* (see pp. 36-39).

• The mercenary will obey orders from superiors unless those orders contravene the Imperial rules of war.

• The mercenary will remain employed by the unit for the duration of the contract (contracts may be for a set period of time or for the duration of a particular ticket), and is to have no other form of employment during this time.

• Either party may terminate a contract by issuing 30 days' notice, although there may be other restrictions.

• The mercenary is subject to military law and the discipline procedures of his unit, and will be punished for infractions in any manner seen fit by his commanders, up to and including death, unless the second clause is violated by such punishment. Orders will be accepted in accordance with the chain of command. The mercenary is not subject to the discipline or orders of local commanders except where specifically agreed by the unit's commander. The unit's complete regulations and discipline procedures must be an appendix to the contract.

These eight clauses are informally known as the "Code of Martin," as it was Martin I, fourth emperor of the Imperium, who legalized the use of mercenary forces within the Imperial borders and granted legal rights to mercenary units. Other clauses normally specify details of payment, such as what currency will be used, what form the payments will take and so on.

TRAINING

Training can be divided into two types: *basic* and *orientation*.

BASIC TRAINING

Basic training takes 6-8 weeks (sometimes more) and is intended to instill or refresh basic skills related to the recruit's military specialty. This stage is often skipped for experienced recruits. The format of basic training is fairly common to most units, and consists of:

Stage 1: Two to three weeks of drill, hard physical training and the like, deliberately made as punishing and spirit-breaking as possible. Twenty-mile runs with dropouts made to clean barracks floors with toothbrushes, parade drill and night-time stand-tos are common. This stage tends to weed out the less determined among the recruits.

To pass the initial stage of training, the recruit must check HT or ST, whichever is higher. Add +3 if the character has previously completed military training. Failure by 3 or less requires a repeat. Failure by more means dismissal.

Stage 2: One to two weeks of combat training involving firearms practice, melee weapons and unarmed combat training. All mercenaries need some familiarity with armed self-defense, even technical specialists and ship's crew. The incompetents and those unwilling to hurt another sophont are sent packing.

To pass the second stage of training, the recruit must check Brawling or another unarmed combat skill, a Weapon skill and HT, and must pass any two to continue. Passing only one means repeating the training. Failing all three means dismissal. Those who have passed previous military training automatically pass this stage.

Stage 3: Two to three weeks of intensive skill training where the recruits learn to carry out their specialist duties to the best of their ability. This period sees fliers constantly in the cockpit or simulator, infantrymen glued to their rifles and spacers living in a vacc suit. The recruits are pushed to their limits, and the ones who don't come up to scratch are dismissed.

To pass stage 3, the recruit must check HT and the highest relevant skill, and pass both to complete training. Passing only one means a repeat of this section. Failure in both means dismissal.

The Icetina Conflict 3: Jumping In

I was on the crowded bridge as we emerged. The task force had formed up in battle array before the insertion jump. We had the merc escort close in. The local escort was beside her freighter charge. It'd looked frighteningly vulnerable as it left port, and I didn't envy the troopers aboard. We had two patrol ships out in front and the auxiliaries to the rear.

When the jump field collapsed, the ships were all over the place. One of the auxiliaries was nowhere to be seen. Apparently she arrived six hours later. We still had our escort, but the other one was maneuvering to avoid a collision with the hospital ship. The skipper took one look at the chaos and nodded sagely.

"Not as bad as I'd expected," he said quietly.

We shook the force out into order. The freighter released her fighters, all except the one that got hung up in the launch cradle. Then the battle board lit up and we knew the fight had begun.

The freighter began spewing missiles from her jury-rigged bay. Our two missile turrets joined in the salvo. I left the bridge, partly to be ready for the assault, but mainly because I was helpless up there and when I have to be helpless I prefer not to see what's incoming.

The troopers were ready when I arrived at the launch bay. Two of our squads jammed into one cutter, my team and a few local troops in the other. We strapped into the crashwebs and waited, just praying to survive long enough to launch.

Once you leave the assault ship, you pray that you'll get down safe. On the ground you pray to survive the action. Then you pray for a successful extraction.

But the trick in staying sane is to only pray for one thing at a time.

– Lieutenant John Milles,
*Mercenary Cruiser **Javelin***

The Icetina Conflict 4: Hitting The Ground

I was foolish enough to watch the space battle while we headed in for landing. It wasn't pretty. Of the seven fighters that'd actually launched, three were destroyed in seconds. One of the patrol ships took a violent hit and started to break up. She had internal fires, too. The hospital ship took a stupid risk and came in to stand by her, transferring crew directly. I saw a pair of Icetinan fighters sweep past, firing, then deliberately sheer off when they realized they were attacking the medical unit. I raised a mental thumb to their competence, that they could still make a no-shoot decision in that maelstrom. Javelin was hit but still firing, her escort doggedly circling her, stopping missiles and fending off fighter strikes. I saw two SDBs trying to intercept our assault ships, missiles coming up from a ground launcher, the other patrol ship exploding.

I turned the screen off and prayed instead. Prayed to the Unheeding God of Foxholes. Then I clutched my laser carbine and swore for a while. I don't remember where I read it, but some old Terran philosopher once said profanity could be as helpful as prayer in some situations.

Finally I heard the sweetest sound in the world, the 30-second klaxon. Just a half minute to touchdown. Half a minute to when the shooting became personal . . .

We hit, hard. I released the straps and led the squad out onto the rocky surface. We took some fire from enemy positions near the missile launchers. The troopers fired back calmly, accurately. The fire stopped. I spoke three words into my comm. The squads began to fan out and advance.

The release of tension was beautiful.

– Lieutenant John Milles,
Pebble Station

Most of those who survive the first week will complete their training period, although the instructors never let up. They will try to find a reason to dismiss a recruit right up to the last minute. People who fail in training will get their comrades killed in battle. It is the instructors' duty to prevent this from happening.

Having passed the basic training, a recruit officially joins the unit, and is given a few days' leave before beginning orientation. The new recruit has the dubious honor of being known as "FNG," "newbie" or "cannon fodder," according to the unit's preference for new-recruit nicknames.

ORIENTATION TRAINING

Even an experienced recruit requires an orientation period upon joining a new unit. Having returned from leave, the new recruit is assigned to an NCO or junior officer, who introduces him to the unit and its procedures. Every mercenary unit is different, with its own way of doing things, and the recruit is expected to learn these customs. Attempting to live by the standards of a previous unit goes down very badly.

Orientation is usually from the time a recruit joins the unit and is given his "purse," to the completion of the first ticket. The recruit is "on probation" during this period, and his performance will be critically evaluated. Mistakes are very dangerous to the unit, and will not be forgiven.

At the end of the orientation period, the recruit's performance is reported to the commanding officer, and a decision is made about his future. There are three possible outcomes:

Dismissal: The recruit is paid up to date and his contract is terminated.

Re-training: The recruit is sent back to repeat part or all of basic training before beginning a new orientation period. He has the option of dismissal instead.

Acceptance: The recruit is offered a permanent position as part of the unit, and is now eligible for promotion.

There is no game mechanic for this, as it depends upon the mercenary character's performance in his first adventure.

MERCENARY UNIT ORGANIZATION

The organizational scheme presented below is based on the old Terran model. The success of the Terran arms against the Vilani Empire and the spread of Terran military government (and the Galanglic language) during the Second Imperium has meant that this model is standard in the Third Imperium, Solomani Confederation and their client states. Nevertheless, they are not ubiquitous by any means and numerous other organizational models exist for different units and on different worlds (see *Vilani Military Traditions,* p. 25).

At high TLs "pure" battalions, regiments, brigades and divisions are rare – most mix infantry, armor, artillery, etc. either through swapping units from like forces or having an organic combined arms unit.

ORGANIZATIONAL COMPONENTS

Ground forces include infantry, artillery, cavalry, support and aerospace ground troops. While not every unit follows the patterns outlined below, most use a close variant. One good reason for this is the sources of recruits. Personnel in mercenary units have often served in the armed forces of the Imperium (or the Solomani Confederation) and would require retraining to use a different organizational structure. The names are suggestions only, and unit organizers are free to use any name(s) they wish for units of their own creation.

Fire Team, Team, Binom

The fire team is the smallest tactical unit, consisting of 2-4 personnel (rarely more), usually armed and equipped very similarly (all armed with rifles, for example). Infantry fire teams normally contain four soldiers, including the team leader. Fire teams are usually led by a very junior NCO (a lance corporal or corporal). The crew of a support weapon or vehicle could be considered to be a fire team, but are not normally referred to as such. A two-man team (such as a sniper and his spotter) is often called a *binom.*

Squad

A squad consists of a number of fire teams (normally 2-3) plus a squad leader (who may double as leader of one of the fire teams). Types of team in a squad might be mixed: for example, two rifle-armed fire teams, a light machine gun team and a squad leader. A light support weapon (grenade launcher or light machine gun) is included at the squad level in many infantry units (and if so, all members of the squad are expected to carry ammunition for the weapon). A squad is commanded by a junior NCO (normally a junior sergeant). Sometimes a single vehicle is considered a squad, and a crew-served weapon such as a howitzer and its crew may be called a squad. Mechanized infantry squads may also include a transport vehicle (a truck, APC or MIFV) and crew.

In some mechanized infantry squads, the vehicle driver and any gunners will normally remain with the vehicle while the squad leader and the rest of the squad dismount to fight as infantry. The vehicle can thus follow along and use its weapon in support of the infantry. In some units, the vehicle's weapon is dismounted and goes with the squad.

Section

A section is an intermediate stage between squad and platoon, and is not used by some armies. A section may consist of two small squads, or may contain from 3-5 fire teams. Sections are often omitted from organizations, especially those which

The Icetina Conflict 5: Close Combat

Pebble Station was some of the worst close-quarters fighting I've ever seen. They fought corridor by corridor, like fanatics. We became disorganized, star mercs mixed in with local troopers. I tried to keep the maps I'd memorized current, keep a coordinated assault going. The biggest obstacle to that wasn't the enemy, but the gung-ho shooting-party captain, who seemed to think that he was leading a bayonet charge or something. His squad had pulled in two others from the reserve to replace casualties that a competent or less reckless leader would not have taken.

I tried to use him as an asset, a distraction to the enemy rather than a large wrench in my assault plan. We pushed on, arriving at the main concourse just as Shooting Party Man tried to charge across it. I managed to keep from cheering as someone shot him in the face with a LAG. The assault stalled, fell back and scattered. The defenders piled across the concourse at us. We shot them to pieces, but they reached us. We found ourselves in a bitter hand-to-hand struggle. A few guys tried to use bayonets and rifle butts before they realized that combat armor really isn't vulnerable to hand weapons. The ones that kept their cool just used their rifles point blank while the fools flailed about.

But that's not saying it didn't hurt.

Some joker managed to smash my head with a rifle butt and somehow tore my laser carbine's power cord out instead. I twisted the quick-release stud for the backpack while he hit me a second time, then shoved him away and drew my gauss pistol. He swung his weapon by the barrel again, denting my helmet and bending his rifle in the bargain. This guy was quite capable of beating me to death if I let him, so I used a Lae Kal trip-and-shove maneuver, put my foot on his chest and emptied the pistol into his faceplate. Technique always wins out over brute force. Especially when firearms backstop your technique.

We continued our advance once the close-quarters combat lesson was over.

– Lieutenant John Milles,
Pebble Station

use the Imperial model. Units with a Solomani influence use the term in its original sense, while many mercenary units use the word to mean any sub-platoon unit that does not fit the squad/fire team model.

In artillery units, a gun and its crew may be called a section.

A section is normally commanded by a sergeant or gunnery sergeant, who may serve as leader of one of the squads or fire teams within the section.

Platoon

A platoon consists of 2-5 squads or 2-3 sections, plus a command group. The command group includes a platoon leader (normally a junior lieutenant), a senior NCO (usually a sergeant), and other personnel, who may be communications operators, runners, a medic or other personnel.

In armored units, the platoon leader also serves as vehicle commander of his own vehicle.

Company, Troop, Battery

A company consists of 3-5 platoons, normally commanded by a captain, who is assisted by a senior NCO and a number of other soldiers serving as clerks, messengers and so on, often organized into a headquarters platoon. Companies may be led by a senior lieutenant or major instead of a captain.

Infantry companies often have a weapons platoon equipped with support or specialist weapons such as mortars, missile launchers or machine guns. The weapons platoon is often split up to support the rifle platoons, in which case there will be as many weapon's sub-units as there are rifle platoons.

Cavalry units of some nations refer to their companies as *troops* (a rare few refer to their cavalry *platoons* as troops and refer to their company-sized units as squadrons). A vehicle company usually has a small headquarters comprising 2-3 vehicles and a staff of no more than 10. Specialist command vehicles are used by some units (these vehicles may have extra commo equipment), while other commanders ride a standard tank (and also serve as vehicle commander) or other vehicle.

Artillery units refer to their company equivalents as *batteries*, generally of 4-6 weapons plus support and communications vehicles. The command unit is a small staff manning a specialist fire direction center (FDC) vehicle, and has several forward observers attached, though these are rarely anywhere near the battery itself.

Battalion, Squadron

A battalion consists of from two to five companies with a command group of eight to 30 soldiers. One of these is the battalion commanding officer, one is the battalion executive officer and one is the unit's senior NCO. The remainder will be headquarters staff, clerks, security troops and other personnel.

In cavalry and armored units the command group is split between various vehicles with the three leading commanders all riding in different vehicles.

A battalion is commanded by a field grade officer, generally no higher in rank than a lieutenant colonel, but normally a major. The executive officer is usually one rank below the commander, so generally is a captain. Cavalry units of some nations refer to their battalions as *squadrons*.

Organizations Above Battalion

Organizations larger than a battalion are beyond the scope of the small-unit actions covered in this book. These are:

Regiment: A regiment consists of several battalions (2-3), plus a smaller headquarters unit (normally a company) and one or more additional units. Regiments are normally commanded by colonels, and are not used in all armies.

A battalion may be formally part of a regiment, but assigned to a brigade on a more or less permanent basis. Some nations refer to their cavalry battalions as regiments.

Brigade: A brigade normally contains 3-5 battalions (or two regiments) and a number of company-sized headquarters and support units. Brigades are normally commanded by a brigadier general, but sometimes by colonels.

Division: A division contains a number of brigades or regiments (typically total-ly about 20 battalions) plus a large battalion-sized divisional headquarters and spe-cialized units of support troops, recon, artillery, MP, medical and so on (normally regiment to battalion-sized). Divisions are normally commanded by a lieutenant general or major general, with an executive officer and a large staff.

Progressively higher organizations such as corps, army, front, theater, and so on also exist, but have no standard organization.

DEEP SPACE ORGANIZATIONS

Deep space mercs are divided into two main types: Ship crews and ground troop-ers. The latter are organized in the same way as ground pounders (usually fire teams, squads and platoons). Ship crews have a different structure, which centers around their use of starships and in some ways mirrors the organization of the Imperial Navy.

Team

A team is the smallest organized unit and consists of from two to six men depending upon the size of ship and task. Any individual team will have a precise job to do within the vessel, such as engineering, gunnery, maintenance etc.

A team is commanded by a spacehand or an NCO (sometimes even an officer) depending on the importance of the job.

On small mercenary vessels, a team may be only one crewmember and is not seen as an organized part of the ship's command structure

Department

A department is a group of teams that take care of one activity on a mercenary vessel. The department is generally referred to by its job title such as *flight, engi-*

neering, command, and so on. For example the typical *Broadsword* class mercenary cruiser has a Flight Department, Medical Department, Engineering Department and Gunnery Department.

A department is commanded by a chief, who again is generally referred to by his department e.g., chief engineer or chief gunner. Other titles for department heads exist, such as gunnery officer, master; commander, and local preference dictates which is used.

Idle Hands Are the Devil's Playground

An old saying describes life in the military as being "Long periods of boredom punctuated by short, brief spurts of abject terror." The question of what soldiers do when they are not fighting deserves some consideration.

A useful discussion of training and practice to avoid skill degradation is on pp. CI114-117.

On the theory that if you do not practice something, you can forget how to do it, soldiers will spend a great deal of time reviewing skills they are already proficient at: target practice, hand-to-hand combat, survival, escape and evasion skills, throwing grenades, identification of enemy equipment, paperwork, equipment issue and re-issue, etc. Drills for every conceivable combat situation will be worked out until they become second nature. And when that's done, there is always something that needs cleaned, oiled, fine-tuned or polished.

Well-run military units can always find something useful for a soldier to do, and thus the phrase "in your copious free time" is a common joke in such organizations – the point being that any free time the soldiers do have is usually spent eating or sleeping (or trying to figure out how to get out of KP).

Crew

A ship's crew consists of all the departments that make up the entire crew of one mercenary ship. The number and size of departments of course varies greatly depending on the type of class and size of vessel.

A ship is commanded by an officer referred to as *captain* (regardless of his actual rank – sometimes, on smaller vessels, he will be a lieutenant or some other rank). Some commanding officers tolerate the nickname "skipper." Some do not.

Sometimes the owner of the ship is not its commanding officer. This person is referred to as the *owner-aboard,* and can make general policy (including the dismissal of crew or even the captain), but must leave the running of the ship to the captain and crew.

Squadron

A squadron is a group of two or more starships of a similar kind operating together to accomplish a certain task. A squadron is commanded by a commodore, who is generally captain of one of the squadron's vessels. The rank commodore lasts only as long as the mercenary squadron exists, which can be two weeks for a convoy ticket or several years for a campaign against the Aslan or Vargr.

There are many types and classes of squadron, but the most common mercenary types are:

Cruiser Squadrons (CruRons) are the most common type of mercenary squadron because of the prevalence of mercenary cruisers, primarily the 800-ton *Broadsword* class.

Escort Squadrons (EscRons) are groups of small mercenary craft usually assigned to a convoy or to a cruiser squadron. These small ships are quick and heavily gunned for their size, and are generally streamlined allowing a variety of operations to be carried out.

Assault Squadrons (AsRons) are composed of troop ships and ground-assault vessels. Their mission is to carry troop units from orbit to a disputed planetary surface. Such squadrons for mercenaries are rare.

Task Force

A mercenary task force consists of any number of squadrons that have been brought together to perform one certain task, such as to retake the mining colony on Gram IV. The component squadrons tend to be of different kinds, but one type will be prominent. For example, the task force sent to Gram IV may well consist of one assault squadron, one escort squadron and two cruiser squadrons.

The task force is commanded by a mercenary admiral, who commands from a flagship not attached on a permanent basis to any one squadron. Like the rank of commodore, the title of mercenary admiral only lasts as long as the task force. Many captains, having once received the title, will continue to use it for as long as possible.

Fleet

The fleet is assembled from a number of squadrons, which have been brought together on a semi-permanent basis to perform a specific task or group of tasks. A fleet contains various types of squadrons, with cruiser squadrons being the most common due to their ability to fulfill many tasks.

A mercenary fleet is very expensive to either run or hire, and therefore such units are quite rare.

AEROSPACE ORGANIZATIONS

Aerospace warriors include aircrew, ground crew and air-defense crew.

Aircrew, Ground Crews

An aircrew or ground crew is the smallest organized unit. In the case of aircrew it may be as small as 1-2 personnel or as large as eight to 10, depending on the requirements of the individual craft. Large crews are divided into teams of two to four men in order to maintain a strict chain of command.

Ground crew vary in size, depending upon the number of personnel assigned to a particular aircraft. Larger ground crews will be subdivided into teams responsible for a specific aircraft system, such as weapons or communications.

Air-defense crews consist of whatever number it takes to properly operate a given air-defense system. Often, air defense will be organized into batteries like ground artillery.

Aircrews are commanded by the aircraft pilot. Ground crews are led by an NCO.

Flight

A flight consists of two to five aircraft and their associated maintenance echelons.

Squadron

The squadron is the basic operating organization for a mercenary air unit. In most cases a squadron is equipped with only one type of aircraft and has a specific mission determined by the type of aircraft. A typical squadron usually contains three to four flights together with several specialist aircraft such as transports or tankers. Squadrons are commanded by a squadron leader assisted by an executive officer of one rank lower. These command officers never crew the same craft.

GMG '98

Identification

Unit nomenclature can be a little confusing. Units may be lettered (Fire Team A), or numbered (Fire Team 2) within their parent unit. They may be informally referred to by the name of their leader, regardless of their formal designation. There are some traditions: fire teams and companies are normally lettered; the rest of the lower units are normally given ordinal numbers (First Platoon, Third Battalion). If they are the only one of their type within a given unit, they may be identified by their function (Weapons Platoon, Headquarters Company). Battalions sometimes get Roman numerals (I Battalion, IV Battalion).

It is seldom necessary to give a unit's full identification – normally all that is necessary is to carry it one or two levels up: a platoon will be identified with reference to the company it is in, and the battalion that the company is in (1st Platoon, B Company, 2nd Battalion). A squad will be identified by its parent platoon and that platoon's parent company (2nd Squad, 1st Platoon, A Company).

Units may be further identified by their type and branch: infantry, cavalry, field artillery and so on (123rd Lift Infantry Regiment, 234th Marine Regiment).

Often it is clear from context which units are being referenced, and a form of shorthand will be used (1st of the 214th, or 1/214 instead of 1st Battalion, 214th Infantry).

Gadgets Vs. Guts

"The Americans, as a race, are the foremost mechanics in the world. America, as a nation, has the greatest ability for mass production of machines. It therefore behooves us to devise methods of war which exploit our inherent superiority. We must fight the war by machines on the ground, and in the air, to the maximum of our ability . . . While we have ample manpower, it is too valuable to be thrown away."

– Gen. George S. Patton

Legal and Admin

The task of running a mercenary unit is complicated, and in no way more so than in the legal sphere. Imperial law must be complied with, contracts must be written and administered, and all obligations faithfully met, or the unit will quickly be closed down. While not the most glamorous part of mercenary work, this is one of the most important. There are several important facets to be considered.

Salaries

As highlighted in the mercenary contract, the mercenary soldier requires a monthly salary. Shortfalls can annul a contract. Salary levels for individual soldiers are fairly standard throughout the Imperium, but talented individuals may be offered salaries 5-10% higher than basic, or more if they are renowned in their field or demand is high.

Most tickets (missions) produce a profit for the mercenary unit, of which up to 50% is taken by the owner and the remainder divided according to a shares system. While salaries of deceased individuals are paid to next of kin until the end of the ticket, only survivors get a share. The unit might choose to withhold the shares of wounded or surrendered personnel if they contributed little to overall success, but normally these are paid. Many units also have a tradition of "heroes' shares," extra shares assigned to particularly deserving troopers, decided by a majority vote among the enlisted ranks after the ticket has ended.

The following tables indicate the typical mercenary salary and share allocation by rank.

Ground Pounders

Rank (GURPS Rank)	Salary (Cr)	Shares
Private (0)	300	1
Lance Corporal (1)	400	2
Corporal (1)	450	3
Lance Sergeant (2)	500	3
Sergeant (2)	550	4
Company Sergeant (2)	600	4
Leading Sergeant (2)	700	5
First Sergeant (2)	800	6
Sergeant Major (3)	1,000	7
Second Lieutenant (3)	1,000	5
First Lieutenant (3)	1,200	6
Captain (4)	1,400	7
Major (4)	1,600	8
Lt. Colonel (5)	1,800	9
Colonel (6)	2,000	10

Continued on next page . . .

Group

A group consists of two or more squadrons, generally of the same role (such large organizations are quite rare, with most support being provided by the hiring state). Groups are commanded by a group captain, who is assisted by an executive officer who holds the rank of squadron leader, and eight to 12 administrative staff.

Ground crew of a group consists of all the units required to operate an airbase, plus administrative personnel.

Wing

A wing is the largest operational aerospace unit and consists of two or more groups. There are no mercenary air wings in the Imperium or the Solomani Confederation. Mercenary units may, however, find themselves "slotted in" to the above organizational structure.

MISSION TYPES

GROUND POUNDERS

The four categories of service for dirtside forces are very similar for infantry, cavalry and deep-space trooper units. Support and artillery units normally undertake cadre tickets, but otherwise are hired for a "support" role, often without a specific mission title.

Cadre Ticket

Mercenaries hired as cadres will provide training personnel for local forces. This is a common ticket on poor worlds. The mercenaries usually provide officers and senior NCOs to lead and advise local units.

Commando Ticket

Mercenaries on commando tickets will be hired to carry out a specific raid, or to serve as a raiding force throughout a campaign.

Striker Ticket

This ticket involves a complete mercenary unit hired to provide a spearhead for an indigenous force.

Security Ticket

Mercenaries are hired to safeguard a specific installation or area for the duration of an anticipated crisis.

DEEP-SPACE SHIP CREWS

Cadre Ticket

Very similar to ground cadre, but once involved in an operation the mercenaries will provide captains and department heads for local vessels.

Raid Ticket

The mercenaries are hired to launch a hit-and-run operation against an enemy base, world or ship.

Striker Ticket

Usually several ships forming a task force are hired to undertake an offworld operation. This is usually a ground attack or seizure of an installation. Worlds occasionally use task forces as a way of cheaply acquiring a short-term navy.

Escort Ticket

The mercenaries are hired to escort a vessel or convoy, protect a route or to act as system-defense vessels.

AEROSPACE WARRIORS

Cadre Ticket

The unit provides instructors and "OPFORS" opponents for training. Cadre missions are similar whatever the unit's type.

Raid Ticket

The unit is hired to launch attacks on enemy forces, installations or logistics. Rarely is a ticket for a single raid. The norm is to hire a force to act as air raiders for the duration of a campaign, hitting various targets as needed.

Air Superiority Ticket

The unit is hired to gain air superiority over local air forces, to free the patron's own nautical or ground forces to undertake their own operations. Defense of local airspace is of course part of this ticket, and air-defense units so hired are tasked to defend key areas or units.

Support Ticket

The unit is hired to transport friendly ground forces or supplies during a campaign.

OTHER TICKETS

As a general rule, nobody hires mercenaries unless they are likely to be needed very soon. The cost is simply too high. Some tickets do not fit into the standard model.

The first of these is the *general ticket*. The general ticket rears its head when a nation or organization is involved in an ongoing conflict or tense situation and feels that troops may be needed. There is no one specific mission in mind; the nation seeks to make use of the mercenaries in whatever way needed.

Legal and Admin (Continued)

The number of shares is determined by adding together all share levels for all soldiers at the time the contract is signed. For example, a unit with 50 privates (one share each, or 50 total), five corporals (three shares each or 15 total), two sergeant majors (seven shares each or 14 total) and a colonel (10 shares) would divide the money 50 + 15 + 14 + 10 = 89 ways (assuming no heroes' shares).

Deep Space

Rank (GURPS Rank)	Salary	Shares
Lackey (0)	350	1
Spacehand (1)	500	2
Third Officer (2)	700	4
Second Officer (3)	900	4
First Officer (4)	1,000	5
Chief (5)	1,500	6
Captain (6)	2,000	8
Commodore (7)	2,000	10
Admiral (8)	3,000	12

The rapid increases in salary reflect the smaller size of deep space units, and the standard of skills needed. While a lackey is merely learning his trade, once he is accepted as a full member of the unit (spacehand) his specialist skills are rewarded by higher pay.

Aerospace

Rank (GURPS Rank)	Salary	Shares
Aircrafthand (0)	250	1
Leading Aircrafthand (1)	350	2
Senior Aircrafthand (2)	400	3
Crew Chief (3)	600	4
Flight Sergeant (3)	650	4
Leading Flight Sergeant (3)	700	5
Master Flight Sergeant (3)	800	6
Flight Sergeant Major (3)	1,000	7
Pilot Officer (4)	1,000	5
Flying Officer (5)	1,250	6
Flight Lieutenant (5)	1,500	7
Squadron Leader (6)	1,750	8
Group Captain (7)	2,000	9
Wing Commander (8)	(No mercenary position)	

Legal Conditions of a Ticket

A ticket is a contract between an employer and a mercenary unit, specifying the mission the employer wants carried out and the payment the employer offers in return. Violation of the terms of the ticket generally leads to some form of legal redress.

All tickets specify certain conditions, including conditions of payment, type of mission, logistic and financial support available to the unit, and the repatriation bond (see p. 39).

Continued on next page . . .

Conditions of Payment

The agreed-upon payment to a mercenary company will be one of two types: "up-front" or "success only."

Up-front tickets generally pay less, as the mercenary unit will be paid whether or not the ticket is a success. Up-front tickets are common in security and cadre missions (especially if the mission is to go on for some time), but for combat missions are offered only to units with a proven record.

Payment in up-front tickets is generally in the form of half now and half on completion. Usually the whole fee is payable whatever the outcome, though the ticket may specify that part of the fee be withheld for failing to complete certain objectives of the mission.

The success-only ticket is more common than the up-front type. The entire payment is deposited in a bank account, to be paid upon successful completion of the mission. It is not uncommon for a percentage to be offered in advance for special outfitting costs, though this is normally refunded if the unit fails in its mission. It is also quite legal to withhold part of the fee for failures in parts of the mission, even if it is successful overall, so long as this is clearly stated in the contract and agreed to by both parties.

The definition of success varies. A unit hired to take out a radar station can measure success by answering a simple question: Is the radar station still functioning?

Units hired on long-term or general tickets present a more difficult legal situation. A unit hired to fight for the Starmalli rebels against their world government may eventually be beaten and surrender. Were they successful? Contract lawyers will argue the case for a while, but will eventually make a decision based on a simple set of questions:

• Did the unit fulfill the conditions of its ticket?

• Did the unit obey orders and serve its employer faithfully?

• Did the unit fight professionally, to an appropriate standard?

Mercenaries are not expected to fight fanatically. A unit that is eventually beaten, but which fights well and hard, has succeeded so long as the contract specified something like "serve the Starmalli rebellion as ground troops." If the mercenaries have clearly done this, they have succeeded. The rebellion may have failed and the leaders all been executed, but the money should be safe in an offworld account, and transferring to the mercs' account as soon as their repatriation bonds (see p. 40) are activated.

Continued on next page . . .

Units on general ticket may find themselves more or less part of the nation's armed forces in a manner similar to the Gurhka units in British service on Terra in the pre-starflight era. They will be deployed like any other unit, receive upkeep and maintenance, and be given combat pay for high-threat duty.

More commonly, a unit will be hired for an entire campaign or crisis and tasked with a string of missions under the one ongoing contract. Thus a grav cavalry unit may see duty in a recon/deterrent role, conducting aggressive recons of a border region to keep hostile incursions at bay, then may be involved in a series of striker missions before switching to a cadre role in a lull. Special negotiations and a complex contract are required for this kind of deployment, and most mercenary commanders view general tickets with distaste.

The other common case is the *retainer*. For example, a number of units are on retainer to the archduke's personal forces. Not all of these contracts are open or public knowledge, giving a level of deniability where needed. A unit "on retainer" may be "standing ready" or "in training" on a long, fat ticket, awaiting deployment. Alternatively, the unit may be on "restricted deployment," allowed to take contracts subject to the approval of the party paying the retainer.

Finally, mercs often refer to the *dream ticket*. This is not any one type of ticket, but is instead whatever most suits a mercenary unit's present needs. A unit needing to rest and recruit after a bloody campaign may consider a long cadre deployment a parsec from their depot to be a dream ticket. The Death's Head Hussars consider any short success-only-ultra-high-threat all-but-suicide-striker mission to be just what they wanted.

Or so they claim.

RESOLVING MISSIONS

Many of the smaller mercenary tickets can be resolved as normal roleplaying sessions. This is especially true for commando raids and cadre tickets. Sometimes the GM will want to determine how an operation is going around the PCs' rifle team, or to find out how many casualties the characters' unit took. The *GURPS Compendium II* mass-combat system (see p. CII112 and p. 44) can be used to resolve battles involving small numbers of troops, but the sheer complexity of the forces deployed makes this impracticable above a certain force level.

The following quick system allows resolution of such operations. The results may be left as they are or used as the basis of a roleplaying session, with the predetermined result giving a general "plot line" for the battle, which may then be influenced by the players' actions.

Note that this is not a wargame. GM "tinkering" with results is necessary. For example, it is possible in certain runaway success scenarios for the enemy's dead+wounded+missing total to exceed 100%. Obviously this means that the wounded have been captured or cannot be located. This will be the case anyway, where an enemy is forced to flee in disorder.

PREPARATION

The forces involved are designated *active force* and *opposing force*. The side instigating the combat or operation, or the side that chooses an aggressive tactic, is the active force. The mercenary force will usually be active. The Game Master has final say, however.

The training level and skills of commanders of both sides will be known, or assigned by the GM. It might be necessary to use an average level of skill for the force as a whole. As a rule of thumb, any newly raised force or civilian mob is Raw, local militia forces and police units are Green, adequately trained regulars and security troops are Average. Mercenary units are almost always at least Seasoned. Elite units are rare, and mainly commando or similar units. Take the following levels for commander's Strategy, Leadership and Tactics skills:

Unit	Commander Skill Levels	Notes
Elite	16+1d	Always High Morale
Veteran	14+1d	May be High Morale
Seasoned	14	
Average	12	
Green	10	May have Shaky Morale
Raw	9	Always has Shaky Morale

There is no reason why a force must be commanded by an officer of the same training level. A Raw conscript unit under an Elite mercenary commander uses the troops' Raw rating for resolution purposes, but skill rolls are made at the commander's levels.

Choose Aggression Level

Each force commander chooses a level of aggression. There are six options:

Extremely Aggressive: This represents an all-out attack, emphasizing speed and maneuver in the hope of overrunning an enemy position and exploiting the breakthrough. Success can reduce the attacker's casualties, but defeat is always very costly. Defeated enemies are vigorously pursued, and suffer heavy casualties.

Aggressive: A little more time is taken in preparation for the attack, but speed and surprise are still paramount. A series of sharp attacks and fast maneuvers unbal-

ances the enemy before a break-through is attempted. Pursuit is vigorous.

Standard: This is a fluid approach, mixing maneuver with artillery preparation. Fixed defenses are used as a pivot point, from which to maneuver. Pursuit is limited.

Cautious: Advances are carefully considered; fixed positions and defended zones are utilized to their full extent. Maneuver forces conduct a staged advance, consolidating positions as they go. Pursuit is very limited.

Defensive: The commander chooses to hold a fixed defensive position or simply avoid the possibility of defeat in an open battle. Maneuver forces conduct limited spoiling and probing attacks. The force will withdraw (early enough to do so in good order) if seriously threatened with overrun. This is the default option of garrisons and security forces.

Extremely Defensive: The defending unit has "DIP" orders (Die In Place). Maneuver forces may make spoiling attacks, but the unit will hold its position at all costs. Overrunning it will be very costly for both sides.

Mercenary forces do not generally use either extreme option, as they are costly in lives and materiel.

Legal and Admin (Continued)

If the contract had specified, "To overthrow the world government and replace it with a Starmalli junta," then the mercs have failed. Their commander should have demanded a much higher fee for such a clause, because the chances of fulfilling it are somewhat narrower.

The actual payment offered to a mercenary unit varies widely. As a guide, the lowest remuneration that a unit will receive is about Cr60,000 per month per ground pounder platoon, assuming up-front money, maintenance taken care of by the employer and a fairly low-threat mission.

Hiring a battalion-sized unit is very, very expensive, especially where armor or sophisticated vehicles are involved.

Bonding Authority: Most mercenary contracts are overseen by a neutral third party known as the *bonding authority*, which ensures a merc unit and employer perform as contracted. Often, a megacorporation specializing in finance or banking will provide this service as part of a standard contract package (including the repatriation bond). Instellarms (see p. BTC15) and Hortalez et Cie (see p. BTC14) are the two firms which are most often involved as bonding authorities, but they are by no means the only ones. In some situations, the Imperium itself may act as a bonding authority, but such instances are rare.

Types of Missions

Mercenaries are hired for a variety of reasons, but broadly speaking there are four categories of mission (or "ticket" as mercenary slang calls it): *cadre, commando, striker* and *security*. These categories are sometimes known by different names depending upon the type of mercenary unit. Deep-space mercs call their mission types: cadre, raid, strike and escort, while aerospace units use similar titles: cadre, raid, air superiority and support.

The difference between these tickets has a drastic effect upon the ticket price, with commando/raid tickets commanding the highest prices. The different tasks associated with these missions are highlighted in the next section.

Continued on next page . . .

Legal and Admin (Continued)

Financial Support

Sometimes a patron undertakes to equip a mercenary unit with specialist equipment for its task. This is referred to as a *long ticket*. Equipment so supplied remains the property of the patron, who will pay a bonus equal to 1-6% of the purchase price for any items of equipment remaining intact at the end of the ticket. Far more common is the situation where the mercenary unit is responsible for supplying its own gear. This is referred to as a *short ticket*.

Upkeep of Forces

Most tickets include the requirement for the patron to provide reasonable living expenses for the duration of the ticket. This is referred to as a *fat ticket,* and involves a payment for all food, water, air and other life-support supplies the unit might need.

A ticket can be a *slim ticket,* where the mercenary unit is responsible for its own living expenses and welfare. Slim tickets are especially common on low-tech worlds with limited resources and finances.

Repatriation Bonds

Nobody wants a bunch of mercenaries, defeated or otherwise, hanging around after the conflict is over. No mercenary wants to be stuck on some backwater world after his ticket expires or his employing government is overthrown. Thus, mission contracts include a repatriation bond clause.

A repatriation bond is a sum posted in a bank account, with sufficient funds to provide at least low passage off-planet for mercenary personnel. Normally, the destination is specified in the mission contract, and is usually the unit's home base. Under the terms of their repatriation bond, mercenaries become non-combatants once it is activated and are given safe transit to the nearest spaceport. One of the most common uses of a repatriation bond is to transport prisoners of war (POWs) off-world.

Since deep-space mercs have ships of their own and their environment is so hostile, repatriation bonds are very rare for them. Some tickets do include a fuel-and-needed-repairs clause, allowing defeated star mercs to at least leave the system.

Note: Technically, a repatriation bond refers to the money deposited in the bank account, but in mercenary parlance, the term has come to mean the coupon (actually a plasticized card similar to some types of ID card) issued to the individual mercenary. See p. 93 and p. 98 for sample bond cards.

Continued on next page . . .

Determine ORS

First, determine the *operational resolution score* (ORS) for the active force. This is determined by a making a Strategy skill check (Tactics skill can be substituted if the operation involves only platoon-size units or smaller) and adding the amount the roll is made by to all applicable modifiers (see the tables below). If the roll is failed, then the amount it failed by is subtracted from the modifiers.

Then, determine ORS for the opposing force. This is determined as for the active force.

It is quite possible for these results to be negative. If the opposing ORS is negative, the result will be even better for the attacker, and vice versa. A critical Strategy roll has no effect until later on, when the casualties and missing are halved after all modifiers. This applies to both sides. A failed Strategy roll doubles the enemy's ORS (or makes it zero if it is negative).

It is quite possible for both commanders to fail and assist each other's efforts by force of sheer incompetence – leaving the ground troops to slug it out in a "soldier's battle."

ORS Modifiers

Force/Equipment Modifiers

Superiority in numbers	+2 per force level greater (e.g., battalion to platoon is 2 force levels, or +4.)
Superiority in TL	+3 per TL greater. (Use TL of most significant combat force; GM rules on which this is.)
Superiority in cavalry/armor	+4
Superiority in artillery	+2; +4 for defensive tactic.
Superior support (logistics, medical, electronics, etc.)	+1
Superiority in mobility	+2
Superiority in air support	+2
Force has combat environment suits for all infantry	+1
Force has combat armor for all infantry	+2
Force has battledress for all infantry	+4
Other superiority	+1 (GM's choice)

The Game Master should subjectively decide if superiority applies. Having the only artillery piece for 200 miles is a superiority. Having 92 men to the opponent's 90 is not. If the superiority is large (three times as much artillery, for example), double the modifier.

Defensive Modifiers

Hastily dug in and defensive tactics	+1
Prepared positions and defensive tactics	+3
Fortified positions and defensive tactics	+5
Extensive fortifications with artillery emplacements	+8

Definitions of prepared or fortified are for the GM to decide. A quick foxhole is hastily dug in.

Rifle pits, wire and a few land mines are prepared. So is a security unit in a built-up area with clear fields of fire.

Fortified positions require bunkers, obstacles and prepared fields of fire.

"Extensive fortifications" might be a purpose-built fortress or bunker, a base built for defense, or the sea of rubble created by carpet-bombing or extensive urban combat.

Other ORS Modifiers

Unit is tired	-2
Unit is exhausted	-5
Unit has shaky morale	-4
Unit has high morale	+2
Unit is suffering a supply shortage	-1d
Unit is raw	-5
Unit is green	-2
Unit is average	0
Unit is seasoned	+2
Unit is veteran	+4
Unit is elite	+6

Supply, tired and exhausted modifiers are applied by the GM. As with all decisions, the players may claim whatever they feel like, but the GM's decision is final.

Determine OOS

Subtract the opposing force's ORS from that of the active force. The result can be positive, negative or zero. This result is the *operational outcome score* (OOS). Consult the appropriate *Outcome Chart,* below.

There are two possible styles of battle: *assault* and *open battle.* Any combat involving urban combat or a fixed defensive position is an assault unless the commander occupying the position chooses an aggressive tactic. Any force standing on a defensive tactic can, given time, create a prepared position, which requires an assault to clear it but a few foxholes do not constitute a defensive position. A force in open country choosing a defensive tactic may well hastily dig in, but without the time to prepare the position the combat is still an open battle.

Outcome Modifiers

Battle is assault	Attacker adds +1 to each Casualty die.
Unit is Raw	Add +1 to each Casualty die.
	Add +3 to each Missing die.
Unit is Green	Add +1 to each Missing die.
Unit is Seasoned	-1 to each Missing die.
Unit is Veteran	-2 to each Missing die.
Unit is Elite	-1 to each Casualty die, -2 to each Missing die.
In prepared position	-1 to each Casualty die.
In fortified position	-2 to each Casualty die.
Extremely Aggressive:	Enemy takes +2 to each Casualty die if you win.
	Enemy takes +3 to each Missing die if you win.
	You take +2 per Casualty die if attacking positions.
	You take extra +2 per Casualty die if you lose.
Aggressive:	Enemy takes +1 to each Casualty die if you win.
	Enemy takes +2 to each Missing die if you win.
	You take +1 per Casualty die if attacking positions.
	You take extra +1 per Casualty die if you lose.
Standard:	None.
Cautious:	You take -1 to each Casualty die.
	Enemy takes -1 to each Casualty die.
	Enemy takes -1 to each Missing die.
Defensive:	Enemy takes +1 to each Casualty die if you win.
Extreme Defensive:	Enemy takes +2 to each Casualty die if you win.
	Enemy takes +1 to each Casualty die if he wins.
	Half your Missing are converted to casualties.
	You take +2 to each Casualty die if you lose.
Critical success on Strategy roll	Your Casualties and Missing are halved after all modifiers.
Failed Strategy Roll	Double the enemy's ORS.

Legal and Admin (Continued)

Prisoners of War

Mercenaries who surrender or are captured become prisoners of war (POWs), and are non-combatants for the remainder of the conflict unless exchanged for opposing POWs.

A mercenary who becomes a POW loses his salary for the rest of the ticket. Shares are also lost in most cases.

In the situation where a mercenary is given permission to surrender by his commanding officer (for example, a unit might be "thrown down" in a hopeless stand to delay an enemy attack, and ordered to resist for at least three hours before surrendering) shares are retained as the decision to surrender was condoned by the CO. Similarly, when a unit surrenders as a whole under orders from the CO, shares and salaries are not lost by individual mercenaries. Whether or not payment from the patron is due after surrender depends upon the ticket conditions.

This process safeguards the lives of surrendered personnel by making their safe return financially attractive to their captors (you use the repatriation bonds to get the hated mercenaries off your world), and helps ensure that mercenaries will fight rather than surrender unless the situation is hopeless.

Treatment of non-mercenary POWs is regulated by the Imperial rules of war. POWs must be sheltered and fed by their captors until an exchange can be negotiated or the war ends. During this time, POWs are non-combatants, and while they are expected to try to escape, are subject to civil laws while they are in custody. For example, a POW who kills a guard during an escape attempt can be tried for murder. A POW who escapes, steals a vehicle and is recaptured can be tried for grand theft.

POWs can be used for labor, but cannot be employed in any war-related tasks (such as working in a munitions factory or constructing fortifications).

Operating Costs

Equipping a unit is relatively easy. Find a few recruits, run through the bureaucratic hassles of obtaining an arms license, purchase equipment at whatever bulk discount you can negotiate. Some kit is hard to obtain, so it is necessary to pay over the list price or develop contacts in the industry. But furnishing equipment is the easy part.

As any logistics officer will tell you, an army marches on its stomach (though most armies manage to wear out an impressive number of boots while they do it). Keeping the fighting force clothed, fed and supplied is the hard part.

It is not enough to pay the troops and divide up their shares. Other costs must also be met. These include:

Consumables (anything that is used up or wears out: ammo, clothing, food, water and even air)
Transport and Fuel
Quarters
Medical supplies and services
Equipment maintenance and repair (including spare parts)
Administrative costs (and bribes)

There is little gaming fun to be had from working out the precise details of logistics costs (the struggle to get supplies to front-line units under fire is rather more interesting, though). The following rough-and-ready system is designed to provide a reasonable set of costs while preventing the logistics of a mercenary campaign from becoming too much like the players' day job.

Costs are worked out per individual, modified by the type of troop in question. The costs listed below are in addition to salary and shares. By totaling the number of troops of each type in a unit, the referee can quickly determine the monthly cost of a mercenary unit's upkeep. For greater simplicity, the player may use the standard-unit costs listed below.

Standard upkeep for one member of a unit is Cr400 per month, plus salary. This includes routine maintenance and minor repairs to personal equipment. If the trooper is part of a unit using heavy weapons, vehicles or technical equipment then the cost is far higher. The first Cr400 goes to feeding the merc, the rest to equipment maintenance.

Continued on next page . . .

Outcome Charts

OOS	Outcome
21+	Runaway success

Active force loses 1d% casualties and 1d% missing.
Opposing force is enveloped and shattered; heavy equipment may be captured; 8d% casualties are taken and 8d% are missing.

OOS	Outcome
13-20	Total success

Active force takes 1d% casualties and 1d% missing.
Decisive breakthrough causes collapse and rout of defenders; heavy equipment may be captured.
Opposing force takes 6d% casualties and 8d% missing.

OOS	Outcome
8-12	Success

Active force takes 3d% casualties and 2d% missing.
Opposing force is decisively beaten and forced to retreat.
Opposing force takes 4d% casualties and 6d% missing.

OOS	Outcome
4-7	Bloody success

Active force takes 5d% casualties and 2d% missing.
Opposing force is beaten and retreats in good order.
Opposing force takes 4d% casualties and 5d% missing.

OOS	Outcome
-3 to 3	Stalemate

Active force takes 5d% casualties and 3d% missing.
Opposing force is unbeaten and may stand or retreat.
Opposing force takes 4d% casualties and 4d% missing.

OOS	Outcome
-4 to -7	Defeat

Active force takes 6d% casualties and 3d% missing.
Active force is beaten and retreats in good order.
Opposing force takes 4d% casualties and 4d% missing.

OOS	Outcome
-8 to -12	Bloody defeat

Active force takes 7d% casualties and 4d% missing.
Active force is beaten and retreats with shaken morale.
Opposing force takes 3d% casualties and 2d% missing.

OOS	Outcome
-13 to -20	Total defeat

Active force takes 7d% casualties and 6d% missing.
Active force is beaten and retreats with shaken morale.
Opposing force takes 2d% casualties and 1d% missing.

OOS	Outcome
-21 or greater	Fiasco

Active force takes 8d% casualties and 9d% missing.
Active force is shattered by counterattack.
Opposing force takes 1d% casualties and 1d% missing.

Aftermath

Casualties: Of casualties taken, 30% are dead, 30% are seriously wounded and 40% are lightly wounded. Half of all seriously wounded cases return to the unit after 2d weeks; the other half retire. Half the lightly wounded return after 1d days, the rest after a week. Single integer casualty levels will require some thought on the part of the Game Master before they are divided into dead, serious wounds and light wounds.

Equipment: Equipment is lost at the same rate as casualties; 30% of this "loss" is destroyed, 30% is salvageable given 1d days and a workshop, and 40% can be repaired in the field once the battle is over (time taken is the GM's call).

Missing: Half the "missing" figure is lost and straggles back in over the next three days. The other half are taken prisoner. If the enemy does not take captives alive or the force fights to the death, the "prisoner" figure becomes extra casualties.

Atrocities are up to the judgment of the Game Master. This system does not take into account non-battle casualties (those caused by disease from poor sanitation in camp, for example) or desertion.

Example

The active force is Peters' Lift Infantry, a 30-strong Veteran TL10 infantry platoon with two armed G-carriers and a grav 80mm RF howitzer as artillery support. The troops are equipped with gauss rifles and combat armor. They have been fighting hard for several days and are both tired and short of ammunition. Lieutenant Peters has a strategy skill of 16. He receives orders to advance and capture a vital river crossing as spearhead to the main advance. Peters consults his satellite recce photos and chooses a cautious aggression level.

The opposing force is three companies of TL7 local militia (green), with a battery of six 105mm towed howitzers (see p. HT122) in support. They are commanded by a local officer, Strategy skill 10. Hasty preparations have been made. While the rank and file are poor, the NCO class is composed of long-service professionals and is very competent. They have been ordered to hold at all costs, but the GM rules that the militia are not sufficiently motivated, and assigns a defensive aggression level instead.

Both sides total up their factors. The active force has a 3 tech level advantage (+9). The player tries to claim that the grav sleds and G-carriers can act as armor, but has to be satisfied with a +2 bonus for mobility (G-carriers) and the normal bonus (+2) for air support (the G-carriers' armament). Other miscellaneous bonuses are combat armor (+2) and satellite reconnaissance (+1). The lift infantry are Veteran (+4) but tired (-2) and short of supply (GM rolls a die and comes up with a -4). The ORS is +14.

The opposing force has three 150-strong companies. The GM doubles the (+2) bonus for force level to +4. This is the same effect as treating three companies and support as a battalion, which is reasonable. The GM refuses to double the +4 for superiority in defensive artillery, as six TL7 105mm howitzers matched against a single TL10 80mm howitzer is not a huge superiority. The militia can also claim +1 for hasty preparations (shallow foxholes and a river in front of the position) and a miscellaneous +1 for the quality of their NCOs. They also suffer a -2 for their Green status. Their ORS is +4.

Both commanders check their skills: Peters rolls a rather poor 14, success by 2. The plan is sound, but there is no devastating surprise attack or other spectacular success. This gives a net ORS of 14+2 = 16 for the mercenaries.

The defending commander rolls 12, failing by 2. ORS is 4-2 for a total of 2. This is subtracted from the attackers' ORS to give 16-2 = 14. The militia are in trouble. Their commander failed to anticipate the mercenaries' tactics.

A 12 on the outcome chart is *success*, but at a price. An additional +1 would put the attack into the *total success* bracket. Suitable actions by PCs among the attackers might suffice.

The mercenaries suffer a base of 1d% casualties. However, the attack was an assault on a defended position, so +1 per die is taken. The advance was conducted at an aggression level of "caution," giving a -1 which cancels out the modifier. The

Operating Costs (Continued)

Troop Type	Cost (Cr)
Infantry	400
Heavy Infantry (Combat Armor)	+200
Heavy Infantry (Battle Dress)	+1,000
Support Team member (MG Gunner)	600
Light Artillery	2,000
Heavy Artillery	3,500
Light Cavalry	5,000
Heavy Cavalry	8,000
Transport: Ground	1,000
Transport: Grav	2,000
Medical/Engineer/Technical	1,000
Ground Crew	2,000
Aircrew	8,000
Air Defense Crew	3,000
Deep Space Troopers	1,000

The cost listed is per individual carrying out each particular function.

For Deep Space mercs, ship operating costs are separate:

Item	Cost (Cr)
Fuel (refined)	500/t
Fuel (unrefined)	100/t
Life Support	2,000/person
Low Berth Life Support	100/person
Routine Maintenance	0.1% of ship's price

Thus, for a fire team of four infantrymen equipped with combat armor, one of whom is equipped with a support weapon, monthly upkeep cost is Cr2,600 plus salaries. (Three men at (400 base+200 for Combat Armor, one at 600 base+200 for Combat Armor).

Game Masters who want to "wing it" can use the following rough numbers:

Each infantry platoon (30 men) costs Cr25,000/month to maintain in the field.

Each complete infantry company (150 men) costs Cr150,000.

An infantry battalion with supporting arms costs Cr750,000.

All units with their own transport cost double to maintain, or four times as much if grav transport.

Light armor, battledress, technical, artillery and aerospace units cost five times as much to maintain.

Heavy armor costs 12 times as much.

Using the Compendium II Mass-Combat System

The normal assignment resolution system can be used to determine the outcome of an operation, or common sense and a feeling for the requirements of the plot can supply the overall result of an operation. If the GM has access to the *GURPS Compendium II* mass-combat system, this can be used to determine the effects of combat upon PC mercenaries.

For almost any force, the "Modern Armies" model can be used (see p. CII113), though some special modifiers should be implemented.

Armor

All armor is TL9+	+1/2 DR

Mobility

Grav vehicles	+ 2×TL
Grav belts	+TL
Battledress	+2

Ranged Weapons

Pistols or short firearms	+3
Rifles or similar	+ TL
Plasma or Fusion Gun	+(TL+2)

Combat Vehicles

Grav Sled	+50
Light Grav Tank	+75
Medium Grav Tank	+150
Heavy Grav Tank	+250

Special Weapons

Support Weapons	+20
High-Tech Artillery (TL9+)	+150
Meson Accelerator	+300

The *Compendium II* system can be used to determine the outcome of the players' small corner of a larger action, or to stand alone.

casualty roll is a 6, giving 6 = 6% casualties. The mercs started with 30 personnel, so actual loss is 1.8 (rounded to 2) casualties. Of these, the GM decides that one is seriously wounded (out of action for seven weeks) and one has a light wound that keeps him out of the line for two days. The force also suffers 1d% missing. This is modified by -2 per die for Veteran status. The roll is a six, which translates to 4% missing, or 1.2 (rounded to one) personnel. Despite the high competence of the unit, one soldier managed to get cut off and finds his way back to the unit later in the day. After a day in their new positions, the platoon is back to 28 effectives but still has not been resupplied. And there's a counterattack on the way . . .

The militia fared rather less well. The mercenaries' success cost the militia 6d% casualties, modified by -1 for the mercenaries' cautious advance. The militia were not sufficiently well dug in to claim a casualty reduction. Casualty roll is (5, 4, 4, 4, 2, 3) at -1 per die (4, 3, 3, 4, 1, 2) giving 17% casualties. For three 150-strong companies this is 76.5 (round to 77) casualties. Of these, 23 are dead, 23 are seriously wounded and 31 are lightly wounded. Lost equipment amounted to 17% – the GM decides one howitzer was destroyed by counterbattery fire. Missing figures are far worse. Despite the lack of a pursuit (the cautious, tired mercs just dug in to keep what they'd taken) the missing figure is 8d%, at +1 per die for Green unit and -1 for a cautious enemy, This gives a straight 8d roll (5, 4, 3, 2, 2, 6, 2, 4) for a total of 28% missing. This is 126 personnel. Of these, half (63) are scattered in the retreat and may be recovered at the end of the day. The rest are prisoners of Peters' Lift Infantry.

The GM should treat this system as open to roleplaying influence. Characters need not be simply swept along in the action. They can influence it by their actions and skills. Appropriate modifiers can be applied for characters' actions, or a defeat may become a stalemate if (for example) the PCs' squad manages to hold out in a desperate rearguard.

CHAPTER THREE

Instruments of Policy

INTRODUCTION

Even in the more peaceable societies, the need for armed defense is generally recognized. What is the point of developing an infrastructure, education system and a fine standard of living if the barbarians tear it down or take it over next week?

Most worlds, nations and states maintain a body of armed personnel for local defense, settlement of disputes and generally "just in case." In situations as varied as civil unrest, natural disaster, fire or flood, trained personnel, loyal to the government and armed to prevent interference with their tasks, are a valuable "crisis resource."

Troops can keep order on the streets or protect the aid convoys from looters or bandits. They can be sent in to rescue hostages or search for earthquake victims. They can prop up a failing regime or bring it down. They can keep the populace in line when they start rioting over last week's interplanetary grapple-ball defeat or they can be used to invade a neighboring state, subjugate the population and strip their resources.

USING THIS CHAPTER

This chapter allows the referee to determine what armament will be available to a mercenary unit or (more importantly) its opposition. Entries are by tech level, allowing a suitable level of armament to be selected at a glance.

The bulk of a state's armed forces are equipped at the nation's (or world's) tech level, as locally produced weaponry is the cheapest option and can be effectively maintained without recourse to imported spares. Crude home-made copies of weapons from the next TL may be issued to some units.

Older, lower-tech gear might be in use by militia or civilian paramilitary use. Such gear is generally left over from some war or other. Even though the rifle rattles when you pick it up, why replace it if it still works acceptably?

As a rule of thumb, elite units serving a nation will be equipped with the very best their TL can provide, and will probably have a considerable amount of higher-technology gear brought in through offworld trade. Maintenance of such high-tech equipment is very difficult, so these weapons are limited to very small quantities and reserved for "special occasions."

The bulk of regular troops will be equipped with reliable standard weaponry from the nation's TL, or brought in if a suitably dependable and cheap supplier can be found. These will be basic weapons of no great sophistication, easy for the troops to maintain and cheap enough to mass-issue. The actual weapon system issued will depend on what the troops are expected to have to do – urban combat, security, desert or arctic warfare – and local preferences for individual excellence, harsh condition tolerance or cost will influence the weapon choice. This locally produced hardware will often be augmented by rugged and "idiot-proof" imports that are plugged into existing systems to create hybrids of variable effectiveness.

For militia, civilian police, reserves and training units, weapons might be of a TL one lower than the nation's listed value. This depends on circumstances. If modern firearms are available, the local police will not be using flintlocks, but a group of backwoodsmen-turned-rebels might. Reservists tend to be issued leftovers, but most governments recognize that while obsolescent equipment is cheap, truly obsolete gear is just a waste of maintenance costs. Large states might still maintain reserves

Unit Sizes

The actual number of soldiers in a unit varies with a number of factors, and all of these are rules of thumb rather than strict guidelines. The larger the organization, the greater proportion of the numbers below that are logistical and administrative troops.

When the text mentions a "company-sized unit" or "several fire teams," refer to this list if you are not sure how many soldiers this means

Fire Team, Team, Binom: 2-4 (4 is most common).
Squad: 8-12.
Section: 20-40.
Platoon: 30-60.
Company: 180-240.
Battalion: 400-600.
Regiment: 1,800+.
Brigade: 2,400+.
Division: 10,000+.

Glossary: A

Abatis: A makeshift barricade of thorny plants, bushes or sharpened tree branches, used to defend a position where more sophisticated defenses are unavailable.

ACR: Advanced Combat Rifle, a sophisticated rifle with built-in electronic sights and links to electronic systems such as heads-up displays.

ACV: Air Cushion Vehicle. A hovercraft or ground effect vehicle.

AD: The abbreviation for Air Defense.

Airborne Infantry: Light infantry intended to be sent to the battle zone in fixed-wing aircraft, arriving by parachute.

Airmobile Infantry: Light infantry force intended to be moved by rotary-wing aircraft, often with helicopter gunships in support. Sometimes referred to as "air cavalry."

APC: Armored Personnel Carrier. APCs may be wheeled, grav-powered, hovercraft (ACV) or tracked. APCs are "battle-taxis," carrying infantry to the combat zone where they will dismount to fight, and usually carry a light support weapon such as a machine gun or autocannon. The same vehicle chassis is often adapted as a weapons carrier, field ambulance and command post or other vehicle.

Armor: (i) Heavy armored fighting vehicles (AFVs), or tanks. (ii) Military formations using heavy AFVs as their main combat capability.

Armored Infantry: Combined-arms force consisting primarily of infantry but including a sizable tank contingent.

Continued on next page . . .

of obsolete weaponry for special purposes, such as to arm sympathetic insurgent forces in an enemy state at minimum expense (during WWII on Terra, the United States armed Burmese guerrillas with weapons almost 75 years out of date).

Unless a world is interdicted or otherwise cut off from trade, quantities of higher-tech weapons will find their way into the hands of the local soldiery. Small arms take up little room in a starship's cargo bay. Such equipment will not be vastly higher-tech than local gear, being mainly TL6 or TL7 rifles and light support weapons.

Some imported items are so useful that they become "must haves" on the ruler's list of offworld trade needs. These items must be rugged enough to survive without much high-technology maintenance and cheap enough to be affordable. Small arms and cheap radio communicators are at the top of this list, usually followed by light support weapons and portable air defense weapons.

The referee needing to quickly generate armed opposition for the players can safely assume that the TL of the world is the TL of the troops, with elite unit equipped one TL higher and militia one lower. If more preparation time is available, the referee has the option of tailoring equipment to the sort of opposition forces he is creating.

Example: Planet Ecks has a TL of 7 (circa 1990). The planet is maintained by a president-for-life who maintains a standing army of TL7 troops, equipped with gear from the low end of the tech level (1950s equivalent). Their rifles are TL7, but their supporting electronics are poor – TL6. The palace guard units have been equipped with TL9 ACRs and body armor bought at great cost offworld. Anti-armor and anti-aircraft gear is TL8.

The cost of maintaining this force, hiring offworld techs to keep the palace defense grid active and so on, has driven taxes up. Two factions are currently waging a guerrilla war against the president. One is a renegade faction of troops, armed with TL7 gear in poor repair and TL6 weapons seized from reserve armories. The other is a group of hillmen who have long opposed the president's regime. Their TL is only 5. Their warriors fight with home-made muskets unless they can capture more modern gear. Such higher-tech equipment is impossible to maintain and ammunition is hard to come by, so the guerrillas' TL remains 5, with a scattering of TL6-7 weapons.

IMPORT POLICY

Most worlds import at least a small quantity of gear, generally of a TL or two higher than can be locally produced. For the vast majority of worlds, the same list of imports appears – small arms, communications equipment, sensors, anti-armor weapons, anti-aircraft weapons – but each state has its own import policy. Some states seem to just buy up whatever is cheap at the time, then try to integrate it with existing systems. This policy usually fails, as a TL7 world cannot for long maintain a force of TL10 interceptors, though for a time the local forces will have gained a powerful asset. Other states buy specific complete systems – for example, a particular armored vehicle or ground-to-air missile system – to equip local troops, while still others just purchase components and build hybrid systems with local technology. It is in these states that ironclads festooned with jamming aerials and missile launchers, or crude jeeps mounting plasma guns, can be encountered.

It is not really feasible to equip an entire state's armed forces with imported weapons. Nor is it desirable, as an interruption in the supply of spares and ammunition would render the weapons useless. This is doubly

true in the case of complex systems. The technical expertise to properly maintain them may be beyond local capabilities (mercenary cadre units are often employed to instill this level of competence). The imported systems are chosen to address a specific need or to enhance the capabilities of a particular unit or branch. Thus, imported gauss sniper weapons might be issued by a TL8 world, or combat armor purchased for the assault units.

One policy is repeated again and again: every government seeks to import enough technology to equip a small guard force to protect the government as well as possible. At TL3 this might mean buying 200 revolvers and a couple of crates of ammunition for the palace guard. At TL8 it might mean an aerospace tracking station and missile launchers to defend the capitol buildings, plus sufficient anti-armor weapons to prevent a small grav cavalry unit from launching a decapitation strike on the government.

One thing, however, always remains constant: nobody is ever satisfied with what they have. However good a nation's weaponry may be, there is always an edge to be gained from importing something. And if there is an edge to be gained, someone will want it.

Individuals within a world's armed forces may well have access to high-tech gear imported for their personal use. Such equipment varies greatly, but usually consists of sidearms and body armor for personal defense, or special equipment such as laser rangefinders or night-vision goggles for specialist troops.

The tools of death and destruction (or defense and deterrence) are, as they have always been, big business.

TECH LEVELS AND TACTICS

As a general principle, the increasing range and lethality of high-tech weapons, combined with advances in communications and mobility, cause soldiers on the battlefield to become increasingly dispersed for survival (partially mitigating the effects of those weapons in the process). Massed formations give way to skirmish lines and eventually to scattered soldiers (or small groups) fighting individually but cooperating to achieve a decisive result.

As the value of defensive armor (particularly for the individual soldier) lags behind the penetrating power and rate of fire of offensive weapons, armies will resort to field fortifications and terrain for protection and concealment. When materials technology or mobility redresses this balance, soldiers will again fight in the open. This is also the effect of a great disparity in sensor technology: battles will be sought on terrain and in circumstances that at least partially negate the advantages of the high-tech force.

Dispersion will also occur in *time,* as outgunned forces will use hit-and-run tactics to offer battle only on favorable terms. These effects will be felt based on the *highest* tech level prevalent in a theater; other forces will adapt their tactics to suit.

Fighting dispersed (and perhaps dug in) places a tremendous burden on the individual soldier, and greatly increases both the level of initiative he is required to exercise and the amount of training he will need to develop it. This usually precludes truly "citizen" irregular forces from being effective in the field, although warrior peoples and cultures may not have problems with this style of warfare, and defensive "home guards" can still free regular forces for offensive operations. Mass armies are still possible, using standardized reaction drills at lower levels for most common situations and orders, and can be quite effective. In most cases, the intent is to substitute the *massed effects* of fire for massed (and highly vulnerable) concentrations of troops.

The usual mercenary ticket involves relatively small, high-tech mercenary forces arrayed against larger, less-well equipped indigenous troops or insurgents (*indigs* in merc slang). In these situations, the advantages to the mercenaries are fairly obvious, those of the indigs less so. First and foremost is the "home field" advantage: the indigs not only can be expected to know their own territory better than any outsider could, but also can blend into the population (whether they enjoy

Glossary: A (Continued)

Army: (i) Ground Force Command, the "dirty feet" part of a world's armed forces. (ii) The Imperial Army, the force maintained for planetary combat of all types and including aircraft, infantry, nautical units, armor, artillery and support personnel.

Artillery: Weapons used for direct and indirect fire support of other troop types. Artillery weapons are characterized by long range and heavy firepower, but relatively poor mobility and close-combat capability. Artillery weapons include mortars, howitzers, tube artillery (traditional guns), guided and unguided missiles, and rockets and meson accelerators.

Arty: Slang term for artillery.

Assault Infantry: Troops equipped and trained for high-intensity close-quarters assaults on enemy positions. Assault troops are usually given weapons of higher firepower than conventional infantry.

Assault Pioneer, Assault Engineer: Infantry specialization. The assault pioneer/engineer clears the path for an assault, removing wire, mines and other obstacles, often using demolitions charges, and often under fire. In some units, the title "engineer" is reserved for officers (enlisted men in such units are called "sappers").

Assault Rifle: A lightweight rifle, capable of burst or full-auto fire. The forerunner of the ACR.

Autocannon: A rapid-fire cannon normally used as an infantry support weapon or as armament on aircraft. Autocannon are typically between 0.6" and 1.6" (15mm to 40mm) in caliber, and may fire AP, HE or HEAT rounds.

Autorifle: Shorthand term for automatic rifle, a mid-tech rifle capable of fully automatic fire.

Glossary: B

Bad War: Mercs' slang for a conflict where the Imperial rules of war (see pp. 20-24) do not apply.

Bastion: (Archaic) A four-sided fortification. (Modern) A heavily defended area. Attempts by enemy units to enter are aggressively countered.

Battledress: Personal powered armor giving enhanced strength and excellent protection to the wearer.

Bayonet: A blade or impaling weapon designed to be attached to a firearm. Various designs exist in different cultures – spike, knife or sword being the most common. Intended to give the infantryman a close-in weapon for assault and hand-to-hand combat.

Book, Boogie, Bug out: Flee, especially in the face of overwhelming force.

Breastwork: Earth parapet for infantry fortification.

Bunker Commando: A soldier whose boasts of his exploits exceed their reality.

Buy the Farm: To die.

Glossary: C

Carbine: Short, light rifle, generally used by vehicle crews.

Cavalry: (Archaic) Troops fighting from animal-back. (Modern) Light armored or airmobile units.

Cheval-de-frise: A barricade made of spikes sticking out of planks or logs. A crude field substitute for barriers of barbed wire or razortape.

COACC: Close-Orbit and Aerospace Control Command. Part of the triad that makes up planetary armed forces (the *army*). COACC forces are the first line of defense for a world, operating SDBs, orbital gunships, aerospace interceptors, air superiority fighters, bombers, and strike, recon and logistics aircraft.

Column: (i) A force on the move; e.g., "armored column." (ii) A designation sometimes used by irregular forces or guerrillas, "the East-Mainland column."

Combat Armor: Unpowered heavy personal armor, pressurized to allow use in vacuum.

Combined Arms: The coordinated use of different troop types (e.g., artillery, AFVs and infantry) to increase the effectiveness of all.

Commandos: (i) Elite units of the Imperial Marines or Zhodani. (ii) Any unit trained for small-unit raiding operations.

Crater: To die, especially in a spectacular manner. Used by drop troops (see *Meteoric Assault,* p. 7).

Crusher: Nickname for provost marshal or military police soldiers.

its support or not) – something offworld mercenaries will almost never be able to manage. This can be used to harass and impede the mercenaries through terrorism and guerrilla operations, by depriving them of any rest or safe haven. Second is the advantage of numbers: if 100 million natives are facing 100 mercenaries (and their native patrons, no doubt), it may well be worth 100 or 1,000 native lives to take out just one mercenary. Finally, although the mercenaries may have a variety of weak points to exploit among their opponents (only some of which will work), the weakest link on their side will almost always be their relationship with their employers. Goading the mercenaries into a few well-publicized atrocities, forcing them to disobey orders to achieve results, sowing doubts about their motives in the minds of their patrons – all these may cut a ticket short and give the indigs their victory.

Other low-tech, high-touch operations (unconventional warfare, psychological operations, propaganda, intelligence and information warfare, politics and economics) can be used equally well on both sides of a conflict. Provoking Imperial intervention is the one thing that will probably be avoided by both sides, because the results are highly variable depending on the personality of the Imperial commander or diplomat in question.

WEAPONS SYSTEMS BY TL

EARLY TL5

Local industry produces reasonable black-powder weapons, but most states choose to import cheap mass-produced firearms from TL6-7 worlds. Generally, TL5 economies are not usually able to purchase large quantities of weapons and cannot maintain complex systems.

Infantry

At early TL5 the main locally produced infantry weapon is a smoothbore flintlock musket (e.g., Brown Bess, p. B209), backed up by a socket bayonet designed to allow the musket to be fired with the bayonet fitted. The musket is sturdy enough to be used at close quarters as a club or with the bayonet as a short pike.

Offworld trade will allow ground troops to be armed with bolt-action or semi-automatic weapons and hand grenades (see p. B209). Body armor is very rare due to cost.

Infantry Support

Very light smoothbore cannon (e.g., galloper gun 3-pounder, p. HT122) are sometimes deployed at the battalion level for close support.

Offworld weapons systems include general-purpose machine guns and infantry mortars (see pp. HT117-121).

Cavalry

TL5 forces do not have access to large numbers of vehicles, and cannot properly maintain those they buy. Cavalry mounted on riding animals is common, equipped with melee weapons such as the saber and the lance (see p. B206). These may be augmented by imported firearms, either pistols and SMGs if the cavalry are to continue in their traditional role, or carbines and rifles if the cavalry are to be used as mobile mounted infantry (see pp. B208-209).

Artillery

Local field artillery consists of smoothbore cannon with a maximum range of a few hundred yards. Crude mortars are available. Rocket batteries are occasionally seen, being reasonably effective in bombardment of large static targets, but very unreliable and occasionally dangerous to the firer (see pp. HT120-122).

Light artillery pieces are often imported, usually crude and rugged light artillery and anti-aircraft guns. Most are fitted to an animal-drawn carriage.

Transport

Infantry marches or travels by water in sailing vessels, boats or canal barges. The local beasts of burden are used to draw wagons, artillery, etc.

A few imported vehicles are used, but fuel availability is a problem unless they are designed to run on alcohol, hydrogen or fusion (in which case maintenance and spare parts will be the bottleneck).

Nautical

Wooden sailing ships with very large cannon are available (see pp. HT 120-122). They can bombard positions very close to the coast, but mainly affect the land action by transport and blockade operations.

Communications

Visual methods of communication such as heliograph or flag signals supplement runners or gallopers. Animals such as trained dogs or carrier pigeons may be used if a suitable species is available and the environment allows their use.

Simple radio equipment (and a large supply of batteries) is among the first imports acquired by low-tech states, often coming before artillery on the "wish list."

Mode of Combat

Local troops will at least be familiar with the capabilities of modern firearms, though the occasional massed bayonet attack or cavalry charge will be attempted. More common will be skirmishing tactics using whatever weapons have been issued (the mercenary soldier should remember that even a musket is deadly in the hands of a skilled sharpshooter), with mounted troops acting as mobile reserves for pursuit and exploitation. Strongpoints will be defended by AA guns and artillery, though the latter will be very slow-moving and only useful in defense.

LATE TL5

The invention of percussion-cap weapons in the middle of the TL5 period and, later, self-contained cartridges makes it possible for local troops to present a credible threat to mercenaries without needing to purchase offworld arms (for examples, see p. HT113).

The enhanced capabilities of higher-technology weapons still make them attractive, however. Greater industrial efficiency enables the late TL5 state to afford better weaponry, or more of it. States are also able to produce copies of imported or captured weapons.

Glossary: D

Dirtsider: Slang term for local planetary forces, from "dirtside" meaning "on a world's surface."

Dragoon: (Archaic) Medium or heavy cavalry, or troops capable of fighting on foot or mounted. (Modern) A term used in unit titles for some medium-heavy armored formations.

Drop Troops: Infantry whose usual means of reaching the combat zone is to be dropped from orbit in a meteoric assault using drop capsules.

Drop Zone/DZ: The area where paratroops or drop troops are to land.

DS: Direct support artillery, a unit or units of artillery assigned to give priority to supporting fire for a specific unit.

Duck Hunter: Slang term for air-defense gunner.

Dustoff: A quick takeoff, sometimes very soon after landing.

Glossary: E

ECCM: Electronic Counter-Counter-measures. Attempts to defeat ECM by similar means.

ECM: Electronic Countermeasures. Jamming or misdirection of enemy weapons and sensors by electromagnetic emissions.

Electronic Warfare: See *EW.*

ELINT: ELectronic INTelligence. Information gained through study of electromagnetic emissions from enemy units, other than communications.

EW: Electronic Warfare, the interruption of enemy communications and sensors, and other manipulations of the electromagnetic spectrum to a military end.

Expense magazine: A small ammunition store placed near an artillery battery, also known as a ready magazine.

Glossary: F

Fascine: A long, narrow bundle (originally of sticks or similar material) for use in filling in enemy trenches or ditches to allow personnel and vehicles to cross. Modern versions use advanced materials, and may make use of expanded foams and the like.

Firing Slit, Firing Port: A hole in a bunker or vehicle wall to allow weapons use from inside. Many MICVs have firing ports for their infantry complement.

Foot: Archaic name for infantry, still occasionally used in unit titles.

Freecorps: Variations of this word (Freikorps, Free Corps) are used as a genteel expression referring to mercenary units.

Glossary: G

Glacis: (Archaic) Artificial slope in front of a fortification. (Modern) Sloped armor plate in the front of an armored vehicle (sometimes called a glacis plate).

Good War: Mercs' slang for a conflict where the Imperial rules of war (see pp. 20-24) apply.

Grav Sled: A small, light or unarmored grav vehicle used as a weapons carrier, recce vehicle or transport.

Grav-Borne Infantry: See *Lift Infantry.*

Grenadier: Archaic term for elite infantry. Occasionally used in unit titles.

Ground Pounder, Grunt: Slang terms for soldiers who normally fight on a planetary surface.

GS: General Support Artillery, artillery whose fire support is parceled out to requesting units on an "as needed" basis.

Guerrilla: Literally "little war." Commonly used to mean an irregular fighter carrying on a patriotic or other "just cause" war.

These copies are sometimes constructed under license or just given a new name. They are usually inferior to higher-tech models, but have the advantage of being cheap.

Infantry

At late TL5, local production is capable of arming infantrymen with a single-shot rifle (e.g., Springfield Trapdoor .45-70, p. HT113), accurate to several hundred yards. The revolver (e.g., Colt .36 "Navy," p. HT109) is a popular sidearm for officers. Snipers use effective but clumsy telescopically sighted rifles, often of very large caliber (e.g., Sharps "Big Fifty," p. HT113).

Imported equipment is generally TL6-7, being mainly semi-auto rifles and SMGs (see pp. B208-209) to provide troops with a measure of automatic fire capability. Robust and simple weapons such as rocket-propelled grenade launchers are popular.

Infantry Support

Rapid-fire weapons such as the Gatling gun or Nordenfeldt .45-70 (p. HT117) are introduced. These are clumsy and unreliable, but deadly under the right circumstances. Imports are so much more mobile and effective that locally produced weapons are only found defending fixed positions if offworld weapons are available in quantity.

Cavalry

Cavalry acts as mounted infantry, dismounting to fight with carbines (e.g., Springfield Trapdoor carbine, p. HT113). Imported vehicles are used to supplement the riding animal, but fuel and maintenance remain problems.

Artillery

Imported artillery pieces of no great sophistication can be properly maintained by local troops. Light tube artillery (howitzers and field guns) is mostly drawn by animals (for examples, see p. HT122).

Transport

Steam ships and the steam railroad make rapid strategic transfer of troops possible. Armed and armored trains are employed on some worlds (although large railway guns do not become common until TL6). Very early steam tractors see use for engineering and artillery transport use. Tactical movement is on foot.

Nautical

Steam vessels begin to carry armor plate and heavy rifled guns. Armored riverine gunboats support infantry operations.

Communications

The telegraph allows the transmission of information very quickly over great distances, and is eventually replaced by the telephone (which is easier to use). Imported radios are vital to effective battlefield communications.

Mode of Combat

Late TL5 troopers fight with relatively crude weapons, but they fight like modern soldiers. Greater familiarity with the capability of firearms has taught the TL5 infantryman that his best friend is his spade or entrenching tool.

Troops are very skilled at using skirmishing tactics, cover and prepared fields of fire. Tactical mobility is not great, though strategically troops are fairly mobile.

EARLY TL6

Local industry is capable of building armored vehicles. Imports can be properly maintained, and local vehicles are often used as weapons carriers to mount imported systems. Local small arms manufacture is adequate for most purposes, so imports tend to be specialist systems and support equipment.

Infantry

Local industry can equip troops with a bolt-action rifle (e.g., M1903 Springfield .30-06, p. B209), a bayonet and crude fragmentation grenades, plus an entrenching tool, gas mask and a steel helmet for protection against shell fragments. Locally made automatic pistols, revolvers, shotguns and crude SMGs are also issued, along with excellent quality sniper weapons to specialists (for examples, see p. HT 77-78).

Imported equipment includes light body armor, NBC protection and light anti-armor weapons such as fire-and-forget missile launchers.

Infantry Support

Infantry are supported at the company level by light mortars (actually early grenade launchers) capable of firing HE and smoke rounds (e.g., Stokes 2 Inch, p. HT120). Locally built machine-guns are very bulky and generally found in defensive positions (the size differences between early TL6 and later machine-guns aren't that great; beyond this point the tradeoff is portability vs. range and striking power). Imported LMGs see heavy use.

Cavalry

Cavalry units operate light scout cars armed with machine-guns in the reconnaissance role. Crude and unreliable tanks can be locally manufactured, but are uncommon. Far more common is a hybrid vehicle built on the chassis of a local scout car or jeep equivalent, mounting an imported machine-gun, recoilless rifle or missile launcher. Such weapons carriers are about as effective as locally made tanks, and more reliable.

Animal-mounted cavalry remains in existence in some places, but is vanishing.

Artillery

Local artillery is fairly good, with rocket and tube systems delivering HE, smoke and gas shells, or armor-piercing shells in the direct fire role (see pp. HT122). Vehicles are available to artillery systems.

Some states import a vehicle chassis or engine to mount or tow locally built guns, while others augment the effectiveness of their own weapons systems with TL7-8 radar and communications equipment.

Transport

The railway, steamship and forced march remain the means by which infantry moves. Artillery tractors using internal-combustion engines become available, but animal power remains common, due to the expense of machines. Large, very long tube railway guns are also available (e.g., Paris Gun, p. HT122).

Nautical

Steel battleships mounting huge guns (see pp. VE194-195) form the backbone of the battle line, and incidentally bombard inland targets. Early submarine and the torpedo craft remain in use, often by nations without a powerful battle line.

Aviation

Crude piston-engined aircraft are used for reconnaissance and artillery observation, while heavier fixed-wing craft and

Glossary: I

Imperial Rules of War: An unwritten set of general rules regulating minor conflicts within (and sometimes outside of) the Imperium. See pp.20-24.

Infantry: Originally foot soldiers, the modern meaning has become blurred by the extensive use of vehicles. Infantry are broadly defined as soldiers who fight on foot. They may be subdivided into groups such as drop troops, lift infantry and armored infantry.

Irregulars: Irregular forces are not formally raised or trained by a state. They are not part of the standing army, serving in time of need before returning to their homes. Examples include patriotic partisans turning out with any weapons they can lay their hands on.

Jäger: An archaic reference to skirmishers, light troops or sharpshooters, occasionally used in unit titles.

Glossary: L

Legion: A small combined-arms unit; e.g., a predominantly infantry battalion with organic artillery and armor, occasionally used in unit titles.

Lift Infantry: Infantry force relying on grav transport.

Loop, Loophole: A hole made in a wall or other obstruction to allow personnel to see or fire through it.

LZ: Landing Zone. Area where airborne troops are to disembark, primarily used in connection with helicopter or grav troop carriers.

lighter-than-air craft are used for bombing raids. Attempts to drive off the scouts and the bombers lead to the creation of the armed fighter plane.

States that import higher-tech aircraft usually find that they are difficult to maintain and deteriorate rapidly. They do, however, provide a significant advantage while they last.

Communications

Radio is available, though sets are bulky and somewhat unreliable. Imports are used to give leaders better tactical communications.

Mode of Combat

Greater reliance on home-built weapons systems means that more troops can be equipped to a level where they present a threat to the modern mercenary unit. Local systems are adequately deadly, though mobility is not great and reconnaissance is a weakness. With the availability of military vehicles, local forces are better able to attempt maneuver warfare, and are less surprised by the mobility of opposing forces.

LATE TL6

States of late TL6 and higher tend to produce almost all of their own weapons. Imported systems are usually specific to a perceived need – an air-defense missile, a light armored vehicle or a communication system – but are sometimes just whatever the last arms dealer to visit had on special.

Infantry

Self-loading rifles (e.g, M1 Garand, p. B208) have replaced the bolt-action rifle, and light automatic weapons (e.g., MG34, p. HT119) are integrated into the infantry squad. The SMG (e.g., MP40, p. B209) is issued to assault troops and vehicle crews. Rifle grenades with various warheads including chemical and anti-armor rounds become available (see p. HT78).

Most infantry units have some means of anti-armor warfare and air defense. These are the most commonly imported systems.

Infantry Support

Light machine-guns and infantry anti-tank weapons (e.g., Bazooka, p. HT122) are issued at the platoon level. Flamethrowers are used in the assault role (they become available at TL3, but only by TL6 are they reliable enough for man portable use, see p. HT121). The light mortar (see p. HT120) and heavy machine-gun (see pp. HT119-120) are the main platoon and company-level support weapons.

Cavalry/Armor

In addition to increasingly effective armored cars, local industry turns out large numbers of track-laying tanks. Light tanks with primarily infantry-support weapons back up advances, while medium and heavy tanks, with heavy armor and large-caliber guns, achieve the shock effect that was once the preserve of heavy cavalry.

Armored vehicles also include specialist engineering vehicles, bridgelayer tanks, flame-thrower tanks and armored personnel carriers. Tank destroyers, a cheaper turretless or thin-skinned alternative to the tank, are deployed by some nations.

Artillery

Traditional towed artillery is supplemented by various anti-tank guns, truck-mounted rocket artillery, and early self-propelled guns (see pp. VE193-194 and HT122). Self-propelled artillery includes anti-tank guns, light autocannon in the air-defense role and armored assault guns for infantry support. Air defense comprises searchlight batteries and heavy AAA emplacements, with imported missile systems defending key installations.

Transport

Some infantry still marches, and some artillery is horse-drawn, but wheeled trucks and other vehicles are used to increase the tactical mobility of infantry forces. Armored personnel carriers mounting light machine-guns are available for elite mechanized forces. Animal transport is almost unknown.

Nautical

The submarine and the aircraft carrier dominate sea combat, with battleships relegated to the role of shore bombardment and air-defense ships. Aircraft also launch strikes against inland positions and naval infantry formations use specialized craft to make beach assaults.

Aviation

Piston-engined aircraft are at their pinnacle of development and are deployed in large numbers. While primitive jets and helicopters can be constructed, it is generally more effective to import a few craft than go through lengthy development processes.

Heavy bombers armed with defensive machine-guns can rain poorly aimed high-explosive and incendiary bombs on ground targets, but are no threat to any unit with more than a token air defense. The difficulty is in hitting an individual unit without hitting your own troops. Most bombers at this TL fly too high to be effectively engaged by ground-based AAA. Higher-TL guided missiles are another story, and might force low-level, high-speed bombing techniques.

Light tactical strike and reconnaissance aircraft assist the ground offensives, often acting as highly mobile artillery for mechanized and amphibious forces, while piston-engined air-superiority fighters battle for air supremacy. Transport aircraft deliver supplies and reinforcements to the front and drop paratroops to make airborne assaults.

Communications

Radio equipment is relatively commonplace, and electronic warfare with it. Early radar is used for fighter control and naval gun-laying.

Missiles and Special Weapons

Unguided missiles and radio-controlled glide bombs are available. These are more nuisance than real threat, but with crude nuclear explosives and biological and chemical weapons available, these systems can be used to deliver weapons of mass destruction.

Mode of Warfare

Mobility is the key, with armored assaults supported by tactical air strikes achieving deep penetration of enemy positions. Armored battles in the open, heavy aerial bombardment of industrial and population centers, and bitter urban fighting are all prevalent at TL6, as at later TLs.

Glossary: M

Marines: Originally infantry carried aboard naval vessels, the Imperial Marines are a modern assault and security force capable of fighting in any environment.

Maritime Force Command: The arm of planetary forces dealing with surface and sub-sea combat. Also known as the "wet navy." MFC is part of the *Army.*

Maroons: Nickname for the ceremonial version of Imperial Marine battledress, primarily distinguished by its deep maroon color (the only form of battledress to which Marines are allowed to attach medals and awards).

MBT: Main Battle Tank. These are heavily armed vehicles carrying a large weapon and intended for use in front-line combat.

Meat in a Can: Slang term for tank crewmembers.

Mechanized Infantry: A combined-arms force consisting primarily of infantry traveling in APCs or similar lightly armored vehicles. Mechanized infantry units generally include a number of tanks for support.

Medevac: Medical evacuation vehicle, usually capable of flight.

Mercenaries, Mercs: Troops who are fighting other than for their "home" government. This term technically includes regular forces such as the Terran Gurkhas in British service, but specifically excludes irregular partisans.

Meteoric Assault: Deployment of troops from orbit in one-use capsules.

MICV, MIFV: Mechanized Infantry Combat Vehicle, also sometimes called Mechanized Infantry Fighting Vehicle. These are APCs with firing slits to enable the infantry they carry to fire from inside the vehicle.

MICV: Mechanized Infantry Combat Vehicle. The next step from the APC is the MICV, which mounts missiles or light guns to support its infantry squad, who may be able to fight from the vehicle, or may dismount. MICVs are often mistaken for tanks by non-military personnel. They lack the armor of MBTs, although they may have similar anti-tank armament.

Mike Force: Slang term for a reserve or relief unit standing by for immediate deployment, usually by airborne means.

MLRS: Multiple-Launch Rocket System. A system designed to fire volleys of rockets simultaneously or in rapid succession, normally mounted on a vehicle

Glossary: N

Naval Infantry: Loose term for the armed force of sailors any Imperial Navy vessel can deploy as infantry. Depending upon the navy, these can be very good or very poor soldiers.

NBC: Nuclear, Biological, Chemical.

OPFORS: OPposing FORceS. The enemy, sometimes used to refer to troops acting as the "other side" in training.

Ortillery: A contraction of ORbital arTILLERY. Meson guns, missiles, kinetic-energy projectiles and the occasional rock used to support ground offensives by bombarding enemy positions.

Glossary: P

Parapet: The lip of a fortification or earthwork, intended to protect personnel from direct-fire weapons.

Platoon: (i) Small unit of infantrymen, consisting of several sections, squads or fire teams, and (occasionally) their transport vehicles. (ii) A tank platoon consists of 3-7 heavy armored vehicles and their crew.

Pongo: Local soldiers, usually non-mercenary.

PROFORS: PROtected FORceS. Troops equipped and trained for hostile-environment combat such as in vacuum or corrosive atmosphere.

Provo: Slang term for a member of a provost marshal or military police unit, plural is provos.

Glossary: R

Rangers: Originally "light troops," current usage is light infantry of high quality capable of undertaking special operations.

Recon, Recce: Both synonyms for reconnaissance.

Redleg: Slang term for an artilleryman.

Redoubt: Originally a detached fortification. Now a strongpoint built in the field.

Regulars: The standing professional army of a state – paid, uniformed and trained to serve the needs of the citizens. Mercenaries are often identical to regulars in equipment and training, but they are not usually considered part of a regular standing army.

Repatriation Bond: Part of almost every contract, the repatriation bond assures the mercenary soldier that he will be transported off-planet to safety in the event of defeat, capture or surrender. The mercenaries' patron will deposit a sum with a large and reputable financial institution to guarantee payment.

TL7

Sophisticated electronics and computers make "smart" weapons possible, greatly increasing the lethality of munitions. Sophisticated night vision devices make "round-the-clock" operations feasible, and convey an enormous advantage over less-well equipped forces. Nuclear explosives and chemical weapons are relatively easy to construct. The guided missile is prevalent in all theaters of war.

Locally made weapons are effective and lethal. Imports are chosen to enhance effectiveness in key areas. Local industry is capable of supporting and maintaining many highly effective high-tech systems. States can thus add Imperial-standard equipment to their arsenal where it is needed, gaining high effectiveness in key areas.

Infantry

The TL7 infantryman counters nuclear fallout, biological agents and chemical weapons by either donning a bulky locally-made NBC suit (hot and uncomfortable to wear, it reduces effectiveness and is thus reserved for special alerts rather than being worn as a matter of course) or importing a combat environment suit.

Body armor, consisting of a flak jacket and ballistic nylon helmet, greatly improves the infantryman's chances of survival. Anti-fragmentation clothing is also available, which is useless against bullets but protects reasonably well against grenade fragments or shell splinters.

The assault rifle (e.g., Colt M16, p. HT115), capable of fully automatic or burst fire and often equipped with telescopic, thermal or low-light sighting, is a deadly personal weapon. It is backed up by a bayonet that rarely sees use in combat anymore, but which makes a handy tool.

Infantry Support

A variety of grenade launchers (e.g., M79, p. HT121) and rifle-launched anti-bunker charges (improved rifle grenades, see p. HT78) are in use at the squad level. The primary infantry support weapon is still the light machine-gun (e.g., M60, p. HT119), with the mortar at company level (e.g., M29 81mm, p. HT121).

Cavalry/Armor

Track-laying tanks are reliable and have good cross-country speed. Armament is generally a 4" (100mm) or higher plus smoothbore or rifled cannon, capable of firing a variety of ammunition (see p. VE196). Guns are stabilized, allowing first-shot kills at 3,000 yards on the move.

MIFVs (Mechanized Infantry Fighting Vehicles) carry and support infantry, using machine-guns, light autocannon (see p. VE193) and missiles (see p. VE203). Lighter vehicles – wheeled and tracked – perform reconnaissance and screening duties, supplemented by a variety of helicopters and VTOL aircraft.

Missile-armed tanks are experimented with, and in some defensively minded states the missile-armed tank destroyer replaces the MBT (Main Battle Tank).

Artillery

MLRS (Multiple-Launch Rocket Systems) allow devastating barrages to be fired by a single vehicle. Counter-battery fire becomes a real threat due to shell-tracking radar, so a shoot-and-scoot policy is adopted, with almost all front-line artillery being self-propelled.

Long-range missiles are used for standoff strikes, and sometimes in the support role.

Missiles and Special Weapons

Support weapons include large ballistic weapons for delivery of massive HE, chemical or tactical nuclear warheads over hundreds of miles. Long-range cruise missiles can carry almost any warhead with impressive accuracy. Such missiles are used to attack installations and to break up enemy formations.

Battlefield tactical missiles (tac missiles) are mounted on vehicles or fired from man-portable disposable launchers. Antitank and anti-aircraft missiles of considerable effectiveness are available (see p. VE203).

Transport

The truck, APC and MIFV provide tactical movement. Helicopters are also used for "vertical envelopment" (airmobile assault) missions, resupply and casualty evacuation.

Nautical

The nuclear-powered attack submarine is a deadly weapon at sea, capable of launching anti-ship or cruise missiles at targets including land installations. Missile subs carrying strategic weapons hide in the deep oceans.

The aircraft carrier dominates sea areas, defended by missile-armed destroyers and sub-hunting frigates. Missile cruisers form the centerpiece of surface action groups. Naval strategy generally revolves around sea area control to allow naval airstrikes, sub hunting and amphibious interventions to be carried out at need. Most ships carry a single medium-caliber gun (3-5 inch) and a mix of surface-to-surface and surface-to-air missiles (see pp. VE194 and VE203).

Aviation/COACC

Jet fighters mount sophisticated missiles and autocannon. Interceptors are capable of reaching high altitude and even of launching anti-orbital weapons.

Strike aircraft deploy "smart" precision munitions to deliver cluster bomblets (bombs that scatter dozens or hundreds of small bomblets or grenades), air-delivered mines, fuel-air explosives (see p. HT26), napalm (see p. HT27) or conventional high-explosive. Strategic bombers carry a vast array of electronic-warfare equipment and can function as missile platforms, launching standoff strikes from hundreds of miles away.

Air missions are supported by airborne tankers and electronic warfare aircraft. Early warning, fighter control and reconnaissance aircraft are all operated.

The attack helicopter, carrying anti-tank missiles, autocannon and rockets, is a lethal tank-hunter. Naval helicopters hunt subs and launch missile strikes against small vessels.

Killer satellites and anti-satellite missiles give a small measure of anti-space defense. Space shuttles and disposable launch vehicles can be converted to carry missile packs, but orbital defense is not truly feasible at TL7 without imported systems.

Communications

Electronic warfare, including jamming of enemy missile control systems, is vital as a "force multiplier." Local communications equipment is vulnerable to jamming and

Glossary: T

Tenaille: An earthen bank constructed in front of a bunker or wall to deflect blast.

Thunderball: Slang term applied to a thermonuclear weapon.

Touch and Go: A type of landing where an aerial transport barely grazes the ground as the troops depart the vehicle.

Trade, The: Insider term for the mercenary business.

Glossary: W

Weapons Carrier: General nonspecific term for a vehicle of any type converted to mount a weapon system it was not specifically designed for; e.g., a jeep retrofitted with a recoilless rifle; a grav sled mounting a heavy mortar.

Weapons of Mass Destruction: Weapons including (but not limited to) nuclear explosives, biotoxins and other biological agents and lethal chemical agents are defined as weapons of mass destruction. They are prohibited by the Imperial rules of war (see pp. 20-24).

Mode of Combat

Control of the air is vital in all-out war. Air attacks on communications and supply centers, interdiction and logistics strikes are used to degrade the capability of the main enemy forces. Heavy losses can be expected to both sides' air forces.

Ground combat is characterized by incredible rates of ammunition and equipment expenditure. The early hours of any war see rapid gains by one side, with massive precision airstrikes and armored exploitation. Urban combat is common, and it is in cities that the close-quarter fighting is bloodiest. Tanks are just big tracked targets for infantry antitank weapons and laser-guided munitions are difficult to use in the confusion; here the infantryman once again dominates the house-to-house fighting. Chemical weapons are a constant threat.

From TL7 onward, the mercenary soldier is fighting in the modern environment. Local weapons are less sophisticated than his, and he still has advantages in communications and reconnaissance, but local forces are a real threat.

TL8

Local industry becomes capable of maintaining grav vehicles at TL8, though locally produced grav equipment is crude and unreliable. Caseless and liquid propellant ammunition (also known as binary propellant) begin to be used in small arms, tank guns and artillery.

Infantry

The TL8 infantryman is dressed in combat armor that provides some fragmentation protection. Vital areas are covered by a flak jacket (see p. GT117) and a light infantry helmet (see p. GT117) helmet with built-in communicator, and a respirator. Armament is the assault rifle, often with a built-in grenade launcher (e.g., M16 with M203 GL, see p. HT115 and 121 or RAM grenades, see p. GT115).

Early laser carbines are available, but are generally reserved for forward observers and elite troops who use their weapons as laser designators.

Some units are equipped for zero-g combat, where the laser comes into its own. Other weapons in common use include the snub revolver and its autopistol variant. Ablative anti-laser armor and early hardened vacc suits (see p. GT118) are issued on an experimental basis.

Infantry Support

The 20mm LAG (Light Assault Gun, see p. GT115) is in use for squad support, as well as the much heavier LSG (Light Support Gun, see p. 63) of the same caliber, for use against light armor and higher-tech troops using battle dress.

Infantry missile launchers are in widespread use at the platoon level, with various battlefield tac missiles available.

Cavalry/Armor

Tracklaying tanks have reached full development, mounting 5-6" (120-150mm) hypervelocity smoothbore cannon capable of delivering nuclear rounds or missiles in addition to standard rounds. Composite armor makes tanks difficult to penetrate with infantry antitank weapons. Infantry assault vehicles, armored like an MBT but carrying infantry and support weapons instead of a main gun, are deployed.

Light wheeled APCs and armored cavalry vehicles are also in common use. Hovercraft strike vehicles mounting missile launchers and light autocannon make an appearance on some worlds, attempting to outmaneuver the armored behemoths.

Artillery

Ortillery (orbital artillery) is available, though the technology is in its infancy. Satellites or spacecraft dispense kinetic-energy rods to home on designated targets.

Tube artillery is largely supplanted by light missile launchers and MLRS systems.

Mass driver guns (electromagnetic accelerators) become more common throughout the period.

Transport

The wheeled or tracked APC and rotary-wing transport are still standard means of moving troops in the tactical environment.

Nautical

The vulnerability of surface vessels to ortillery drives most from the oceans. Those few surface ships remaining are armed with laser or particle accelerator weaponry to defeat incoming missiles and with mass driver guns in addition to their own missile armament. Submersible vessels are common, however, surfacing only when necessary for the mission.

Aviation/COACC

Hypersonic aerospace interceptors capable of reaching low orbit launch missiles at enemy vessels, while orbital stations are used to launch unstreamlined combat spacecraft and missiles for beyond-atmosphere intercepts.

Air-superiority aircraft can mount laser weapons in addition to missiles. Strike aircraft are capable of using a ballistic trajectory to reach distant targets, though this relies on a lack of interception capability.

The helicopter is supplemented by a jet-powered vehicle using rotary wings for takeoff before locking them for rapid flight.

Communications

Secure microwave and laser comms go some way to offsetting the advances in electronic warfare being made. However, these depend upon direct-line relays such as satellites, which are vulnerable to attack. Interception of sidelobes from tight-beam communications yields dividends in the signals intelligence field. The portable battlefield computer system makes collation of information automatic, greatly simplifying the command process.

Missiles and Special Weapons

The infantry missile comes with a variety of warheads – anti-bunker, anti-armor, anti-air, antipersonnel, bomblet and so on. Each warhead incorporates appropriate guidance systems to its task, allowing the infantry platoon to counter most threats with one weapon system.

Mode of Combat

Most TL8+ combat falls into one of two categories: either close-quarters fighting in urban or other confined areas or else fluid actions in the open, dominated by aerospace craft and contests for control of the "high ground" – close orbit. Close Orbit and Aerospace Control Command (COACC) replaces the Air Force of many nations.

Aerospace combat dominates the ground and water theaters. Close-orbit craft are used for reconnaissance and bombardment of anything that stands still long enough.

Installations are very well hidden or else have impressive aerospace defenses. Combat is three-dimensional in high-intensity areas.

I don't expect you to understand this, and you'll probably think I'm crazy, but I do what I do because war is the single most exciting thing you can ever do. I've tried the so-called action sports, and all of them . . . every single one . . . fails to give the adrenaline rush you get from being shot at. If you live through a firefight, you come out of it with a feeling of being truly, 100% alive, and everything else in the universe pales to insignificance next to that. "

– Anonymous mercenary officer, TNS interview, Efate, 217-1114

"I don't know who that Omlette guy was who invented ham, but that was the only halfway decent ready-to-eat ration we ever got. Everybody I knew threw away the dehydrated beer — it was Vilani beer to start with and being desecrated . . . dissected . . . whatever . . . didn't help it at all."

– Anonymous mercenary officer, TNS interview, Efate, 217-1114

Against insurgents and in built-up areas (including space vehicles and installations), small units of infantry are still the primary means of taking and controlling ground.

TL9

At TL9 and above, worlds can construct their own grav sleds (a generic term for transport and utility grav vehicles) and grav tanks. Imports are mainly key components rather than whole systems. Electrothermal weapons begin to replace those with earlier propulsion systems.

Infantry

The TL9 infantryman is armed with the ACR (Advanced Combat Rifle) with its sophisticated built-in sighting and RAM grenade launcher capability (see p. GT115). He wears a combat environment suit (see p. GT118) as standard, which offers light ballistic protection and is sealed against gas and other chemical agents. Heavier body armor is sometimes issued for wear over the suit. This armor may incorporate reflec for anti-laser protection.

Units deployed for low-G operations are issued accelerator rifles or laser rifles.

Infantry Support

At the squad level, the ASW (Advanced Support Weapon, see p. 63) is in use. This is simply a heavier variant of the ACR, having many components in common. The LAG sees common use, and the ARL (Assault Rocket Launcher, see PML p. UT126) is introduced for assault troops.

The mortar is gradually replaced by disposable remote-controlled rocket launchers. Grav sleds mounting direct-fire support weapons are sometimes integrated at the platoon level.

Cavalry/Armor

Early grav tanks mounting beam lasers, gauss guns or basic plasma weapons form the backbone of armored forces, supported by grav sleds serving as APCs and weapons carriers. Fast wheeled vehicles are still in use, but the tracklaying tank has largely disappeared.

Artillery

Mass drivers and MLR systems are common. VRF gauss mounts are used for point defense.

Transport

Most tactical transport is by contragrav vehicles, with wheeled vehicles and hovercraft rapidly being superseded.

Nautical

Only submarines remain viable as nautical combat vessels. Many installations lurk in the deep ocean, and subs are the means to neutralize them without resorting to weapons of mass destruction.

Aviation/COACC

Line-of-sight anti-air weapons make low-level capability essential for strike aircraft. Grav vehicles replace helicopter gunships, being capable of far greater speeds, and merge with contragravity-equipped armor until any distinction is effectively lost. Air-superiority craft are grav powered, allowing orbital interceptions, though craft designed for atmosphere are less efficient in space, and vice versa.

Surface missile and beam emplacements are common.

Communications

Advanced broadcast radio-frequency, laser and microwave communicators are in use. Countermeasures still manage to achieve a measure of interception and jamming of broadcast media, and direct attacks upon communication relay devices can disrupt tight-beam comms.

Mode of Combat

The battlefield is completely three-dimensional, with any region reachable by fast gravitic craft. Grav tanks are capable of reaching orbit, though they routinely stay low to avoid becoming easy targets. Maneuver is the key to vehicular warfare – anything staying still is an artillery or ortillery target, or else will be intercepted by aircraft. Infantry survives by being too small to detect and individually too insignificant to earn a high priority for destruction, but can carry tac missiles capable of useful battlefield effects.

Urban combat remains the commonest theater of warfare, whether defense of built-up areas in major war or low-intensity counterinsurgency warfare.

TL10

This is the average Imperial level of technology.

Infantry

While most TL10 infantrymen are dressed in advanced versions of the combat environment suit, some units are clothed in combat armor (see p. GT118). The ACR is the standard infantry weapon, though gauss rifles (see p. 64) are on issue in small numbers for specialist troops. RAM grenade launchers remain in common use.

Infantry Support

Crude plasma guns such as the PGMP-10 (see p. GT115) are integrated at the platoon level. Squad support is still the advanced support weapon and LAG.

Cavalry/Armor

Fast grav tanks mounting heavy plasma guns or missile racks and support sleds mounting gauss weapons operate in conjunction with grav APCs (G-carriers).

Artillery

Plasma weapons are deployed in the air defense role, along with VRF gauss weapons. Missiles and ortillery have mostly supplanted conventional artillery, though some highly mobile mass-driver guns and rocket batteries remain in service.

Transport

The grav APC or G-carrier remains the tactical transport of choice. Mounting a VRF gauss gun or missiles, it doubles as a support vehicle.

Communications

Communications systems constantly improve to deal with developments in the electronic warfare field.

Aviation/COACC

Advanced aerospace interceptors engage space vessels more evenly.

Plasma support guns on fast grav gunships are the standard air support weapons, though the distinction between air support and armor is increasingly blurred.

Mode of Combat

This follows the standard Imperial model (see p. 19) for all TLs 10 or higher.

(see p. GT118) ... (see p. 64) ... (see p. GT115) ... (see p. 19)

Medics

Death and injury is an accepted occupational hazard for mercenaries (and for soldiers in general), however, they expect reasonable steps to be taken to minimize these risks. Thus military units will have adequate medical services available. Units smaller than a platoon will try to have one or more members with First Aid skill. Most platoons will have one or two medics (medical technicians, see p. GT96). These may be part of the organization or attached temporarily. A clearing station with a medical doctor (see p. GT96) plus two or three medical technicians will normally be present at company/battalion level and an aid station (one or two medical doctors supported by five to eight medical technicians with facilities for minor surgery at battalion level or higher. Failure to provide adequate medical personnel (roughly 1 person with medical training per forty personnel) will have an adverse affect on the unit's morale (reduce morale by 2 in *GURPS Compendium II* mass combat).

Under most circumstances medics are considered non-combatants, and are not to be fired upon. As such, medics (and wounded) are sometimes granted some latitude, and are often allowed to cross enemy lines unhindered. This is not a universal convention, however (during the Ziru Sirka, the Vilani did not regard medics as non-combatants), and often in the heat of battle identifying medical personnel takes a low priority. Often, medics will arm themselves with an inconspicuous sidearm such as a pistol, which they keep concealed and use only for self-defense.

Improvised Anti-Vehicle Weapons

Irregular forces (and regular forces to a lesser extent) often make use of improvised anti-vehicle weapons, especially in heavily wooded or urban areas where opportunities for ambush are greater than in more open combat environments.

Improvised weapons generally involve flame weapons, homemade explosives or try to interfere with a vehicle's vision/sensors/communication.

Flame Attacks: At TL 6 and below, vehicles are vulnerable to fire, especially improvised napalm and similar compounds. At TL7 and higher, vehicles become increasingly resistant to such attacks. Any armored vehicle designed to operate in an NBC or vacuum environment can resist most fire attacks. This ability increases with higher tech levels, and improvised fire weapons are more effectively applied in attacks against barracks, supply and repair depots, and other rear area installations.

Explosives: A large enough explosion can damage or destroy any vehicle. At higher tech levels, however, armor, sealed environmental systems and gravitic compensation help vehicles survive almost any explosive charge a single person can carry. Command detonated mines, fougasses, and emplaced demolition charges can still damage or destroy almost anything (drop a building on a passing grav tank can be very effective). Improvised shaped charges remain a danger to vehicles of all tech levels, but they almost always require hand placement.

Sensors and Communication: The earliest tanks had no radios, and communication required leaving the tank (or at least opening a hatch). Vision was accomplished through simple slits in the armor (the vehicle's driver, gunner, and commander all needed to be able to see). Between tech levels 5 to 8, view slits acquired panels of bullet resistant glass (becoming stronger as technology improved), and radios became commonplace. Advancing technology provided replacements for windows and radios became more resistant to damage. Nevertheless, vehicles of all tech levels are vulnerable to "blinding" by paint bombs and the like.

The *GURPS Basic Set* covers damage from fire and explosives in general.

GURPS Vehicles and *GURPS High-Tech* have more specific rules on napalm, fuel area explosives, and so on. Game Masters will need to make their own rulings when players improvise for paint bombs, mud on the viewports, and the like.

TL11

Worlds of TL11 and higher do not need to import weapon systems. They are the source of the imports sought by lower-tech worlds.

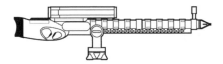

Infantry

Most first-line infantrymen are now encased in combat armor and armed with gauss rifles (often using RAM grenade launchers). Specialist assault units are armored in battledress (see p. GT118) and equipped with either early fusion guns (FGMP-11, see p. GT115) or advanced plasma weapons (PGMP-11, see p. GT115).

Infantry Support

Non-battledress equipped units employ gauss machine-guns at the squad level and missile launchers or heavy pulse lasers at the platoon level. Battledress units use the plasma or fusion weapons.

Cavalry/Armor

Light grav tanks mount rapid-fire plasma guns while heavy versions carry powerful fusion weapons capable of engaging orbital targets. Grav vehicles have replaced all forms of ground transport.

Artillery

Nuclear dampers make possible the use of very short half-life materials held in stasis before use. Weapons firing 20mm californium rounds are used aboard remotely piloted drones, the round having sufficient mass to go critical and cause a small nuclear explosion upon impact (see p. 66). Heavy direct-fire fusion guns are employed on the battlefield.

COACC

Advanced aerospace craft utilize wings for lift as well as grav propulsion. Response times are very short, and weapons are comparable with small spacecraft.

TL12

The meson accelerator takes its place as the ultimate battlefield weapon system. Nuclear dampers remove the nuclear threat.

Infantry

Most troops are equipped with combat armor and gauss rifles.

Battledress is worn by all elite and some specialist regular units, who employ grav belts and fusion guns (FGMP-12) for devastating individual firepower.

Cavalry/Armor

Grav tanks and G-carriers continue to operate as at lower TLs, but become even more advanced.

Artillery

Damper fields render all forms of nuclear munitions useless within their range and are deployed by all major forces. Meson accelerators are deployed for battlefield support. They are expensive and bulky, but incredibly deadly.

COACC

Aerospace interceptors are still in use, and have reached high levels of sophistication.

The deep-site meson gun, buried deep inside a planet's rocky crust, is the ultimate ground-defense weapon for those militaries that can afford it.

CHAPTER FOUR

Ironmongery

The old *Traveller* book *Mercenary* used the word *ironmongery* to describe the eclectic collection of equipment, weapons, vehicles and space ships that might be used by a mercenary unit. An ironmonger is another name for blacksmith, and the name dates from a time when blacksmiths made most military equipment.

Heavy Plasma and Fusion Gun "Hot Shots": For reliability reasons, plasma and fusion guns with 6,400 KJ or more output possess an over-engineered magnetic containment system; a gunner can override this and fire a "hot shot" with 1.5 times normal damage. A hot shot drains four times as much power as usual, so the weapon must either be connected to an appropriate power source or drain four times as many shots from its power cell energy bank. When firing hot shots, the weapon's Malfunction chance increases by 1 (e.g., a weapon that would malfunction on a critical miss malfunctions on a 16+ when firing a hot shot).

Thermal-Superconducting Armor: This is limited to a maximum DR bonus of +250 in designs for the *Traveller* universe.

Meson Weapons: The minimum size of meson weapons is 1 terajoule (1 billion kj) at the TL of introduction divided by 10 for each successive tech level. This brings meson weapons more into line with their behavior in the *Traveller* universe.

COMBAT EQUIPMENT

COMMANDO BATTLEDRESS (TL12)

This is a stealthy battledress specially designed for use by the Imperial Marine commandos (see p. 21). It is capable of 70 mph ground speed and has the strength of five normal humans. With an attached flight pack (see below) it is capable of flight.

- **Subassemblies and Body Features:** Head (Limited Rotation Turret), Arms (L, R), Legs (L, R).
- **Propulsion:** Legged drivetrain (Legs, HP 12, 80 kW).
- **Instruments and Electronics:** Short range meson communicator (Head, 2,000 mile, HP 3 , 0.1 kW), Short range laser communicator (Head, 10,000 miles, HP 1, 0.1 kW), Medium range radio (Head, 10,000 miles, HP 1, 0.1 kW), 10 mile AESA (Head, scan 17, HP 1, 2.5 kW), 5 mile PESA (Head, scan 15, HP 1, neg.), 1 mile passive sonar (Body, scan 11, HP 2, neg.), 0.5-mile geophone (L leg, scan 9, HP 1, neg.), 2-mile radscanner (Head, scan 12, HP 1, neg.), 0.1-mile gravscanner (Head, scan 5, HP 1, neg.), Level 10 surveillance sound detector (Head, HP 1, neg.), Inertial navigation system (Body, HP 2, neg.), Military GPS (Body, HP 1, neg.), HUDWAC, Deceptive Jammer (Body, rating 4, HP 2, neg.), Advanced radar/ladar detector, (Body, HP 3, neg.), Minicomputer (Body, complexity 8, HP 2, neg.), Terminal (Body, HP 4, neg.).
- **Miscellaneous Components:** ST 50 arm motors (RA/LA each: HP 1, 0.25 kW).
- **Controls:** Computer.
- **Crewstations:** Pilot, Battledress crew station, grav web (HP 3, 0.5 kW).
- **Occupancy:** Short.
- **Accommodations:** Battledress crew station.
- **Environmental Systems:** Full life support (Body, HP 6, 0.1 kW).
- **Power:** 100 kW NPU (Body, HP 3), 540 MJ rechargeable power cell (RL, E cell, HP 2, 1 hour, 45 minutes).
- **Empty Space:** H 0.3975 cf, B 0.215 cf, RA 0.15 cf, LA 0.15 cf, RL 0.4 cf, LL 0.5 cf.
- **Volume:** H 1 cf, B 6 cf, RA 0.4 cf, LA 0.4 cf, RL 2.6 cf, LL 2.6 cf.
- **Surface Area:** H 6 sf, B 20 sf, RA 4 sf, LA 4 sf, RL 12 sf, LL 12 sf.
- **Structure:** Heavy advanced.
- **Hit Points:** H 18, B 60, RA 24, LA 24, RL 36, LL 36.
- **Armor:** PD 4 DR 1.200 Advanced laminate.
- **Surface features:** Basic emissions masking, basic sound baffling, basic stealth, instant chameleon, thermal superconductive armor, improved suspension.

- **Statistics:** Empty weight: 1,845 lbs., Usual Payload: 200 lbs., Loaded Weight: 2,045 lbs. (1.02 tons), Vehicle Volume: Total 13 cf, Size Modifiers: H -2, B 0, RA -2, LA -2, RL -1, LL -1.
- **Price:** KCr380.
- **Health:** HT 12.
- **Ground Performance:** Top Speed: 70, Accel: 7, GMr: 2.75, GSr: 1, Decel: 20, Ground Pressure: Low (1,065), Off-Road Speed: 56.

GMG '98

Flight Pack (TL12)

This unit is intended to be attached to commando battle-dress in order to give it flight capability. It is not designed for use by itself.

- **Propulsion:** 2×2,000 lb. vectored reactionless thrusters (ea. HP 7, 100 kW).
- **Aerostatic Lift:** 2×2,000 lb. Contragrav (ea. HP 2, 2 kW).
- **Controls:** Computerized.
- **Crewstation:** Harness crewstation for pilot.
- **Environmental Systems:** 1×Total life support (HP 15, 0.1 kW).
- **Power:** 210 kW NPU (HP 4), 540,000 kJ Energy Bank (E cell, HP 2, 44 Minutes).
- **Access, Cargo and Empty Space:** Empty Space: 0.45 cf.
- **Volume:** 8 cf.
- **Surface Area:** 24 sf.
- **Structure:** Advanced Heavy.
- **Hit Points:** 72.
- **Armor:** PD 4, DR 1,200 Advanced Laminate.
- **Surface features:** Basic Emissions Masking, Basic sound baffling, basic stealth, instant chameleon, thermal superconductive armor.
- **Statistics:** Empty weight: 835 lbs., Usual External Payload: 2,045 lbs., Loaded Weight: 2,880 lbs. (1.44 tons). Vehicle Volume: Total 8 cf, Size Modifier: +0.
- **Price:** Cr120,000.
- **Health:** HT 12.
- **Ground Performance:** Top Speed: 60, Accel: 6, GMR: 2.75, GSR: 1, Decel: 20, Ground Pressure: Extremely low (149), Off-Road Speed: 60.
- **Submerged Performance:** Top Speed: 17, Accel: 30, WMR: 1.25, WSR: 5, Decel: 140, Crush Depth: 12,100 (6.8 miles).
- **Air Performance:** Top Speed: 600, Accel: 30, AMR: 6, ASR: 3, Decel: 24.
- **Space Performance:** Accel: 1.39, SMR: 1.39.

Drop Capsule (TL12)

This is a disposable atmospheric reentry capsule for meteoric assaults. It holds one Marine in battledress, and up to 250 lbs. (5 cf) of additional equipment and supplies. The ablative armor on the capsule allows reentry to take place in 2-3 minutes rather than the 10-20 required for the stealthier landing the battledress/flight pack is capable of by itself.

- **Propulsion:** Uses battledress' flight pack.
- **Aerostatic Lift:** Uses battledress' flight pack.
- **Miscellaneous Components:** Shell is fitted as a vehicle bay (holds battledress plus 250 lbs. 5 cf of equipment).
- **Controls:** None.
- **Crewstations:** Uses battledress'.
- **Volume:** 30 cf.
- **Surface Area:** 58 cf.
- **Structure:** Super light advanced.
- **Hit Points:** 9.
- **Armor:** PD 4 DR 4,000 expensive fireproof ablative.

- **Surface features:** Fair streamlining.
- **Statistics:** Empty weight: 1,856 lbs., Usual Internal Payload: 3,130 lbs., Loaded Weight: 5,238 lbs., Vehicle Volume: Total 30 cf, Size Modifier: +1.
- **Price:** Cr11,000.
- **Health:** HT 5.
- **Air Performance:** Top Speed: 600, Accel: 15, AMR: 6, ASR: 3, Decel: 24.
- **Space Performance:** Accel: 0.76, SMr: 0.76.
- **Cargo Modifications:** With the addition of two 1-ton contragrav units, a 1-ton vectored reactionless thruster, a mini computer, an inertial navigation system, and an E cell (provides power for 1 hr and 26 min.), the capsule can be sent down as an unmanned cargo container. Add the following to the standard capsule: Weight: +122 lbs., Cost: +Cr25,250. Cargo capacity is 1,250 lbs. (25 cf).

Decoy Capsule (TL12)

This capsule carries a powerful active jammer, and is deployed during meteoric assaults to cover the descent of manned capsules using chaff and other electronic countermeasures. It disrupts radar and radio communication over a 750-mile radius (this includes the radios of the descending drop troopers, but this is not a major disadvantage, as it is normal to maintain radio silence during a drop anyway).

- **Propulsion:** 2,000 lbs. reactionless thruster (HP 5, 100 kW).
- **Aerostatic Lift:** 2×2,000 lbs. Contragrav (ea. HP 2, 2 kW).
- **Instruments and Electronics:** Short-range meson communicator (2,000 mile, HP 3, 0.1 kW), Level 15 Active Jammer (Rating 15, HP 36, 3,750 kW), Inertial navigation system (Body, HP 2, neg.), Military GPS (Body, HP 1, neg.), HUDWAC, Minicomputer (Body, complexity 8, HP 2, neg.).
- **Miscellaneous Components:** Chaff Discharger (HP 6), 9×Chaff reloads (HP 16).
- **Controls:** Computer.
- **Power:** 110 kW NPU (HP 3), 12.42 GJ Energy Bank (23 E cells, 55 minutes for jammer).
- **Access, Cargo and Empty Space:** Empty Space: 0.065 cf.
- **Volume:** 30 cf.
- **Surface Area:** 58 sf.
- **Structure:** Very expensive heavy.
- **Hit Points:** 174.
- **Armor:** PD 4 DR 1,700 Advanced composite.
- **Surface features:** Thermal superconductive armor, fair streamlining.
- **Statistics:** Empty weight: 2,980 lbs., Usual Internal Payload 0 lb. Loaded Weight: 2,980 lbs. Vehicle Volume: Total 30 cf, Size Modifier: +1.
- **Price:** Cr360,000.
- **Health:** HT 12.
- **Air Performance:** Top Speed: 600, Accel: 27, AMr: 6, ASr: 3, Decel: 24.
- **Space Performance:** Accel: 0.76, SMr: 0.76.

WEAPONS

Descriptions are provided only for weapons not described in *GURPS Traveller.*

SMALL ARMS

Snub SMG: A submachine gun designed to use the same 10mm ammunition as the snub pistols (see p. GT111).

ACR-ETC, 7mm (TL9): An advanced version of the 7mm advanced combat rifle (see p. GT111) using electrothermal propulsion.

ACR-ETC, 9mm (TL9): An advanced version of the 9mm advanced combat rifle (see p. GT111) using electrothermal propulsion.

SUPPORT WEAPONS

LAG-ETC (Light Assault Gun, ElectroThermal-Chemical, TL9): An advanced version of the 20mm light assault gun (see p. GT111) using electrothermal propulsion, and firing 35 shots on a rB cell built into the magazine.

LSG (Light Support Gun, TL8): A squad support version of the 20mm LAG (see p. GT111).

LSG-ETC (Light Support Gun, ElectroThermal-Chemical, TL9): An advanced version of the 20mm light support gun using electrothermal propulsion, and firing 25 shots on a rB cell built into the magazine.

ASW-9mm (Advanced Support Weapon, TL8): A squad support variant of the 9mm advanced combat rifle, incorporating a heavier barrel, a bipod and a larger capacity magazine (the ASW can use ACR magazines, but not vice versa).

ASW-ETC (Advanced Support Weapon, ElectroThermal-Chemical, TL9): A squad support variant of the 9mm advanced combat rifle ETC, incorporating a heavier barrel, a bipod and a larger capacity magazine (the ASW can use ACR magazines, but not vice versa). This weapon fires 360 rounds from a pair of rC cells built into the magazine.

HEAVY WEAPONS

VRFGG-9, VRFGG-10 (Very Rapid Fire Gauss Gun): A heavy machine gun version of the conventional 4mm gauss gun, modified for an extremely high rate of fire. The version at TL10 incorporates a longer barrel, resulting in higher damage, lower cost and greater range.

The weapon is normally used as vehicle-mounted ordinance, but manpacked versions are available for infantry support. A tripod for the manpacked version weighs 29 lbs. and is Cr290.

VEHICLE WEAPONS

PD xaser (TL10): An X-ray laser used as a point-defense weapon on vehicles. Versions are available at both TL10 and 11.

10 MJ RF plas (TL10): A plasma gun used as a main weapon on AFVs.

80mm RF howit (TL10): A rapid fire howitzer used as a main weapon on vehicles.

360 Xaser (TL10): An X-ray laser used as a point defense weapon on vehicles.

540 Lt Plasma Gun (TL10): A plasma gun used as a main weapon on AFVs, including the Instellarms light grav tank.

945 Med Plasma Gun (TL10): A plasma gun used as a main weapon on AFVs, including the Instellarms medium grav tank.

1,350 Hvy Plasma Gun (TL10): A plasma gun almost exclusively used as a main weapon on AFVs.

Fusion/10 (TL11): This weapon is the main armament of the Imperial *Astrin* class grav APC.

Fusion/2300 (TL12): This ferociously powerful weapon is the main armament of the Imperial *Intrepid* class grav tank.

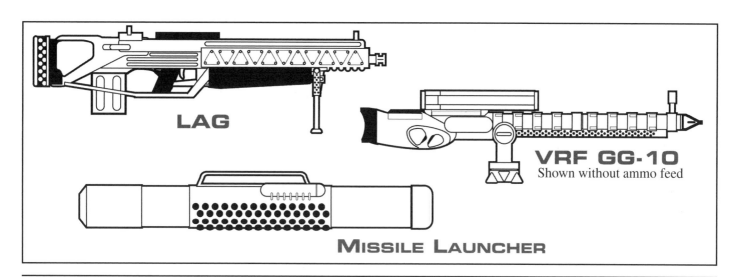

LAG

VRF GG-10
Shown without ammo feed

MISSILE LAUNCHER

CONSOLIDATED WEAPONS TABLES

These tables contain the weapons from *GURPS Traveller* and new weapons introduced in this book combined into a single table for ready reference.

PISTOLS

Weapon	Malf	Type	Damage	SS	Acc	1/2D	Max	Wt	Rof	Shots	ST	Rcl	Cost	LC	Hld	TL
Revolver, 5mm	Ver.	Cr.	1d	10	2	75	1,100	0.7	3~	6	8	-1	57	3	0	6
Revolver, 7mm	Ver.	Cr.	1d+2	10	3	130	1,500	1.4	3~	6	8	-1	63	3	0	6
Revolver, 9mm	Ver.	Cr.	2d	10	4	150	1,600	2	3~	6	8	-1	68	3	0	6
Magnum Revolver, 9mm	Ver.	Cr.	3d-1	10	3	185	2,034	3	3~	6	10	-2	100	3	-1	7
Snub Revolver, 10mm	Ver.	var.	var.	9	2	80	1,100	0.96	3~	6	8	-1	280	3	+1	8
Auto Snub Pistol, 10mm	Ver.	var.	var.	9	2	80	1,100	0.96	3~	20	8	-1	280	3	+1	8
with HEAT		Exp.	2d(10)													
with HEC		Exp.	1d													
with CHEM		Spcl.*	Spcl.*													
Body Pistol, 5mm	Ver.	Cr.	2d-1	10	2	100	1,467	1.25	3~	6?	8	-1	75	3	+2	7
Auto Pistol, 7mm	Ver.	Cr.	2d-1	10	2	175	1,700	1.25	3~	7	10	-1	75	3	0	6
Auto Pistol, 9mm	Ver.	Cr.	2d+2	10	3	150	1,867	2.5	3~	15	9	-1	400	3	0	7
Gauss Pistol, 4mm	Ver.	Cr.	6d(2)	10	7	500	3,200	1.65	8*	15/A	8	-1	1,300	2	0	10

* Covers most of a hex (0.75 hex diameter) with sleep gas (0.125 doses) – see *GURPS Space*.

RIFLES AND CARBINES

Weapon	Malf	Type	Damage	SS	Acc	1/2D	Max	Wt	Rof	Shots	ST	Rcl	Cost	LC	Hld	TL
Carbine, 7mm	Ver.	Cr.	5d+1	14	10	500	3,200	9.2	3~	10	9	-1	120	4	-5	6
Rifle, 7mm	Ver.	Cr.	7d	14	11	1,000	4,655	11	3~	20	11	-2	550	4	-6	7
Rifle, 9mm	Ver.	Cr.	7d-1	14	10	540	3,400	10	3~	10	12	-2	750	4	-6	7
Rifle, 13mm	Ver.	Cr.	13d+1	17	15/16	1,200	5,400	31	2~	10	14/12B	-2	4000	3	No	8
Assault Rifle, 5.5mm	Ver.	Cr.	5d	12	11	500	3,843	8	12*	30	9	-1	540	1	-5	7
Assault Rifle, 7.5mm	Ver.	Cr.	7d	14	11	1,000	4,655	11	11*	20	11	-2	900	1	-6	7
ACR, 7mm	Ver.	var.	var.	12	10	Var.	Var.	7.6	10*	20	10	-2	1,274	1	-5	9
with Solid	Ver.	Cr.	6d+1			740	4,000									
with APS	Ver.	Cr.	6d+7(2)			1,100	6,000									
ACR-ETC, 7m	Ver.	Cr.	9d+2	12	12	1,100	5,100	7.6	16	20C	10	-2	2,000	1	-5	9
w/APS			12d(2)			1,700	7,700									
ACR, 9mm	Ver.	var.	var.	12	10	var.	var.	8.9	10	20	11	-2	1,364	1	-6	9
with solid	Ver.	Cr.	7d-1			540	3,400									
with APS	Ver.	Cr.	7d+6(2)			840	5,100									
with HEC	Ver.	Exp.	1d+1			(540)	3,400									
ACR-ETC, 9mm	Ver.	Cr.	10d	12	12	840	4,300	8.8	16*	20C	10	-2	2,100	1	-6	9
Gauss Rifle, 4mm	Ver.	Cr.	8d+1(2)	12	12	900	4,500	6.2	20*	40/2A	9	-1	3,029	0	-4	10

The weight and cost for the ACRs and gauss rifles include an empty RAM grenade launcher that can be loaded with one TL8-9 RAM grenade (ACR) or TL8-10 RAM grenade (gauss rifle). They both also have integral laser sights and gyrostabilization. For the 9mm ACR HEC round, 1/2D is in parenthesis to note that damage is not halved but Acc is still lost (see p. UTT124).

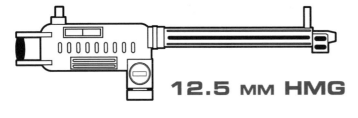

12.5 MM HMG

SNIPING ACR

SUBMACHINEGUNS

Weapon	Malf	Type	Damage	SS	Acc	1/2D	Max	Wt	Rof	Shots	ST	Rcl	Cost	LC	Hld	TL
SMG, 9mm	Ver.	Cr.	3d-1	10	7	160	1,900	9.5	10*	32	10	-1	150	2	-4	7
SnubSMG	Ver.	Cr.	1d+2	9	2	100	1,300	2.6	16*	40C	8	-1	720	2	-4	8
w/HEAT	Ver.	Exp	1d(10)													

SHOTGUNS

Weapon	Malf	Type	Damage	SS	Acc	1/2D	Max	Wt	Rof	Shots	ST	Rcl	Cost	LC	Hld	TL
Shotgun	Ver.	Cr.	4d	12	5	25	150	8	3~	5	12	-3	235	4	-5	6
Auto-Shotgun	Ver.	Cr.	4d	12	6	27	160	12	10*	10	12	-2	570	1	-6	8

ENERGY WEAPONS

Weapon	Malf	Type	Damage	SS	Acc	1/2D	Max	Wt	Rof	Shots	ST	Rcl	Cost	LC	Hld	TL
Laser Pistol-9	ver.	imp	2d	10	10	580	1,200	2.8/3	4~	50/5C	7	0	1,300/500	2	-1*	9
Laser Carbine-8	ver.	imp	2d+2	12	18	2,700	5,400	9/6	4~	50/D	7	0	1,900/500	1	-6*	8
Laser Carbine-10	ver.	imp	2d+2(2)	12	19	4,000	8,000	6/6	4~	50/D	7	0	1,475/500	0	-4*	10
Laser Rifle-9	ver.	imp	4d	12	19	3,300	6,600	10/12	4~	100/2D	8	0	2,100/1,000	0	-6*	9
Laser Rifle-10	ver.	imp	4d(2)	12	20	4,900	9,200	9/12	4~	100/2D	8	0	1,875/1,000	0	-6*	10
Laser Pistol-10	ver.	imp	2d(2)	10	11	870	1,700	1.9/3	4~	50/5C	7	0	1,095/500	0	0*	10
PGMP-10	ver.	exp	6d×8	12	14	460	920	7.2/6	1	46/D	12	-3	16,675/500	0	No	10
PGMP-10A	ver.	exp	6d×15	17	15	740	1,500	19/120	1	450/5E	19	-3	36,175/2,500	0	No	10
PGMP-11	ver.	exp	6d×15	17	15	740	1,500	20/156	1	750/6E	9	-3	72,675/3,500	0	No	11
FGMP-11	ver.	exp	6d×25	17	16	1,100	3,300	17/192	1	500/8E	22	-4	63,175/3,000	0	No	11
FGMP-12	ver.	exp	8d×20	15	12	1,100	3,300	22/48	1	80/2E	10	-4	65,475/1,500	0	No	12

Holdout figure is for laser weapon only. Power packs are separate items. A laser pistol power pack is -3 to Holdout; all others are -5.

SUPPORT WEAPONS

Weapon	Malf	Type	Damage	SS	Acc	1/2D	Max	Wt	RoF	Shot	ST	Rcl	Cost	LC	Hld	TL
LAG, 20mm	Ver.	var	var.	17	10	var.	var.	18	2~	5	15	-3	1,100	0	No	8
with APDS		Cr.	12d(2)			630	4,350									
with HE		Cr.	1d+2(2d)			420	2,900									
with Beehive		Imp.	2d-1			420	2,900									
LAG-ETC	Ver.	Var	Var	17	10	630	3,600	18	2~	5	14	-3	2,200	0	No	9
w/APDS		Cr.	18d(2)													
w/HE		Exp.	2d+1[2d]													
LSG	Crit	Var	Var	17	10/11	630	3,600	26	1	5	12B	-1	1,200	0	No	8
w/APDS		Cr.	15d(2)													
w/HE		Exp.	1d+2[2d]													
LSG-ETC	Ver.	Var	Var	17	11	940	4,600	26	1	5	12B	-1	2,500	0	No	9
w/APDS		Cr.	6d×4(2)													
w/HE		Cr.	2d+1[2d]													
ASW-9mm	Ver.	Cr.	8d	12	11/12	840	4,300	21	20*	var	11B	-1	2,000	0	No	8
w/APS		Cr.	10d(2)			1,300	6,500									
ASW-ETC	Ver.	Cr.	12d	12	11/12	1,300	5,500	22	20*	var	11B	-1	2,200	0	No	9
w/APS		Cr.	16d(2)			1,900	8,300									
VRFGG-9	Ver.	Cr.	15d(2)	20	9/14	1,500	7,200	29	100*	var	18T	-1	26,000	0	No	9
VRFGG-10	Ver.	Cr.	18d(2)	20	10/15	2,300	9,200	29	100*	var	18T	-1	13,000	0	No	10
12.5mm HMG	crit.	Cr	12d+	20	16	1,200	5,000	84/128	8	100	39T	-1	1,000/14,000	0	No	6

RAM GRENADES

Weapon	Type	Damage	SS	Acc	1/2D	Max	Wt	Rof	Shots	ST	Rcl	Cost	LC	Hld	TL
4cm RAM-8 HEAT	exp	8d(10)	*	10	250	510	0.88	1/6	1	–	0	19	0	-3	8
4cm RAM-8 HE	exp	6d(4d)	*	10	250	510	0.88	1/6	1	–	0	18	0	-3	8
4cm RAM-10 HEAT	exp	6d×2(10)	*	10	250	1,500	1.1	1/6	1	–	0	13	0	-3	9
4cm RAM-10 HE	exp	9d(4d)	*	10	250	1,500	1.1	1/6	1	–	0	12	0	-3	9

Holdout figure is for the grenade alone. Attaching the grenade to a weapon lowers the weapon's Holdout by -2. All Malf. are ver.

VEHICLE ARMAMENT

Name	Type	Damage	SS	Acc	1/2D	Max	Wt	RoF	Cost	WPS	PPS	CPS	TL
4mm VRFGG	Cr.	18d(2)	20	15	2,300	9,200	29	100*	13,000	0.0021	13K	0.13	10
20mm ETC chain	Cr.	6d×5	20	16	2,300	8,000	90	20*	14,000	0.24	120	0.6	9
w/APFSDS		6d×10(2)		17	3,400	12,000				0.16		9.6	
PD xaser	Imp.	6d×4(2)	20	25	16 mi	48 mi	250	16*	120,000	–	6M	–	10
10 MJ RF plas	Exp.	5d×40	25	20	3,300	9,900	700	8*	67,000	–	20M	–	10
80mm RF howit	Cr.	6d×12	20	16	2,500	8,500	290	4*	49,000	3.8	960k	30	10
w/HE	Exp.	6d×24[6d]								2.5		60	
w/HEDP	Exp.	6d×20(5)[6d]								2.5		90	
w/HEAT	Exp.	6d¥20(10)								2.5		90	
w/Chem		Spcl 24 yard radius								2.5		var	
w/ICM		Spcl 48 yard radius								2.5		180	
360 xaser	Imp.	6d×50	30	32	200mi	600mi	6700	1/2	MCr1.8	–	900M	–	10
540 lt plasma	Exp.	6d×250	30	25	7 mi	20 mi	2800	1/2	900,000	–	1080M	–	10
945 med plas	Exp.	8d×250	30	24	9 mi	27 mi	4700	1/2	730,000	–	1.8G	–	10
1350 hvy plas	Exp.	6d×400	30	25	11 mi	34 mi	7000	1/2	MCr2.1	–	2.7G	–	10
Fusion/10	Exp	5d×50	25	20	3,600	10,800	700	8*	23,000	–	20M	–	11
Fusion/2300	Exp	6d×750	30	25	17mi	50mi	6T	1/2	MCr1.8	–	4.6G	–	12
PD xaser	Imp.	6d×5(2)	20	25	16 mi	47 mi	200	20*	27,000	–	3,840	–	12
10 Gj Meson Gun	Exp.	8d×1000	30	23	400mi	1,200mi	35T	1/2	MCr1.7	–	20G	–	12

Malfunction for all vehicle armaments is ver., Legality Class is 0; Holdout is "No."

2CM CALIFORNIUM ROUNDS

These rounds are found only in Imperial service, as their use could be considered a violation of the rules of war (see pp. 20-24). Californium rounds are based on the *GURPS Vehicles* "micronuke" (see p. VE110). Use the stats for the 0.001 kiloton warhead, which is available in 20mm at TL11, but since the *Traveller* californium rounds are less advanced (they require dampers) they become available at TL10. Note, however, that californium rounds as described in *Striker* are not as reliable as those in *Vehicles*. To simulate this, roll 1d: on a 1-2 it does full damage, on a 3-5 it does 1/4 damage, and a 6 it does 1/10 damage.

Damper boxes to store the ammunition in cost MCr1, hold three tons of ammunition and are available at TL10.

CONSOLIDATED AMMUNITION LISTS

These include ammunition entries for weapons in *GURPS Traveller* and new weapons introduced in this book, combined into a single listing for ready reference.

20mm LAG/LSG: A 10 round clip is 0.87 lb.; Cr26 for APDS, Cr10 for HE. ETC is 0.68 lb.

18.5mm Shotgun: A box of 100 is 12 lb. and Cr48.

13mm Rifle: A box of 10 is 1.6 lb. and Cr6.5.

10mm Pistol: A box of 100 is 0.8 lb. and Cr5 for ball, 0.53 lb. and Cr15 for HEAT. A 40-round clip is 0.13 lb. empty, 0.45 lb. with ball, 0.34 lb. with HEAT.

9mm ACR: A box of 100 is 4.6 lbs. and Cr18 with ball, 3.1 lbs. and Cr90 with APS. A 20-round clip is 0.37 lb. empty, 1.3 lb. with ball, 1 lb. with APS.

9mm Magnum: A box of 100 is 2.7 lb. and Cr5.40.

7.5mm Rifle: A box of 100 is 5.3 lb. and Cr11; a 20 round detachable clip is 1.5 lb. (.4 lb. empty).

7mm Rifle: A box of 100 is 2.1 lb. and Cr8.4 for ball, 1.4 lb. and Cr42 for APS. ACR/ETC is 1.7 lb. for ball, 1.1 lb. for APS (prices the same). A 20-round clip is 0.17 lb. empty, 0.6 lb. with ball, 0.45 lb. with APS.

7mm Carbine: A box of 100 is 1 lb. and Cr6. A 10-round clip is 0.17 lb. (0.07 lb. empty).

5mm Pistol: A box of 100 is .5 lb. and Cr1.

4mm Gauss: A box of 100 is 0.16 lb. and Cr1.30, or 0.11 lb. and Cr6.5 for APS. A 40 round clip is 0.09 lb., a 100 round clip is 0.25 lb.

4mm VRFGG: A case of 2,500 is 5.3 lbs., Cr325; it is normally paired with a rC cell, which will be completely drained by firing.

BOMBS AND MINES

GURPS Vehicles covers aerial bombs and land mines on pp. VE130-131. *GURPS Ultra-Tech* and *Ultra-Tech II* contain descriptions of a few advanced mines and other fiendish devices.

Basically, both bombs and land mines are treated as an artillery shell of the appropriate size, with a trigger of some sort (contact, time, impact, etc.). Antitank mines are taken from AP shells, antipersonnel mines from HE, beehive or ICM shells.

Here are a few special cases:

Antipersonnel Mine (e.g., M25 APERS): This small mine contains a 1/3-oz. tetryl shaped charge directed straight up. It is normally carefully concealed after being emplaced, and detonates on contact. Damage is 1d+1(10) and is inflicted only to the foot of the person who steps on it. It ignores boot DR (2-4 range), and cripples the average foot about 2/3 of the time. This mine's effects are best simulated using the advanced injury rules on p. CII154-158. These mines are sometimes known as "toe-poppers."

"Bouncing Betty" Mine (e.g., M16A1 APERS): This type is also carefully concealed after being emplaced, and is normally detonated by trip wire. When triggered, it leaps to waist height and detonates, unleashing a shower of steel pellets potentially lethal out to 30 yards. A single projectile should inflict 7d-1 cr damage. The base to-hit roll is 14 or less minus the range penalty. Make the roll and consult the table on p. VE190 for the number of hits. E.g., at close range (2 yards, penalty 0), an average roll of 10 will result in 4 hits. This almost guarantees a hit at 10 yards or less, making this mine extremely deadly.

Claymore Mine (e.g., M18A1 APERS): This mine has command and trip-wire triggers. It is 1.5 lbs. of C4 in a curved sheet with 700 steel balls in front of it. Treat it as a huge shotgun round that attacks everything in a 60° cone in front of it at 14 or less minus range penalties (in addition, it also attacks anything outside of the arc but within 10 yards – you can't clamp it to your chest). Damage should be cr 6d+2, out to 220 yards.

TDX: Some early *Traveller* adventures made use of TDX, a gravitationally polarized shaped charge that directed its explosive force in a plane at right angles to the pull of gravity. This would be especially useful in "bouncing betty" land mines, or in artillery shells with proximity fuses set to detonate 2-4 feet off the ground. Treat TDX explosives as inflicting twice the damage on anything intersected by the "plane" of the detonating charge, and multiply the burst radius by 1.5. TDX shells and mines cost four times as much as their ordinary equivalents.

TDX (Two Dimensional eXplosive) is a term and concept created by novelist James Blish in his *Cities in Flight* series.

Starships and Spaceships

Mercenaries use a wide variety of star- and spacecraft, both combat and troop-carrier vehicles.

Deck plans are provided (pp. 68-71) for the *Broadsword* class 800-ton mercenary cruiser, as described on p. GT139.

Design Adaptations

Since there is no entry for a 300 ton hull on the design table, the following values were interpolated for the *Puller* class 300-ton assault ship design:

Class	Volume	Area	TL10 Mass	TL12 Mass	Cost	Size Modifier
300	150,000	20,000	20	10	1/2.4	+9

Also, several additional modules were created using *GURPS Vehicles:*

Bunkrooms: Bunks for 16 personnel with life support and slice of a galley. Imperial ships usually only load 4 troops aboard giving a comfortable safety margin in the life support.

Drop Capsule Launcher: A pair of 700mm missile launchers in a fixed mounting. Rate of fire is 1/10 each so in one space combat phase the pair can launch 240 Capsules. This module can also function as a pair of one-man airlocks.

Capsule Rack: 16 capsules stored in ready racks with room for maintenance and loading.

"Morgue": 20 sets of battledress (with or without flight packs) and room for maintenance.

External Cradle: Allows other ships to be carried *externally.*

Plasma Gun (TL10): 422 MJ Plasma Gun in fully stabilized universal mount.

Fusion Gun (TL12): 689 MJ Fusion Gun in fully stabilized universal mount.

Weapon	Dam	SS	ACC	1/2D	Max	1/2D (Space)	Max (Space)
Plasma Gun	6d×272	30	28	94,000	282,000	2,700 mi*	8,000 mi (0 hex)
Fusion	6d×411	30	29	129,000	387,000	3,700 mi (0 hex)	11,000 mi (1 hex)

*PD only

Modules	Space	Mass	Cost	Modules	Space	Mass	Cost
Bunkrooms TL10	4	4.8	0.018	Morgue	1	28.75	–
Bunkrooms TL12	4	1.92	0.018	External Cradle	1*	12.5*	0.25*
Drop capsule launcher	1	12	0.15	Plasma Gun	1.5	15.8	7.426
Capsules	1	16.86	–	Fusion Gun	1.5	13.5	21.574

*per 125 tons of *Mass* to be carried. External cradle modules count against the turret-mounted weapons limit at a rate of 3 modules per 1 turret.

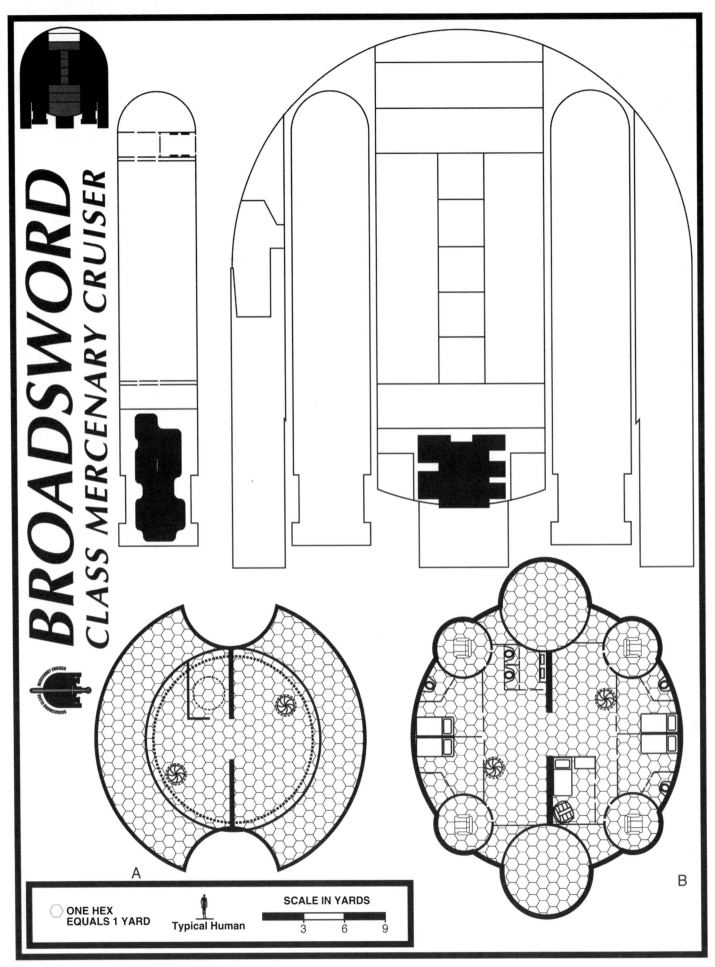

BROADSWORD
CLASS MERCENARY CRUISER

A

B

ONE HEX
EQUALS 1 YARD

Typical Human

SCALE IN YARDS

3 6 9

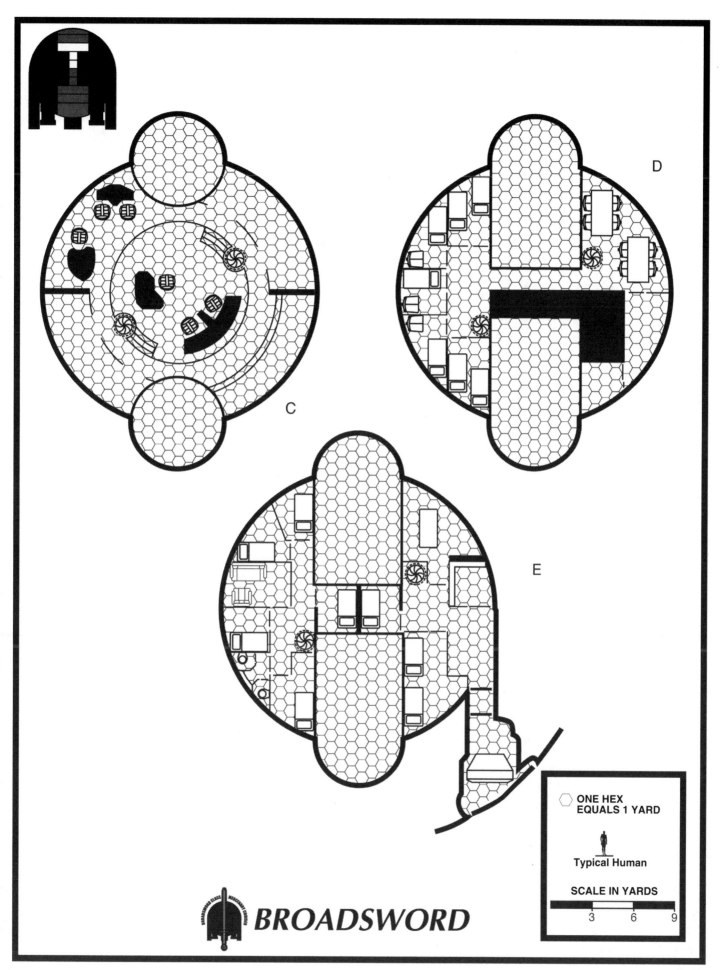

C

D

E

ONE HEX
EQUALS 1 YARD

Typical Human

SCALE IN YARDS

3　　6　　9

BROADSWORD

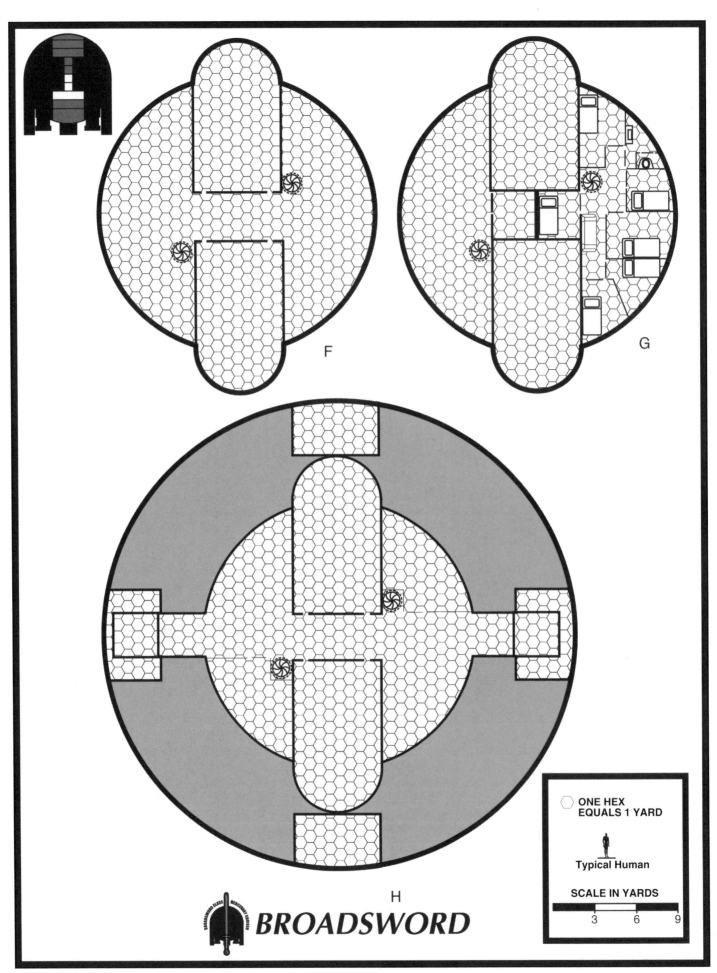

F

G

H

ONE HEX
EQUALS 1 YARD

Typical Human

SCALE IN YARDS

3   6   9

BROADSWORD

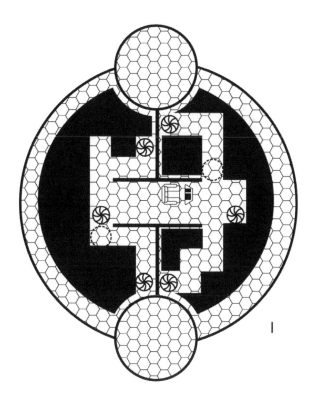

I

J

Deck Plan Symbols

✗	Iris Valve
⭕	Iris Valve, Overhead
✸	Iris Valve, Floor
✸	Iris Valve, Floor and Overhead
▦	Acceleration Couch
☌	Fresher
– – –	Sliding Door
▬ ▬ ▬	Folding Airtight Partition
▬▬▬	Armored Partition
────	Airtight Bulkhead
└─┘	Access Panel

BROADSWORD

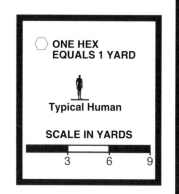

⬡ **ONE HEX EQUALS 1 YARD**

Typical Human

SCALE IN YARDS

3   6   9

Assault Rider

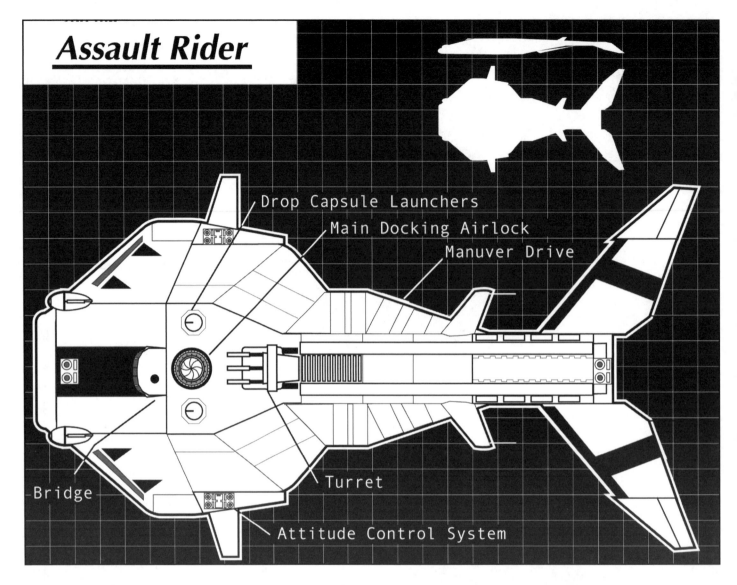

Drop Capsule Launchers
Main Docking Airlock
Manuver Drive
Bridge
Turret
Attitude Control System

PULLER CLASS 300-TON ASSAULT SHIP (TL12)

This ship is intended to transport a platoon-sized unit from one world to the surface of another. It is capable of discharging troops in drop capsules as well, and if doing so, carries fighters or cargo in the vehicle bays.

Crew: Captain (Leadership/Tactics), Pilot (Pilot [Small Starship]/ Astrogation), Electronics Tech (Electronics Operations [Sensors], Electronics Operations [Commo]), Engineer (Engineering [Starship]), 3 Gunners (Gunner [Beam] or [Drop Capsule]).

300-ton SL Hull, DR 100, Radical Stealth, Radical Sensor Masking,Hardened Basic Bridge, Engineering, 17 Maneuver, 12 Jump, 90 Fuel, 6 Staterooms, 14 Bunkrooms, Sickbay, Utility, 6 Vehicle Bays (Heavy Tank), Drop Capsule Launcher, 4 Drop Capsule, 3 Morgue, 2 Turrets, 4 689 MJ Fusion Guns, 0.3 cargo.

■ **Statistics:** EMass: 594.745, LMass: 1,796.245, Cost: MCr182.7736, HP 30,000.

■ **Performance:** Accel: 0.95 Gs, Jump: 3, Air Speed: 2,430, Size: +9.

With APCs carried instead of tanks:

■ **Statistics:** EMass: 594.745, LMass: 686.245, Cost: MCr182.7736, HP: 30,000.

■ **Performance:** Accel: 2.48 Gs, Jump: 3, Air Speed: 2,430, Size: +9.

ERINYES CLASS 200-TON ASSAULT RIDER (TL12)

This vessel was designed for the same function as the *Puller* class assault ship described earlier, but without jump capacity. As such, it requires a separate carrier for interstellar travel, but the omission of a jump drive means that the ship can be made smaller and do the same job.

Crew: Captain(Leadership/Tactics), Pilot (Pilot [small starship]/astrogation), Electronics Tech (Electronics

Operations [Sensors], Electronics Operations [Commo]), Engineer (Engineering [Starship]), 3 Gunners (Gunner [Beam] or [Drop Capsule]).

200-ton SL Hull, DR 100, Radical Stealth, Radical Sensor Masking, Hardened Basic Bridge, Engineering, 35 Maneuver, 6 Staterooms, 14 Bunkrooms, Sickbay, Utility, 6 Vehicle Bays (Heavy Tank), Drop Capsule Launcher, 4 Drop

Capsule, 3 Morgue, 2 Turrets, 4 689 MJ Fusion Guns, 0.3 cargo.

■ **Statistics:** EMass: 477.795, LMass: 1,679.295, Cost: MCr126.076, HP 22,500.

■ **Performance:** Accel: 2.08 Gs, Jump: 0, Air Speed: 4,183, size +8.

Young Class 5,000-ton Assault Tender (TL12)

Young class carriers are designed to jump with six *Erinyes* class assault riders and a number of smaller raft (cutters, fighters, or other surface interface craft) in the ship's two space docks. *Young* class vessels (also known as rider carriers) can defend themselves, but are not front-line combat ships, and require escort vessels if spaceborne opposition is expected. Staterooms are single occupancy for captain, executive officer and chief engineer, double for the rest of the ship's crew, quadruple for troops.

Crew: Captain (Leadership/Tactics), Executive Officer (Leadership/Tactics), 3 Pilots (Pilot [starship]), 3 Navigators (astrogation), 6 Sensor Techs (Electronics Operations [Sensors]), 12 Commo Techs (Electronics Operations [Commo]), 9 Engineers (Engineering [Starship]), 22 Gunners (Gunner [Beam], [Missile] or [Drop Capsule]), 9 Medics (First Aid, Physician), 42 Small Craft Crew.

5,000-ton SL Hull, DR 1,000, Radical Stealth, Radical Sensor Masking, Total Compartmentalization, 2 Hardened

With APCs carried instead of tanks:

■ **Statistics:** EMass: 477.795, LMass: 569.295, Cost: MCr126.076, HP 22,500.

■ **Performance:** Accel: 6.15 Gs, Jump: 0, Air Speed: 4,183, Size: +8.

Command Bridge, Hardened Basic Bridge, 2 Engineering, 420 Maneuver, 248 Jump, 1860 Fuel, 5 low berth, 90 Staterooms, 8 Sickbay, 10 Utility, 2 Space Docks (Holds 900, 6 Doors), 6 External Grapples (Holding 1750 tons each) 4 nuclear Damper (15 mile range), 22 Turrets, 30 405 MJ Lasers, 15 Missile launchers, 21 Sandcasters, 167 cargo.

■ **Statistics:** EMass: 9,844.825, LMass: 24,179.825, Cost: MCr1,507.0926, HP 165,000.

■ **Performance:** Accel: 1.74 Gs, Jump: 3, Air Speed: USL, Size: +11.

After dropping Riders:

■ **Statistics:** EMass: 9,844.825, LMass: 13,679.825, Cost: MCr1,507.0926, HP 165,000.

■ **Performance:** Accel: 3.07 Gs, Jump: 3, Air Speed: USL, Size: +11.

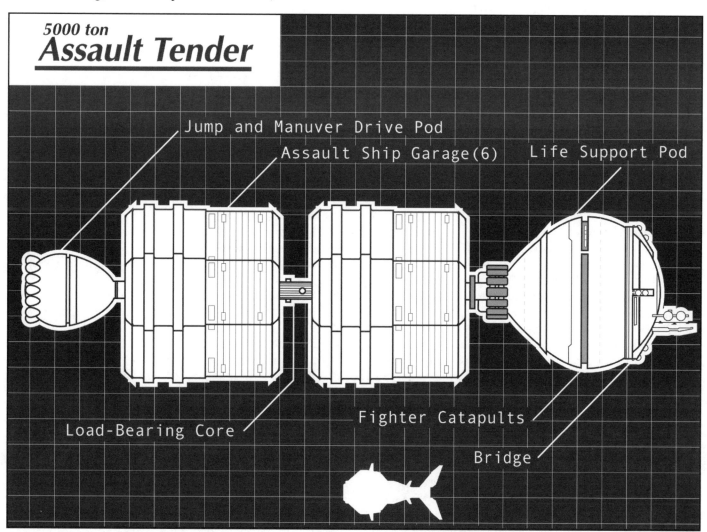

5000 ton **Assault Tender**

Jump and Manuver Drive Pod

Assault Ship Garage (6)

Life Support Pod

Load-Bearing Core

Fighter Catapults

Bridge

VEHICLES

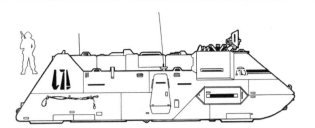

UTILITY GRAV SLED (TL9)

This vehicle is a typical light transport vehicle at TL9, and is basically a civilian model with military fittings.

- **Body and Subassemblies:** No subassemblies. Body has very good streamlining.
- **Drivetrain:** 2×100 kW vector ducted fan (0.2 MW, 800 lbs. thrust), TL13 contragrav with 10T lift.
- **Instruments and Electronics:** 2×long range scrambled radios, 5 mile (scan 15) Radar, ×5 magnification LLTV (forward), ×1 magnification LLTV (back), radar/laser detector, IFF, terrain-following radar, micro-computer (C×3), one terminal.
- **Programs:** Datalink, computer navigation, Pilot-12.
- **Misc. Equipment:** Compact fire suppression.
- **Controls:** Computerized controls.
- **Crew:** one roomy crewstation, "driver."
- **Occupancy:** Short.
- **Passengers:** One roomy passenger seat.
- **Environmental Systems:** Environmental control.
- **Safety Systems:** Crashwebs for driver and passenger.
- **Power Systems:** 2×115 kW fuel cell power all systems, use 26.5 gph lhd. 212 gallon self-sealing fuel tank (-4 fire) lasts 8 hours.
- **Spaces:** 26.14 cf access space, 440 cf cargo space, 7.96 cf waste space.
- **Volume:** 750 cf body, size +4.
- **Area:** 500 sf body.
- **Frame:** Cheap.
- **Hit Points:** body 750.
- **Armor:** PD 3/DR 5 expensive metal, additional DR 50 open-frame expensive metal on front, rear, and belly.
- **Cargo:** 120 lbs. hydrogen fuel, two passengers, 4.5 tons cargo.
- **Statistics:** weight 4,914 lbs. unloaded, 14,434 lbs. (7.2 tons) loaded, HT 12.
- **Price:** Cr 59,220.
- **Performance:** No ground performance. No water performance. Stall speed 0, can fly. Motive thrust 800 lbs., drag 100, aMax 240, aAcc 1 mph, aMR 3, aSR 5, aDec 12 mph.
- **Variants:** Passenger variant would add twelve medium seats, leaving 80 cf cargo.

IMPERIAL MESON SLED (TL12)

Hated by other units for its stealth, this vehicle can submerge (roughly neutral density with power off; CG sufficient to rise out of water). The meson gun is poorly suited to anti-spacecraft fire, though since meson guns are unaffected by atmosphere its atmospheric range is fairly good. This is the standard meson-gun vehicle for the Imperial armed forces.

- **Body and Subassemblies:** One full-rotation turret.
- **Drivetrain:** 3×15 ton vector super thrusters, 2×TL13 contragravs, with 115T lift each.
- **Weapons:** 10 GJ meson gun (BoF), with full stabilization. 1,440 kJ point defense xaser (TuF), with full stabilization and a universal mount.
- **Instruments and Electronics:** Very long range scrambled radio, 2×long range scrambled radios, 2×long range lasercomm (100,000 miles), long range meson comm (100,000 miles), 1,000 mile (scan 29) PESA (TuF), 4×2 mile (scan 13) PESA (band about body), 1,000 mile (scan 29) radscanner, 2×IFF, HUDWAC w/pupil scanner, 2×Inertial Navigation System, 2×terrain following radar, deceptive jammer/10, 8 dischargers, 32 reloads, hardened genius dedicated microframe w/target +10, hardened minicomputer (C×7), 4×terminal
- **Programs:** Datalink-1, computer navigation-2, targeting +8 ×2, transmission profiling, damage control, encryption/7, translation.
- **Equipment:** Compact fire suppression, 1-person airlock.
- **Controls:** Computerized, duplicate.
- **Crewstations:** Four roomy, designated "driver" "gunner," "commander," "electronics."
- **Occupancy:** Short.
- **Passengers:** None.
- **Environmental Systems:** Full life support.
- **Safety Systems:** Crashwebs.
- **Power Systems:** 80 megawatt fusion power plant powers all systems but weapons, with 75 megawatts excess power. 162 gigajoule energy bank is sufficient for 8 meson shots, and the power plant will recharge another shot every 4.5 minutes.
- **Spaces:** 432.5 cf access space, 0.6 cf waste space in turret, 10.99 cf waste space in body.
- **Volume:** Body 2,750, turret 20. Total 2,770, size +5
- **Area:** Body 1,200, turret 40, total 1,240.
- **Frame:** Very heavy.
- **Hit Points:** Body 7,200, turret 240.
- **Armor:** PD 4/DR 1,250 expensive metal armor.
- **Surface features:** Sealed, instant chameleon, radical emissions, basic stealth, radical sound suppression.
- **Statistics:** Weight 177,096 lbs. unloaded, 177,896 lbs. (89.9 tons) loaded, HT 12.
- **Price:** Cr6,984,000.
- **Performance:** No ground performance. Flotation 173,125, cannot float. Submerged drag 3,100, submerged thrust 90,000 lbs., sMax 20 mph, sAcc 10 mph. Stall speed 0, can fly. Motive thrust 90,000 lbs., drag 2,720, aMax 500 mph, aAcc 10 mph, aMR 4, aSR 6, aDec 16 mph. Space performance 0.5 Gs.

IMPERIAL ASTRIN CLASS GRAV APC (TL12)

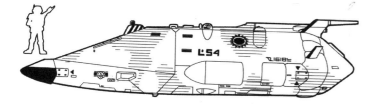

The *Astrin* was developed to accompany the *Intrepid* class grav tanks into battle. It entered service in 1112, and equips units of the Imperial Marines, the Imperial Army, and a few planetary armed forces.

- **Body and Subassemblies:** Body with 60° frontal slope, one full rotation turret with 60° frontal slope.
- **Drivetrain:** 4×7,500 lbs. vector super reactionless thruster, 2×TL13 contragrav, 20T lift each.
- **Weapons:** 10 MJ RF fusion gun (Tu) with full stabilization and a universal mount. 4mm VRF gauss gun (Tu) with full stabilization, a universal mount, and 12,000 rounds of ammunition.
- **Instruments and Electronics:** Very long range scrambled radio, 4×long range scrambled radios, long range laser-comm (100,000 miles), 20 mile (scan 19) PESA (Tu), 4×2 mile (scan 13) PESA about body, 100 mile (scan 23) radscanner, 25 mile laser rangefinder (Tu), 2×IFF, HUDWAC w/pupil scan for gunner, 2×Inertial Navigation System, 2×Terrain Following Radar, 4 dischargers (2 blackout, 2 chaff) with 16 reloads, hardened minicomputer (C×7) with 3 terminals.
- **Programs:** Datalink, computer navigation, Piloting-15, Targeting +7 ×2, transmission profiling, damage control, encryption/6, translation. Cannot run targeting for both weapons simultaneously, nor in combination with encryption.
- **Misc. Equipment:** Compact fire suppression.
- **Controls:** Computerized, duplicate controls.

- **Crewstations:** 3 medium, designated "driver," "gunner," "commander."
- **Occupancy:** Short.
- **Passengers:** 10 large passenger seats. *Note:* Troops in battledress fit in large seats as if they were small seats.
- **Environmental Systems:** Full life support for 13.
- **Safety Systems:** Crashwebs for passengers and crew.
- **Power Systems:** 1.555 MW NPU power all systems but fusion gun. 2,250 MJ energy bank is sufficient for 112 fusion gun shots.
- **Spaces:** 25.6 cf access space, 0.6 cf waste in turret, 1.99 cf waste in body, 180 cf cargo in body.
- **Volume:** Body 960, turret 31, total 991, size +4.
- **Area:** Body 600, turret 60. Total 660 sf.
- **Frame:** Extra-heavy, cheap.
- **Armor:** PD 4/DR 550 advanced metal. Slope increases this to 6/1,100 on turret and body front.
- **Body features:** Sealed.
- **Surface features:** Instant chameleon, basic emissions cloaking, basic stealth.
- **Statistics:** weight 22,432 lbs. unloaded, 30,657 lbs. (15.3 tons) loaded, HT 8.
- **Price:** Cr936,000.
- **Performance:** No ground performance. Flotation 23 tons, can float. Stall speed 0, can fly. Motive thrust 30,000 lbs., drag 660, aMax 580, aAcc 20 mph, aMR 4.5, aSR 5, aDec 18 mph. Space performance 0.99 Gs.

Variants: Cargo variant removes 10 seats and relevant life support, giving 620 cf total cargo space. No significant cost change; it matches the stats above with a 4 ton load.

Damper variant, as above, but adds one crewstation, a 5 mile radius nuclear damper, a 1 megawatt auxiliary power system to run the damper, and 300 cf of waste space. Adds MCr4.08; fully loaded it is 23.5 tons, reducing acceleration to 15 mph and space performance to 0.65 Gs. Other stats are not generally affected.

Other variants (command, FDC, computer, communications, and so on) do not signifigantly alter the APC statistics or performance.

IMPERIAL INTREPID CLASS GRAV TANK (TL12)

The *Intrepid* is the standard Imperial grav tank, and is an excellent example of what TL12 military technology can actually accomplish (with a nearly unlimited budget). It entered service in 1109 and equips units of the Imperial Marines, the Imperial Army, and a few planetary armed forces, but is very rare in mercenary units.

- **Body and Subassemblies:** Body with 60° frontal slope. One full-rotation turret on body with 60° frontal slope. One full-rotation "cupola" turret on top of main turret.
- **Drivetrain:** 4×50 ton vector super reactionless thruster, 2×TL13 contragrav with 240 tons lift each.
- **Weapons:** 2.3 GJ MJ RoF 1/2 compact fusion gun, with full stabilization and a universal mount, in turret. 1440 kJ point defense xaser, with full stabilization and a universal mount, in cupola. 4mm VRF gauss gun, with full stabilization, a universal mount, and 30,000 rounds of ammunition, in cupola.
- **Instruments and Electronics:** Extreme range scrambled radio, 4×long range scrambled radios, 4×long range lasercomm (100,000 miles), medium range meson comm

(10,000 miles), 2,000 mile (scan 31) PESA in turret, 500 mile (scan 27) PESA in cupola, 4×5 mile (scan 15) PESA in band about body, 4,500 mile (scan 33) AESA in cupola, 1,000 mile (scan 29) radscanner, 2×IFF, 2×HUDWAC w/pupil scanner, 2×Inertial Navigation System, 2×terrain following radar, deceptive jammer/10, 4 dischargers in turret, 4 dischargers and 16 reloads in body, hardened genius dedicated microframe with targeting +10 for fusion gun, hardened genius dedicated microframe with gunner-17, 3×hardened microframe (complexity 8), 4×terminal.

- **Software:** Datalink, computer navigation, targeting (C7) for all weapons, transmission profiling, damage control, encryption (C8), translation, driver (skill 16).
- **Misc. Equipment:** Compact fire suppression.
- **Controls:** Computerized, with duplicate controls.
- **Crewstations:** Four medium, designated "driver," "gunner," "commander," "electronics."
- **Occupancy:** Short.
- **Environmental Systems:** Full life support.
- **Safety Systems:** Gravity webs and crashwebs.
- **Power Systems:** 30 megawatt fusion power plants powers all systems but weaponry with 8.5 MW excess power. 186 gigajoule energy bank is sufficient for 40 shots from the main gun; point defense weapons fire uses up one shot per 60 seconds. One shot is recharged every 9 minutes under normal operating circumstances.
- **Spaces:** 410 cf access space, 0.14 cf waste space in cupola, 0.5 cf waste space in turret, 5.85 cf waste space in body.
- **Volume:** Body 1,460, turret 520, cupola 30, total 2,010, size +5.
- **Area:** Body 800, turret 400, cupola 60, total 1,260.
- **Frame:** Extremely heavy, cheap.
- **Hit Points:** Body 4,800, turret 2,400, cupola 360.
- **Body features:** Heavy compartmentalization, sealed.
- **Armor:** PD 4/DR 10,000 advanced metal on body and turret, increases to PD 6/DR 25,000 on front. PD 4/DR 5,000 advanced metal on cupola.
- **Surface features:** Sealed, instant chameleon, radical emissions cloaking, radical stealth, basic sound suppression.
- **Statistics:** Weight 381,023 lbs. unloaded, 381,848 (191.9 tons) loaded, HT 8.
- **Price:** Cr15,600,000.
- **Performance:** No ground performance. Flotation 44 tons, cannot float. Crush depth 140 miles. Stall speed 0, can fly. Motive thrust 400,000 lbs., drag 1,260, aMax 600, aMR 4, aSR 6, aAcc 20 mph, aDec 16 mph. Space performance 1.04 Gs.

Grav APC (TL10)

This design is typical of a number of 10-ton, export grade APCs made by various manufacturers, normally carrying eight passengers and three crew. It is resistant to small-arms, and has weaponry suitable for killing other vehicles in its same general class, or for killing battledress or other relatively light armor. A wide variety of variants exist – if you remove the seats the vehicle has slightly over 400 cf of free space, sufficient for large amounts of cargo, a repair shop, surgical theater, etc.

- **Body and Subassemblies:** Good streamlining, 30° frontal slope, one full rotation turret with 60° frontal slope.
- **Drivetrain:** 4×1 ton vector super reactionless thruster, 2×TL13 contragrav, 15T lift each.
- **Weapons:** 10 MJ rapid pulse (Tu) with full stabilization and a universal mount, VRF gauss gun (Tu) with full stabilization and a universal mount, 12,000 rounds 4mm (Tu).
- **Instruments and Electronics:** Very long range scrambled radio, 4×long range scrambled radio, long range laser-comm, PESA/10 (Tu), 4×PESA/1, radscanner/20, 25 mile laser rangefinder (Tu), 2×IFF, HUDWAC w/pupil scanner, 2×Inertial Navigation System, 2×terrain following radar, 4 dischargers with 12 reloads, hardened mini-computer (C×5), 3×terminal.
- **Programs:** Datalink-1, computer navigation-2, targeting +6 (separate for fusion gun and VRF; does not run both at the same time), transmission profiling, damage control, complexity 5 encryption.

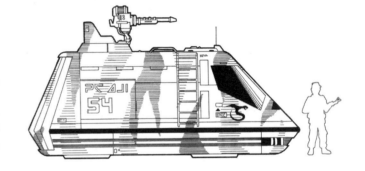

- **Misc. Equipment:** Compact fire suppression.
- **Controls:** Computerized, with duplicate controls.
- **Crewstations:** 3 medium, designated "driver" "gunner," "commander," in normal crewstations.
- **Occupancy:** Short.
- **Passengers:** 8 medium seats.
- **Safety Systems:** All crewstations and seats have crashwebs.
- **Environmental Systems:** NBC for 11, 11 man-days limited life support.
- **Power Systems:** 455 KW NPU powers all systems except weaponry, 1.8 GJ energy bank lasts for 90 fusion gun shots, or consumes equivalent of one shot every 15 seconds of VRF fire. If parked, the energy bank can be fully recharged in somewhat over an hour.
- **Spaces:** 18 cf short-term access space, 160 cf cargo space, 0.7 cf waste in turret, 1.47 cf waste in body.

Air/Space Defense (TL10)

This is not a terribly common vehicle – it's mostly used to discourage light spaceships from intervening in a battle, as it has similar weaponry and is impervious to turret-based lasers. It is also suitable for long-range defense against aircraft.

- **Body and Subassemblies:** One full-rotation turret (Tu) on body. One full-rotation turret (Cupola), on main turret.
- **Drivetrain:** 4×3-ton vector reactionless thruster, 2×TL13 contragrav with 115T lift each.
- **Weapons:** 360 MJ compact starship xaser (TuF) in a fully stabilized universal mount. VRF gauss gun (Cup) in universal stabilized mount with 12,000 rounds of ammunition.
- **Instruments and Electronics:** Extreme range scrambled radio, 4×long range scrambled radios, 4×long range lasercomm (100,000 miles), medium range meson comm (10,000 miles), 5 mile (Scan 15) PESA in cupola, 4×5 mile PESA cover 360° about vehicle, 1000 mile (Scan 29) PESA in turret, 4500 mile (Scan 33) AESA with the air search option in turret, 200 mile (Scan 25) radscanner, two IFF, two HUDWACs with pupil scanning, two inertial navigation system, deceptive jammer/8, 8 dischargers with 32 reloads (normally 6 blackout, 2 chaff), genius dedicated mainframe with C×8 targeting (+9, for xaser), 3×hardened microframes, 3×terminals.
- **Software:** datalink, computer navigation, targeting +7 ×2 (for xaser and VRF; xaser not normally used)), transmission profiling, damage control, encryption/6.

- **Misc. Equipment:** Compact fire suppression.
- **Controls:** Computer controls, duplicate controls.
- **Crewstations:** Three medium, designated "driver," "gunner," "commander/sensors."
- **Occupancy:** Short.
- **Environmental Systems:** Full life support.
- **Safety Systems:** Crashwebs on all crewstations.
- **Power Systems:** 10 megawatt fusion powers all systems but laser with 7.44 MW power remaining. 72 GJ energy bank is sufficient for 80 laser shots. Recharges 1 shot per 2 minutes under normal operating conditions.
- **Spaces:** 120 cf access space, 1.58 cf waste in turret, 1.4 cf waste space in body, 6 cf cargo space in body.
- **Volume:** Body 510, turret 260, cupola 1.35, total 771.35. Size +4.
- **Area:** Body 400, turret 250, cupola 8, total 658.
- **Frame:** Extra-heavy, cheap.
- **Hit Points:** Body 2400, turret 1500, cupola 48.
- **Armor:** PD 4/DR 500 advanced metal overall. Increased to PD 4/DR 3,000 on turret and body front and top.
- **Surface features:** Sealed, instant chameleon, radical emissions cloaking, radical stealth.
- **Statistics:** Weight 93925.5 unloaded, 94600 (47.3 tons) loaded. HT 10.
- **Price:** Cr7,787,035.
- **Performance:** Flotation 24 tons, cannot float. Crush depth 20,000 yards. Stall speed 0, can fly. Motive thrust 24,000 lbs., drag 658, aMax 520, aAcc 5 mph, aMR 4, aSR 5, aDec 16.

- **Volume:** Body 750 cf, turret 31 cf, size +4.
- **Area:** Body 500 sf, turret 60 sf.
- **Frame:** Heavy, good streamlining.
- **Hit Points:** Body 1500, turret 90.
- **Armor:** PD 4/DR 250 expensive laminate armor. Slope increases this to 5/375 on the body front, 6/500 on the turret front.
- **Surface features:** Sealed, instant chameleon, basic emissions cloaking, basic stealth, basic sound suppression.
- **Statistics:** Weight 14,865 unloaded, 20,290 (10.2 tons) loaded (including 1.6 tons cargo), HT 12.
- **Price:** Cr855,205.
- **Performance:** No ground performance. Flotation 18 tons, can float. Stall speed 0, can fly. Drag 186, motive thrust 8000 lbs., aMax 570 mph, aAcc 8 mph, aMR 4, aDec 16, aSR 5. Space performance 0.4 Gs.

Variants: Removing the seats gives 400 cf of cargo space, sufficient for about around 4 tons of cargo; this ups loaded weight to around 12 tons, reducing acceleration to 6 mph, but does not otherwise affect performance.

An ambulance variant can fit two medics and eight stretchers; the conversion Cr1,000 plus Cr7,500 each for ESUs.

The most common weaponry variant is to replace the fusion gun with a rapid-fire 80mm electromagnetic howitzer (usable for direct or indirect fire) and a 400 round ABS magazine. This variant is sometimes called a support sled, and cuts 310 lbs. off the unloaded weight, and subtracts Cr17,000 from the price, but adds 690 lbs. to the loaded weight.

Instellarms Light Grav Tank (TL10)

Instellarms manufacturers its grav tanks under a variety of names, and licenses its production to other companies. It is not an especially advanced design, but the price is reasonable, and it can hold its own against most lighter vehicles.

- **Body and Subassemblies:** Body with 60° frontal slope. One full-rotation turret with 60° frontal slope, on body.
- **Drivetrain:** 4×3 ton vector reactionless thruster, 2×TL13 contragrav with 65T lift each.
- **Weapons:** 540 MJ light plasma cannon (TuF) with a universal mount and full stabilization, 4mm VRF gauss gun (TuF) with universal mount and full stabilization, and space for 12,000 rounds.
- **Instruments and Electronics:** Very long range scrambled radio, 2×long range scrambled radios, 2×long range lasercomm (100,000 miles), 50 mile (scan 21) PESA (TuF), 4×5 mile (scan 15) PESA in band about body, 300 mile (scan 26) AESA with air search option, 200 mile (scan 25) radscanner, 2×IFF, 2×HUDWAC with pupil scan, 2×inertial navigation system, 2×terrain following radar, deceptive jammer/8, 6 dischargers (4 blackout, 2 chaff) plus 18 reloads, hardened genius microframe with targeting/7 (+8 to plasma gun), 3×hardened microframe (C×6), 3×terminal.
- **Programs:** Datalink-1, computer navigation-2, targeting +7 ×2, transmission profiling, damage control, encryption/6
- **Misc. Equipment:** Compact fire suppression.

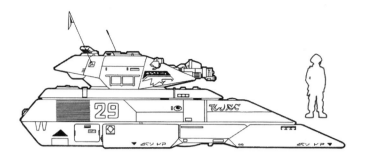

- **Controls:** Computerized, duplicate.
- **Crewstations:** Three normal, designated "driver," "gunner," "commander."
- **Occupancy:** Short.
- **Environmental Systems:** 6 man-days limited life support, NBC for 3.
- **Safety Systems:** Crashwebs for all crewstations.
- **Power Systems:** 1,405 kilowatt NPU (lasts 2 years) powers all systems except weaponry. 27 GJ energy bank supports

25 shots from main gun or essentially unlimited VRF fire. If parked, can renew 1 main-gun shot every 13 minutes.
- **Spaces:** 53.5 cf access space, 0.45 cf waste in turret, 0.15 cf waste in body.
- **Volume:** Body 350, turret 120, total 470, size +4.
- **Area:** Body 300, turret 150, total 450.
- **Frame:** Extra-heavy, cheap.
- **Hit Points:** Body 1,800, turret 900.
- **Armor:** Overall PD 4/DR 2,750 advanced metal. Body and turret front have PD 6/DR 8,000 advanced metal.
- **Surface features:** Instant chameleon, basic emissions cloaking, basic stealth, basic sound suppression.
- **Statistics:** Weight 95,095 unloaded, 95,757 (48 tons) loaded, Cr4,010,000, HT 9.
- **Performance:** Flotation 14 tons, cannot float. Crush depth 34 miles. Stall speed 0, can fly. Motive thrust 24,000 lbs., drag 450, aMax 600, aAcc 5 mph, aMR 4, aSR 5, aDec 16 mph. Space performance 0.25 Gs.

INSTELLARMS MEDIUM GRAV TANK (TL10)

Instellarms' next step up from the light grav tank, this vehicle is more expensive, but with a built-in point defense gun, better electronics and heavier armor.

- **Body and Subassemblies:** Body with 60° frontal slope. One full-rotation turret with 60° frontal slope, on body. One full-rotation point defense turret, on main turret.
- **Drivetrain:** 4×15,000 lbs. vectored reactionless thruster, 2×TL13 CG units with 115 tons lift each.
- **Weapons:** 945 MJ plasma gun (TuF), with full stabilization and a universal mount. 2250 kJ point defense xaser (PD) with full stabilization and a universal mount. 4mm VRF gauss gun with full stabilization, a universal mount, and 30,000 rounds of ammunition.
- **Instruments and Electronics:** Extreme range scrambled radio, 4×long range scrambled radios, 4×long range lasercomm (100,000 miles), medium range meson comm (10,000 miles), 100 mile (scan 23) PESA (TuF), 4×5 mile (scan 15) PESA in band about body, 50 mile (scan 21) PESA (PD), 2000 mile (scan 31) AESA with the air search option (PD), 2×HUDWAC w/pupil scanner, 2×inertial navigation system, 2×terrain following radar, deceptive jammer/10, 6 dischargers (4 blackout, 2 chaff) with 18 reloads, genius dedicated microframe with targeting +8, genius dedicated mainframe with gunner/16, 3×hardened microframe (C×6), 3×terminal.
- **Programs:** Datalink-1, computer navigation-2, targeting +7 ×3, transmission profiling, damage control, encryption/6.
- **Misc. Equipment:** Compact fire suppression.
- **Controls:** Computerized, duplicate.
- **Crewstations:** Three normal, designated "driver," "gunner," "commander."
- **Occupancy:** Short.
- **Environmental Systems:** 6 man-days limited life support, NBC for 3.
- **Safety Systems:** Crashwebs.

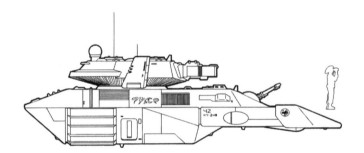

- **Power Systems:** 10 MW fusion power plant powers all systems but laser and fusion guns with 6.3 MW excess power. 72 gigajoule energy bank lasts for 38 main gun shots or drains equivalent of one shot per 18 seconds of point defense fire.
- **Spaces:** 175 cf access space, 3.64 cf waste in turret, 1.8 cf waste in body, 20 cf cargo in body.
- **Volume:** Body 750, turret 210, PD 24, total 974, size +4.
- **Area:** Body 500, turret 250, PD 50, total 800.
- **Frame:** Extremely heavy, cheap.
- **Hit Points:** Body 3,000, turret 1,500, PD 300.
- **Armor:** Body and turret have PD 4/DR 3,300 advanced metal, with PD 6/DR 9,600 advanced metal on the front. Point defense turret has PD 4/DR 2,000 advanced metal armor.
- **Body features:** Sealed, heavy compartmentalization for body.
- **Surface features:** Instant chameleon, basic emissions and stealth, basic sound suppression.
- **Statistics:** Weight 196,843 unloaded, 197,905 (99 tons) loaded HT 8.
- **Price:** Cr8,200,000.
- **Performance:** No ground performance. Flotation 30 tons, cannot float. Crush depth 40 miles. Stall speed 0, can fly. Aerial thrust 60,000 lbs., drag 800, aMax 600, aAcc 6 mph, aMR 4, aSR 5, aDec 16 mph. Space performance 0.3 Gs.

Instellarms Heavy Grav Tank (TL10)

This design is similar to the medium tank, but incorporates upgraded armor and an additional crewmember.

- **Body and Subassemblies:** Body with 60° frontal slope. One full-rotation main turret with 60° frontal slope, on body. One full-rotation point defense turret on main turret.
- **Drivetrain:** 4×20 ton vector reactionless thruster, 2×TL13 contragrav with 240T lift each.
- **Weapons:** 1,350 MJ RoF 1/2 compact plasma gun (TuF) with full stabilization and a universal mount, 2,250 kJ point defense xaser (PD) with full stabilization and a universal mount. 4mm VRF gauss gun (TuF) with full stabilization, a universal mount, and 30,000 rounds of ammunition.
- **Instruments and Electronics:** Extreme range (5,000,000 mile) scrambled radio, 4×long range (50,000 mile) scrambled radios, 4×long range lasercomm (100,000 miles), medium range meson comm (10,000 miles), 100 mile (scan 23) PESA (TuF), 4×5 mile (scan 15) PESA in band about body, 50 mile (scan 21) PESA (PD), 2,000 mile (scan 31) AESA with the air search option (PD), 200 mile (scan 25) radscanner, 50 mile laser rangefinder (TuF), 2×HUDWAC w/pupil scanner, 2×inertial navigation system, 2×terrain following radar, deceptive jammer/10, 6 dischargers (4 blackout, 2 chaff) in turret, 6 dischargers (4 blackout, 2 chaff) in body, 18 reloads, genius dedicated microframe with targeting +8 (main gun), genius dedicated mainframe with gunner/16 (gatling xaser), 3×hardened microframe (C×6), 4 terminals.
- **Programs:** Datalink-1, computer navigation-2, targeting +7 ×3, transmission profiling, damage control, encryption/6

- **Misc. Equipment:** Compact fire suppression.
- **Controls:** Computerized, duplicate.
- **Crewstations:** 4 medium, designated "driver," "gunner," "commander," "electronics."
- **Occupancy:** Short.
- **Environmental Systems:** full life support.
- **Safety Systems:** crashwebs.
- **Power:** 20 megawatt fusion power plant powers all systems except weapons with 12.2 MW of excess power. 72 gigajoule energy bank lasts for 26 main gun shots, or drains one shot per 30 seconds of xaser fire. One shot is recovered every 4 minutes of normal operation.
- **Spaces:** 370 cf access space, 2.24 cf waste space in turret, 2.1 cf waste space in body, 40 cf cargo space in body.
- **Volume:** Body 1,350, turret 300, PD 24. Total 1,674 cf, size +5.
- **Area:** Body 800, turret 300, PD 50, total 1,150.
- **Frame:** Extremely heavy, cheap.
- **Hit Points:** Body 4,800, turret 1,800, PD 300.
- **Body features:** Sealed, heavy compartmentalization in body.
- **Armor:** PD 4/DR 4,750 advanced metal on body and turret, increases to PD 6/DR 12,000 on front. Point defense turret PD 4/DR 2,000.
- **Surface features:** Instant chameleon, basic emissions cloaking, basic stealth, basic sound suppression.
- **Statistics:** Weight 381,695 unloaded, 382,557 (191.3 tons) loaded, HT 8.
- **Price:** Cr12,580,000.
- **Performance:** No ground performance. Flotation 42 tons, cannot float. Crush depth 55 miles. Stall speed 0, can fly. Aerial motive thrust 160,000 lbs., drag 1,150, aMax 600 mph, aAcc 8 mph, aMR 3.5, aSR 6, aDec 4 mph. Space performance 0.4 Gs.

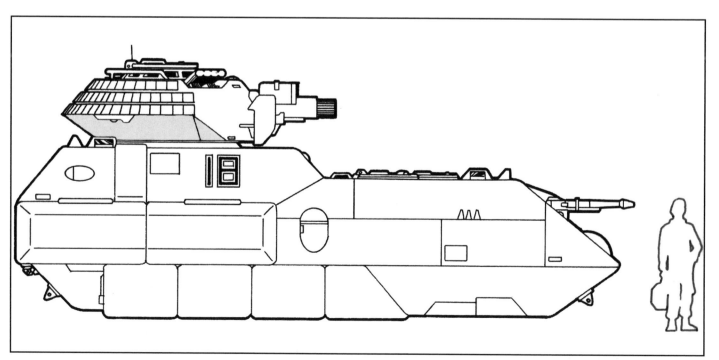

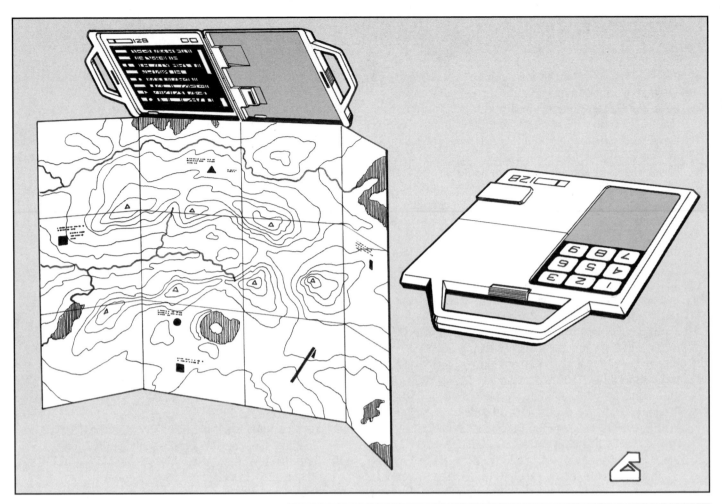

OTHER EQUIPMENT

Artificial Gill: Works by electrolysis to extract oxygen from water for 24 hours on a C-cell. Cr2,000, 20 lbs.

Backpack: With frame (holds 150 lbs.) Cr200, 5 lbs.

Canteen: Holds one quart (2 lbs.) of water. Cr10, 3 lbs. (full).

Chemsticks, IR: Five IR-only chemsticks, with blackout cover. Cr15, 0.5 lbs.

Chemsticks: Five chemsticks, 24 hr duration, with blackout cover. Cr5, 0.5 lbs.

Clothing, Summer Uniform: Shorts, t-shirt, shoes, etc. Cr30+, negligible weight.

Clothing, Ordinary Uniform: Cr50+, 2 lbs.

Clothing, Dress Uniform: Cr100+, 3 lbs.

Clothing, Winter: PD0, DR1, +2 to HT to resist cold weather. Cr100+, 2 lbs.

Clothing, Arctic: PD0, DR2, +5 to HT to resist cold weather. Cr200+, 4 lbs.

Emergency Blanket: Aluminized "space" blanket with fluorescent orange and camouflaged sides. Cr5, 0.5 lbs.

Entrenching Tool: A folding shovel, uses Axe skill, does Swing-1 cutting. Cr15, 2 lbs.

Fire Extinguisher, Personal: One-use item for small fires. Cr10, 0.5 lbs.

Filtration Canteen: Filters one quart of water pure enough for drinking in 30 minutes. Cr175, 3 lbs.

Laser Designator: Illuminates the target for laser-homing projectiles, giving a +5 to hit. Cr1,000, 2 lbs.

Laser Rangefinder: This device is used to give accurate range and movement, adds +2 to hit Cr3,000, 2 lbs.

Machete: Sw+1 cut, Reach 1, Min ST 10. Cr50, 3 lbs.

Map Box: A hardened computer running a Computer Navigation program, +2 to skill Cr4,500, 1 lbs.

Medkit, Individual:+1 to First Aid Cr300, 2 lbs.

Medkit, Medic's: +2 to First Aid, Physician, Surgery, and Diagnosis at no penalty. Cr1,500, 15 lbs.

Medkit, Vehicle: +2 to First Aid, +1 to Surgery, Physician and Diagnosis. Cr5,000, 50 lbs.

Mess kit, Personal: Small cooking kit for one man, with can opener, fork, knife, cup, and spoon. Cr15, 0.5 lbs.

Mine, Bouncing Betty: See p. 67. Cr100, 5 lbs.

Mine, Claymore: See p. 67. Cr200, 5 lbs.

Rations, Tube: Concentrated rations for one week, water required. Cr50, 2 lbs.

Rations, MRE: Military rations, water required. Cr5, 1.5 lbs.

Rations, Tablets: 30-day supply of tablets provides all nutrients, water required. Cr50, 2 lbs.

Sleeping Bag, Cold-Weather: +5 to HT rolls in cold weather. Cr200, 5 lbs.

Sleeping Bag, Standard: Cr100, 3 lbs.

Tripod, VRFGG: Cr290, 29 lbs.

CHAPTER FIVE

Character Templates

To the casual glance, it might seem that these templates duplicate those on pp. GT100-105. The character templates in *GURPS Traveller*, however, mostly represent former members of the military, whereas these templates are changed slightly to represent serving military characters or mercenaries. Marines use the Marine templates from pp. GT102-103, Marine commandos use the Marine Special Operations templates from pp. GT103-104.

Character templates and their use in character creation are discussed on p. GT86.

INFANTRY   60 POINTS

Attributes: ST 11 [10], DX 12 [20], IQ 11 [10], HT 10 [0].

Advantages: A total of 15 points in: Combat Reflexes [15], Fit or Very Fit [5 or 15], Hard to Kill 1-2 [5 or 10], Toughness (DR1) [10], High Pain Threshold [10], Alertness [5/level].

Disadvantages: A total of -20 points in: Bloodlust [-10], Berserk [-15], Callous [-6], Chummy [-5], Code of Honor (Mercenaries) [-5], Overconfidence [-10], Post Combat Shakes [-5], and Sense of Duty (Comrades) [-5].

Primary Skills: Either Beam Weapons (any) or Guns (any) both (P/E) DX+2 [2]-14, plus Gunner (any) (P/A) DX [1]-12, Stealth (P/A) DX [2]-12, Tactics (M/H) IQ-1 [2]-10, Thrown Weapon (Grenade) (P/E) DX [1]-12.

Secondary Skills: Savoir-Faire (Military) (M/E) IQ [1]-11, Armory (Small Arms) (M/A) IQ [2]-11, Camouflage (M/E) IQ [1]-11, Electronics Operation (Commo) (M/A) IQ-1 [1]-10, First Aid (M/E) IQ [1]-11, Hiking (P/A; HT) HT-1 [1]-9, Orienteering (M/A) IQ-1 [1]-10, Survival (any)

(M/A) IQ-1 [1]-10, a total of 2 points in Brawling (P/E), Judo (P/H), Knife (P/E) and Spear (P/A).

Background Skills: A total of 6 points in Scrounging (M/E), Administration, Demolition, Forward Observer, Leadership, Merchant, Streetwise, Electronics Operation (Commo), (all M/A); Engineer (Combat) (M/H); Beam Weapons (other), Guns (other), or Parachuting (all P/E); and Battlesuit, Driving (any), Pilot (Grav) or Gunner (any) all (P/A).

CAVALRY   65 POINTS

Attributes: ST 11 [10], DX 12 [20], IQ 11 [10], HT 10 [0].

Advantages: A total of 15 points in: Combat Reflexes [15], Fit or Very Fit [5 or 15], Hard to Kill 1-2 [5 or 10], Toughness (DR1) [10], High Pain Threshold [10], Alertness [5/level], Animal empathy [5].

Disadvantages: A total of -20 points in: Bloodlust [-10], Berserk [-15], Callous [-6], Chummy [-5], Code of Honor (Mercenaries) [-5], Overconfidence or Glory Hound [-10 or -15], Post Combat Shakes [-5], and Sense of Duty (Comrades) [-5].

Primary Skills: Either Beam Weapons (any) or Guns (any), both (P/E) DX+2 [2]-14, plus Gunner (any) (P/A) DX [1]-12, Either Pilot (Grav) or Riding (any) or Driving (any) all (P/A) DX [2]-12, Stealth (P/A) DX [2]-12, Tactics (M/H) IQ-1 [2]-10, Thrown Weapon (Grenade) (P/E) DX [1]-12.

Secondary Skills: Savoir-Faire (Military) (M/E) IQ [1]-11, Armory (Small Arms) (M/A) IQ [2]-11, Camouflage (M/E) IQ [1]-11, Electronics Operation (Commo) (M/A) IQ-1 [1]-10, Electronics Operation (Sensors) (M/A) IQ-1

ARTILLERY   55 POINTS

Attributes: ST 10 [0], DX 11 [10], IQ 12 [20], HT 10 [0].

Advantages: A Total of 15 points in: Combat Reflexes [15], Fit or Very Fit [5 or 15], Hard to Kill 1-2 [5 or 10], Toughness (DR1) [10], High Pain Threshold [10], Alertness [5/level].

Disadvantages: A total of -20 points in: Bloodlust [-10], Berserk [-15], Callous [-6], Chummy [-5], Code of Honor (Mercenaries) [-5], Overconfidence or Glory Hound [-10 or -15], Post Combat Shakes [-5], and Sense of Duty (Comrades) [-5].

Primary Skills: Either Beam Weapons (any) or Guns (any), both (P/E) DX+2 [1]-13*, plus Gunner (any) (P/A) DX+2 [4]-14*, Either Pilot (Grav) or Driving (any) (all P/A) DX [2]-11, Forward Observer (M/A) IQ [2]-12.

Secondary Skills: Savoir-Faire (Military) (M/E) IQ [1]-12, Armory (any) (M/A) IQ [2]-12, Mechanic (any) (M/A) IQ-1 [1]-11, Camouflage (M/E) IQ [1]-12, Electronics Operation (Commo) (M/A) IQ-1 [1]-11, Electronics Operation (Sensors) (M/A) IQ [2]-12, First Aid (M/E) IQ [1]-12, Orienteering (M/A) IQ-1 [1]-11, Survival (any) (M/A) IQ-1 [1]-11, a total of 1 point in Brawling (P/E), Judo (P/H), Knife (P/E).

Background Skills: A total of 8 points in Scrounging (M/E), Administration, Demolition, Leadership, Merchant, Streetwise (all M/A); Tactics, Engineer (Combat) (M/H); Beam Weapons (other), Guns (other), (all P/E); Pilot (any) or Gunner (any) all (P/A).

*Includes bonus for IQ.

[1]-10, First Aid (M/E) IQ [1]-11, Orienteering (M/A) IQ-1 [1]-10, Survival (any) (M/A) IQ-1 [1]-10, a total of 3 points in Brawling (P/E), Judo (P/H), Knife (P/E), Sword (P/A), Spear (P/A), Veterinarian (M/H), and Mechanic (any).

Background Skills: A total of 8 points in Scrounging (M/E), Administration, Demolition, Forward Observer, Leadership, Merchant, Streetwise, No-Landing Extraction (all M/A); Engineer (Combat) (M/H); Beam Weapons (other), Guns (other), or Parachuting (all P/E); Battlesuit, or Gunner (any) all (P/A); and Hiking (P/A; HT).

ARMOR   60 POINTS

Attributes: ST 10 [0], DX 12 [20], IQ 12 [20], HT 10 [0].

Advantages: A total of 15 points in: Combat Reflexes [15], Fit or Very Fit [5 or 15], Hard to Kill 1-2 [5 or 10], Toughness (DR1) [10], High Pain Threshold [10], Alertness [5/level].

Disadvantages: A total of -20 points in: Bloodlust [-10], Berserk [-15], Callous [-6], Chummy [-5], Code of Honor (Mercenaries) [-5], Overconfidence or Glory Hound [-10 or -15], Post Combat Shakes [-5], and Sense of Duty (Comrades) [-5].

Primary Skills: Either Beam Weapons (any) or Guns (any), both (P/E) DX+2 [1]-14*, plus Gunner (any) (P/A) DX+2 [2]-14*, either Pilot (Grav) or Driving (any) all (P/A) DX [2]-12, Tactics (M/H) IQ-2 [1]-10.

Secondary Skills: Savoir-Faire (Military) (M/E) IQ [1]-12, Armory (any) (M/A) IQ-1 [1]-11, Mechanic (any) (M/A) IQ [2]-12, Camouflage (M/E) IQ [1]-12, Electronics Operation (Commo) (M/A) IQ-1 [1]-11, Electronics Operation (Sensors) (M/A) IQ [2]-12, First Aid (M/E) IQ [1]-12, Orienteering (M/A) IQ-1 [1]-11, Survival (any) (M/A) IQ-1 [1]-11, a total of 1 point in Brawling (P/E), Judo (P/H), Knife (P/E).

Background Skills: A total of 7 points in Scrounging (M/E), Administration, Demolition, Forward Observer, Leadership, Merchant, Streetwise (all M/A); Engineer (Combat) (M/H); Beam Weapons (other), Guns (other), all (P/E); Pilot (any) or Gunner (any) (all P/A).

*Includes bonus for IQ.

HEAVY WEAPONS SPECIALIST

Attributes: ST 12 [20], DX 12 [20], IQ 11 [10], HT 10 [0].

Advantages: A total of 15 points in: Combat Reflexes [15], Fit or Very Fit [5 or 15], Hard to Kill 1-2 [5 or 10], Toughness (DR1) [10], High Pain Threshold [10], Alertness [5/level].

Disadvantages: A total of -20 points in: Bloodlust [-10], Berserk [-15], Callous [-6], Chummy [-5], Code of Honor (Mercenaries) [-5], Overconfidence [-10], Post Combat Shakes [-5], and Sense of Duty (Comrades) [-5].

Primary Skills: Either Beam Weapons (any) or Guns (any), both (P/E) DX+1 [1]-13, plus Gunner (any) (P/A) DX+3 [4]-15, Gunner (Other) (P/A) DX [1]-12, Stealth (P/A) DX [2]-12, Tactics (M/H) IQ-1 [2]-10.

Secondary Skills: Savoir-Faire (Military) (M/E) IQ [1]-11, Armory (Small Arms) (M/A) IQ-1 [1]-10, Camouflage (M/E) IQ [1]-11, Electronics Operation (Sensors) (M/A) IQ+1 [4]-12, First Aid (M/E) IQ [1]-11, Hiking (P/A; HT) HT-1 [1]-9, Orienteering (M/A) IQ-1 [1]-10, Survival (any) (M/A) IQ-1 [1]-10, a total of 1 point in Brawling (P/E), Judo (P/H), Knife (P/E).

Background Skills: A total of 8 points in Scrounging (M/E), Administration, Demolition, Forward Observer, Leadership, Merchant, Streetwise, Electronics Operation (Commo), (all M/A); Engineer (Combat) (M/H); Beam Weapons (other), Guns (other), or Parachuting (all P/E); and Battlesuit, Driving (any), Pilot (Grav) or Gunner (any) (all P/A).

SNIPER

75 POINTS

Attributes: ST 10 [0], DX 12 [20], IQ 12 [20], HT 10 [0].

Advantages: A total of 15 points in: Combat Reflexes [15], Fit or Very Fit [5 or 15], Hard to Kill 1-2 [5 or 10], Toughness (DR1) [10], High Pain Threshold [10], Alertness [5/level].

Disadvantages: A total of -20 points in: Bloodlust [-10], Berserk [-15], Callous [-6], Chummy [-5], Code of Honor (Mercenaries) [-5], Overconfidence [-10], Post Combat Shakes [-5], and Sense of Duty (Comrades) [-5].

Primary Skills: Either Beam Weapons (any) or Guns (any), both (P/E) DX+5 [8]-17*, Stealth (P/A) DX+2 [8]-14, Tactics (M/H) IQ [4]-12, Camouflage (M/E) IQ+2 [4]-14.

Secondary Skills: Savoir-Faire (Military) (M/E) IQ [1]-12, Armory (Small Arms) (M/A) IQ-1 [1]-11, Electronics Operation (Sensors) (M/A) IQ [2]-12, First Aid (M/E) IQ [1]-12, Hiking (P/A; HT) HT-1 [1]-9, Orienteering (M/A) IQ [2]-12, Survival (any) (M/A) IQ [2]-12, a total of 2 points in Brawling (P/E), Judo (P/H), Knife (P/E).

Background Skills: A total of 4 points in Scrounging (M/E), Administration, Demolition, Forward Observer, Leadership, Merchant, Streetwise, Electronics Operation (Commo), (all M/A); Engineer (Combat) (M/H); Beam Weapons (other), Guns (other), or Parachuting (all P/E); and Battlesuit, Driving (any), Pilot (Grav) or Gunner (any) all (P/A).

*Includes bonus for IQ.

ASSAULT TROOPER　　65 POINTS

Attributes: ST 10 [0], DX 12 [20], IQ 11 [10], HT 11 [10].

Advantages: A total of 15 points in: Combat Reflexes [15], Fit or Very Fit [5 or 15], Hard to Kill 1-2 [5 or 10], Toughness (DR1) [10], High Pain Threshold [10], Alertness [5/level].

Disadvantages: A total of -20 points in: Bloodlust [-10], Berserk [-15], Callous [-6], Chummy [-5], Code of Honor (Mercenaries) [-5], Overconfidence [-10], Post Combat Shakes [-5], and Sense of Duty (Comrades) [-5].

Primary Skills: Either Beam Weapons (any) or Guns (any), both (P/E) DX+2 [2]-14*, plus Gunner (any) (P/A) DX [1]-12, Stealth (P/A) DX+1 [4]-13, Tactics (M/H) IQ-1 [2]-10, Thrown Weapon (Grenade) DX [1]-12.

Secondary Skills: Savoir-Faire (Military) (M/E) IQ [1]-11, Armory (Small Arms) (M/A) IQ-1 [1]-10, Electronics Operation (Sensors) (M/A) IQ-1 [1]-10, First Aid (M/E) IQ [1]-11, Hiking (P/A; HT) HT-1 [1]-10, Orienteering (M/A) IQ-1 [1]-10, Survival (any) (M/A) IQ-1 [1]-10, a total of 5 points in Brawling (P/E), Judo (P/H), Knife (P/E), Spear (P/A) and Battlesuit (P/A).

Background Skills: A total of 8 points in Scrounging (M/E), Administration, Demolition, Forward Observer, Leadership, Merchant, Streetwise, Electronics Operation (Commo), All (M/A); Engineer (Combat) (M/H); Beam Weapons (other), Guns (other), or Parachuting all (P/E); and Battlesuit, Driving (any), Pilot (Grav) or Gunner (any) all (P/A).

COMBAT ENGINEER, PIONEER, SAPPER   65 POINTS

Attributes: ST 11 [10], DX 11 [10], IQ 12 [20], HT 10 [0].

Advantages: A total of 15 points in: Combat Reflexes [15], Fit or Very Fit [5 or 15], Hard to Kill 1-2 [5 or 10], Toughness (DR1) [10], High Pain Threshold [10], Alertness [5/level].

Disadvantages: A total of -20 points in: Bloodlust [-10], Berserk [-15], Callous [-6], Chummy [-5], Code of Honor (Mercenaries) [-5], Overconfidence [-10], Post Combat Shakes [-5], and Sense of Duty (Comrades) [-5].

Primary Skills: Either Beam Weapons (any) or Guns (any), both (P/E) DX+2 [1]-13*, plus Gunner (any) (P/A) DX+1 [1]-12*, Engineer (Combat) (M/H) IQ [4]-12, Demolition (M/A) IQ [2]-12.

Secondary Skills: Savoir-Faire (Military) (M/E) IQ [1]-11, Armory (Small Arms) (M/A) IQ-1 [1]-10, First Aid (M/E) IQ [1]-12, Orienteering (M/A) IQ-1 [1]-11, Survival (any) (M/A) IQ-1 [1]-11, Camouflage (M/E) IQ [1]-12. Driving (any) or Pilot (Grav) (P/A) DX [2]-11, Battlesuit or Exoskeleton (P/A) DX [2]-11.

Background Skills: A total of 7 points in Scrounging (M/E), Administration, Forward Observer, Leadership, Merchant, Streetwise, Electronics Operation (Commo), Electronics Operation (Sensors), All (M/A); Tactics (M/H); Brawling , Beam Weapons (other), Guns (other), Knife or Parachuting all (P/E); and Battlesuit, Driving (any), Stealth, Spear, Pilot (Grav) or Gunner (any) all (P/A); Judo (P/H).

*Includes bonus for IQ.

MILITARY POLICE, PROVOST

Attributes: ST 10 [0], DX 12 [20], IQ 12 [20], HT 10 [0].

Advantages: A total of 15 points in: Combat Reflexes [15], Fit or Very Fit [5 or 15], Hard to Kill 1-2 [5 or 10], Toughness (DR1) [10], High Pain Threshold [10], Alertness [5/level], Legal Enforcement Powers [5, 10 or 15].

Disadvantages: A total of -20 points in: Bloodlust [-10], Berserk [-15], Callous [-6], Chummy [-5], Code of Honor (Mercenaries) [-5], Overconfidence [-10], Post Combat Shakes [-5], and Sense of Duty (Comrades) [-5].

Primary Skills: Either Beam Weapons (Pistol) or Guns (Pistol), both (P/E) DX+2 [2]-14*, plus Gunner (any) (P/A) DX [1]-12* or Beam Weapons (any) or Guns (any) both (P/E) DX+1 [1]-12*, Holdout (M/A IQ+1 [4]-13, Interrogation (M/A) IQ [2]-12.

Secondary Skills: Savoir-Faire (Military) (M/E) IQ [1]-12, Electronics Operation (Commo) (M/A) IQ-1 [1]-11, Electronics Operation (Sensors) (M/A) IQ-1 [1]-11 First Aid (M/E) IQ [1]-12, Orienteering (M/A) IQ-1 [1]-11, Survival (any) (M/A) IQ-1 [1]-11, a total of 2 points in Brawling (P/E), Judo (P/H), Knife (P/E) and Spear (P/A).

Background Skills: A total of 3 points in Camouflage, Scrounging (M/E), Administration, Demolition, Forward Observer, Leadership, Merchant, Streetwise, all (M/A); Engineer (Combat), Tactics (M/H); Beam Weapons (other), Guns (other), Thrown Weapon (Grenade), or Parachuting all (P/E); and Battlesuit, Driving (any), Pilot (Grav), Stealth or Gunner (any) all (P/A).

*Includes bonus for IQ.

MEDIC

Attributes: ST 11 [10], DX 10 [0], IQ 12 [10], HT 11 [10].

Advantages: A total of 15 points in: Combat Reflexes [15], Fit or Very Fit [5 or 15], Hard to Kill 1-2 [5 or 10], Toughness (DR1) [10], High Pain Threshold [10], Alertness [5/level], Empathy [10].

Disadvantages: A total of -20 points in: Bloodlust [-10], Berserk [-15], Callous [-6], Chummy [-5], Code of Honor (Mercenaries) [-5], Overconfidence [-10], Post Combat Shakes [-5], and Sense of Duty (Comrades) [-5].

Primary Skills: Stealth (P/A) DX [2]-10, Physician (M/H) IQ-1 [2]-11, First Aid (M/E) IQ+2 [4]-14.

Secondary Skills: Either Beam Weapons (any) or Guns (any), both (P/E) DX+2 [1]-12, Savoir-Faire (Military) (M/E) IQ [1]-12, Electronics Operation (Commo) (M/A) IQ-1 [1]-10, Hiking (P/A; HT) HT-1 [1]-9, Orienteering (M/A) IQ-1 [1]-11, Survival (any) (M/A) IQ-1 [1]-11, a total of 2 points in Brawling (P/E), Judo (P/H), Knife (P/E) and Spear (P/A).

Background Skills: A total of 4 points in Scrounging (M/E), Administration, Demolition, Forward Observer, Leadership, Merchant, Streetwise, Electronics Operation (Commo), (all M/A); Engineer (Combat), Tactics (M/H); Beam Weapons (other), Guns (other), or Parachuting (all P/E); and Battlesuit, Driving (any), Pilot (Grav) or Gunner (any) (all P/A).

NCO

Advantages: Add 1-2 levels of rank [5/level].

Skills: Add 1-2 points to tactics (+1 to skill level), Leadership (M/A) IQ [2], Administration (M/A) IQ-1 [1] or IQ [2].

CHAPTER SIX

Sample Tickets

The following sample missions are all set in the Spinward Marches, but could easily be transplanted to similar worlds elsewhere in the Imperium. Missions are categorized by the type of mercenary units required and by the size of the unit. The information presented in *Background* and *Mission* sections is available to the mercenary characters. Any other information is available only at the Game Master's discretion.

GROUND MISSIONS

SPECIALIST/INDIVIDUAL MISSIONS

Cadre Ticket

Background: Keng (see p. BTC 83) is a warm, heavily forested world controlled by an oligarchy of Imperial nobles. The nobles live in high-tech reservations guarded by household security forces (equipped to TL6 to 7 standards), but Keng overall is only TL5.

Recently, the long-standing dispute between Baron Mirakru and Baronet Sequille over ownership of the Dorgrandre Forest (a major belt of keng oaks and of no small economic importance) has become an outright feud. A ruling by the Imperium prevents the two lords from deploying their household forces or bringing in offworld mercenary units, but a loophole allows the two lords to raise local forces to challenge for ownership. Early attempts to field local militia have proven to both lords that some experienced leadership is necessary. Baronet Sequille has opted to exercise some discretion and hire a specialist to train and lead his levies. Baron Mirakru has taken the direct route of placing himself at the head of the locals, applying his own theories of bush warfare to the situation. By bringing only a couple of his household guards (and calling them "attendants") he hopes to avoid official censure.

Mission: The mercs are offered command positions (major or captain rank to no more than three individuals) at double standard salaries for the duration of the conflict plus a success bonus of Cr500,000 if Baronet Sequille gains control of the Dorgrandre Forest. The mercenaries are to raise, train and lead a force to drive Baron Mirakru's workers and troops from the region. They have a free hand to do as they think is necessary, and a budget of MCr5 to outfit their force. This money must be used to purchase weaponry and ammunition – the baronet will supply food and shelter.

If the mercs want equipment of higher than TL5, it must be bought offworld and shipped in, with a delay of three to four weeks. Cost will be two to five times the list price, to account for the back channels that must be used and shipping costs incurred.

Game Master's Information: The villages and towns loyal to Sequille make a reasonably productive recruiting ground, but the supply is not infinite. Recruiting will become progressively harder once more than about 100 troops have been raised and very difficult once there are more than 1,000 under arms. These troops will be raw villagers armed with bolt action rifles, and will require training to be anything other than an armed mob.

In the thick forest, vehicles are of little use. The local *cardin* (a large, deer-like herbivore) makes a docile and reliable mount/beast of burden, but cannot carry much (they are equivalent to large mules; see pp. B144-145).

Cardin can be had at most villages, and as a rule of thumb one is available for every two villagers recruited. Most of the action will be raids on logging stations and forward bases. It will be a war of endless patrol and encounter, ambush and counter-ambush. Victory will be determined by whose side gets tired and refuses to enter the forest (to fight or to work) first.

Maintaining morale will be perhaps the most important task the mercs have on their hands. Wholesale slaughter of villagers will bring Imperial retribution, but taking over a village or scattering a work party will be considered legitimate.

The private estates are nowhere near the war zone, and the two nobles' private forces will not (and legally, cannot) be engaged. The GM can make up a map of a large, heavily forested wilderness area, or use an existing map of a state park or forest preserve (with the names and scale changed if necessary).

Resolving the Mission: Mirakru is fairly skilled in military matters (his Strategy skill level is 15) but he is reckless, and will often attack when his forces are not completely ready. Thus the mercs may have several sudden attacks to deal with, which may alarm them. Eventually the pattern will emerge and they will realize that Mirakru is not as strong as they feared. They may even be able to use his recklessness against him.

Whatever forces the mercenaries raise, Mirakru can field about 30% more, plus himself and two bodyguards in combat armor. He will first try to raise a force of light infantry and equip them to TL8 with assault rifles smuggled in for the purpose. He will then try to create a small force of "Rangers" (about a dozen highly skilled individuals with TL10 gear) and an assault unit equipped with close-quarters weapons (supplied with locally manufactured grenades, rifles and revolvers). Finally he will expand the light infantry force until he thinks he has enough to overrun the opposition. All the time, Mirakru will launch aggressive raids on enemy positions to keep them off balance and frighten Sequille's workers out of the forest.

The GM should run a series of minor patrol encounters as each side trains its forces and feels out the opposition, launching the odd mission to capture key logging camps, sawmills and villages. Finally one side will gain enough of an advantage to drive directly on the other's headquarters. Even with the private estates well out of the fight, losing his main base of operations in the region will cause either lord to give up.

Security Ticket

Background: Dinom (see p. BTC85) is a tidally locked world, with cities scattered across the world's equatorial "twilight" zone. The world's economy is based around mining, with camps in both the hot northern region and the frozen south. Government is by a "Workers' Council," a ramshackle gathering of the leaders of the Workers' Revolution of 1106, which has lurched from crisis to disaster for the past 14 years. Dinom is an armed camp, wracked by internal disputes and beset by fears of another offworld takeover bid.

The situation on Dinom is deteriorating still further, with the Workers' Council finding it increasingly difficult to ensure the flow of supplies to the more distant mining installations.

Mission: The Workers' Council is offering standard salaries plus a success bonus of Cr15,000 each, for a security team to escort an important shipment of spare parts to the mining site at Haldi Crater on the frozen south face of Dinom. The shipment will be landed at the starport in the city of Rhylan and transferred to Medianne City by monorail. From there the mercs will convey the shipment by ATV to the mining site, pick up a small cargo of high-value materials, and return by the same route. There are two suitcase-sized boxes of spares (the mercs will be shown them and they are entirely as presented – expensive but mundane spare parts for life-support and mining machinery). The return cargo is of a similarly size.

While the council does not expect trouble, the mercs are expected to watch the spares and the return cargo closely, as there has been trouble with pilfering in the past. There exists a small chance that someone may attempt to steal the spare parts shipment outright.

Nobody on Dinom would bat an eyelid at a party equipped with combat armor, laser rifles and a gauss or two working security for an installation in the outback. However, in towns and on the monorail the rule is sidearms or shotguns only and no heavy armor. There have been too many disputes ending in firefights recently, and collateral damage has been high.

Game Master's Information: Upon arrival, the mercs will be given government patches to wear on their suits and clothing. Wearing them attracts hostility from personnel aggrieved at the Workers' Council (not wearing them attracts hostility from almost everyone – offworlders are viewed with deep suspicion on Dinom).

While the locals are surly, there is no real difficulty in reaching Medianne. The tracked ATV is waiting for the characters. The mining camp is 750 miles south across mountainous terrain followed by icy plains in the latter stages.

The drive will take a couple of days and will be very tiring. The characters may encounter some minor hazards along the way (*Traveller* grognards may like to haul out the long out-of-print *Across the Bright Face* one more time for specifics, but this is not necessary), but these will be connected with the dangers of travel across ice plains on an airless world in a vehicle that is not in the best state of repair.

At the camp, the mercenaries find about 300 personnel operating a large installation. Vacc-suited security patrols meet the mercs with open suspicion, which turns gradually to guarded warmth. Once the supplies are delivered, the mercs will be invited to rest up for a day before heading back, and fed the same rather bland fare the miners live on. It is obvious that things are difficult. Some components of the meal are obviously recycled, and equipment everywhere (from the monorail onward) is battered. Finally the return crates (the mercs are told they contain high-value mineral samples, which could really make a difference if the bosses can get them to a decent market) are loaded and the ATV sets off. All they have to do is reach Medianne and board the monorail.

Halfway back to Medianne, the mercs' ATV will be ambushed. Two ATVs containing a total of 10 vacc-suited hostiles have deployed on their route. The hostiles are employees of a rival mining operation, and want to prevent the "mineral samples" reaching market. They would prefer to disable the mercs' ATV and demand their surrender (the mercs will be disarmed and held in a survival shelter for 48 hours before being released unharmed). If the mercs will not surrender the hostiles will shoot to kill. They have laser carbines and ACRs.

Assuming the mercs escape this first attack, there will be a second attempt on the monorail. The rival corporation would prefer to simply pilfer the crates, which will be carried in a cargo compartment on the monorail. If the mercs are guarding the crates (as they should be), a party of six thugs equipped with concealed body armor and pistols will attack them. One of the thugs has an SMG.

The mercs should not have their heavy armor or weapons available (such equipment is packed into locked crates by the monorail staff). While the mercs will have the keys to these crates, they will not be permitted to travel in the same rail car.

Resolving the Mission: The "mineral samples" are in fact zuchai crystals, a natural formation of great use in the construction of jump drives. They are rare and valuable. The mercs' patron will be very pleased that his shipment made it, and will add 10% to his proposed bonus.

Small Unit Missions

Commando Ticket

Background: Hofud (see p. BTC72) is an agricultural world, with scattered communities numbering around 60,000 inhabitants. Despite its low population, Hofud is one of the most troubled planets in the entire Domain of Deneb. The local officials simply cannot cope with the continual outbreaks of insurgency, and government authority has broken down in many distant regions. Certain government officials are thought to be actively supporting the insurgents, and gaining a power base in the outback. The area around the starport is heavily patrolled and relatively secure, but the rest of the planet is in a state of disorganization.

Mission: The mercs are offered a success-only ticket: Cr175,000 for a small unit (squad or section size) to attack and destroy a training camp which is thought to exist in the

Kralspine Range, an area of rugged hills about 3,000 miles from the starport. The camp is close to a number of small farming villages, whose inhabitants may be rebel supporters or may have been intimidated into cooperation. It is possible that the insurgents are employing offworld troops to train their personnel.

The camp is thought to have about 30 personnel at any one time, of whom six to ten are instructors and can be considered skilled opponents. The remainder will be local volunteers of low training level. Insurgent weaponry seems to be mostly civilian hunting weapons, but lax law levels have allowed some automatic weapons to be brought in.

The mercenaries are to be inserted at night by grav transport about 30 miles from the objective to avoid detection by local sympathizers, and will cover the remaining distance in their own vehicles. The camp is to be destroyed. A bonus is payable for the capture of instructors, whose testimony could be used to incriminate local government officials. Civilian casualties are to be avoided.

Game Master's Information: The locals mostly just want to be left alone, and do not actively support the insurgents. There are a few sympathizers who will turn out to warn or assist their comrades if there is time. If the mercenaries strike quickly, these will not be a factor, but delay may bring three or four fire teams of locals armed with rifles. Roll 9+ on 3d every 30 minutes for this to happen, stopping when the rebels are defeated or once 12 fire teams have appeared.

The insurgents have two fire teams of Sword World troops acting as instructors. These are Seasoned troops equipped with ACRs and combat armor. Their leader is in command of the base, with a Strategy skill level of 14.

The local rebels have four *service units* (each equivalent to a squad of eight). One unit contains Raw recruits armed only with semiautomatic rifles and pistols. Two are Green troops with rifles and one is Average with light flak jackets, helmets and autorifles.

The rebels also have a heavy machine gun (12.7mm HMG, see p. VE43) emplaced in a sandbagged position and two truck-mounted rocket launchers (equivalent to a Katyusha, see p. HT122).

Attempts to keep the operation secret have been successful. The rebels will be taken by surprise unless local sympathizers warn them. This will not occur unless the mercs are very slow in moving to the camp from their drop-off point.

Resolving the Mission: The rebels as an overall force should be represented as a Green platoon-sized unit at TL8, with possible modifiers for artillery, high quality leaders and a prepared position.

Commando Ticket

Background: Squallia (see p. BTC74) is a chilly world of moderate size, with a very thin atmosphere and 80% surface water. The 32 city-states of Squallia are all self-ruling, with a population of approximately 100,000 each. Recently Aslan ihatei (landless second sons and their dependents) have landed on the planet and begun to carve out their own little enclaves.

The citizens of the city-state of Dasas are concerned that the ihatei landings are the thin edge of a very large wedge. The ihatei have taken possession of the ruined settlement of Sendei, abandoned a decade ago after one of Squallia's increasingly common military clashes. The government of the neighboring city-state of Dasas fears that the ihatei will be able to set up a community very quickly using the ready resources of the old town. Within a few years there will be thousands of Aslan pouring into the new territory, and conflict will certainly ensue. Their ruling council has decided to dislodge the squatters by using mercenaries rather than local forces.

Mission: The government of Dasas is offering a success-only ticket for a platoon-sized mercenary outfit to attack and dislodge the ihatei presence. Cr250,000 is offered, success-only.

The platoon will launch a strike on the Aslan community with the primary aim of destroying installations and equipment and thus rendering the settlement unviable. The Aslan will resist, naturally, and any casualties they sustain should further persuade them that their presence is not wanted.

The Aslan community is about 120 miles from the Dasas border. The platoon will be provided with wheeled or tracked ATVs (GM's choice) to transport them to within strike range. Drivers are also available but they will not enter combat.

The Aslan community numbers around 400, with a higher than usual proportion of males – 200 or so – all potential combatants. Weapons are small arms with a few heavy weapons. The ihatei have a lightly armed vessel grounded at the settlement. It is not to be damaged, as they will need it if they are to leave (and the last thing the Dasas government wants is to strand the Aslan on Squallia).

Game Master's Information: The ihatei have heard of other attempts to dislodge similar bands, and maintain a high level of watchfulness. This takes the form of small patrols around the perimeter of their settlement, and occasional recon/hunting forays farther out from the settlement.

The ihatei can be considered to have about 10 weak platoon-sized units of males organized along family or warband lines. Six such platoons are Average troops with no body armor and a mix of TL9 small arms, mainly assault rifles and SMGs. Three platoons are equipped to TL10 standards, with ACRs, flak jackets and helmets. One warband is Seasoned and equipped with ACRs, combat environment suits and a couple of light machine guns (see p. HT120). This is the ihatei leader's personal following. The leader has a Strategy skill level of 14.

In desperation, the 200 females (armed with pistols and rifles) will be ferocious (if untrained) fighters.

Resolving the Mission: The Aslan as an overall force should be represented as two Average companies of light infantry with no artillery support. The mission will be quite complicated if the objective to destroy equipment is observed rather than simply trying to kill the ihatei.

Striker Ticket: Commando

Background: Bularia (see p. BTC48) is a client state of the Imperium, a somewhat dry world with a population of about 4,000,000. The main export of Bularia is agricultural produce grown at considerable effort in the river valleys. Government is by a ramshackle participating democracy, which is notorious for inefficiency.

The megacorporation Naasirka has invested heavily in the world's fledgling electronics industry and has brought in its own troops to defend the subsidized starport and surrounding industry.

Mission: A faction among Bularia's farmers are concerned that the megacorporation is taking over their world and dragging their conservative culture into modern society rather more quickly than is desirable. There have already been incidents of sabotage, and a coalition of farmers has managed to scrape together the resources to make an effective strike.

The Conservative Agricultural Alliance (as the farmers' coalition calls itself) is seeking a platoon-sized unit to lead a strike on one of the Naasirka manufacturing centers. A core of perhaps 200 farmers armed with various small arms will undertake the strike and some diversionary operations, but they recognize the need for a hard core of skilled troops to make the main assault. Cr230,000 is offered on a success-only basis. The strike force will seize the warehouses and manufacturing plant situated in the town of Castira-Lakeside and remove the stored components before destroying the production equipment and withdrawing. The components and mercenaries will be transferred to a waiting transport vessel and taken offworld, where the components will be sold to finance other CAA operations if any are necessary.

Naasirka has a battalion-sized security force at the port, with a few light grav vehicles for patrol work. The plants are known to be guarded by platoon-sized units, with a full company on call at any time. The security forces have stepped up their alert status in response to the CAA unrest, but have not the forces available to undertake proper sweeps into the countryside. Patrols consisting of a single air/raft are common near the port area.

Game Master's Information: The rebels' information is partially correct. In fact the Naasirka troops are of somewhat lower quality than commonly encountered, having become complacent in their long-term security duties. Even at a heightened alert status the force is less effective than it should be. However, the Naasirka executive is aware of this and has begun to remedy the situation. A mercenary light cavalry unit, Spooner's Squadron, has been hired to act as a response force. This consists of four troops, each of wheeled ATVs mounting TL7 20mm autocannons (see p. VE191) and machine guns. The unit is a relatively new mercenary outfit and is of only Average quality. Captain Spooner has a Strategy skill of 14.

Also assigned to the response team is the executive's personal guard, a nine-man squad of infantry equipped to TL11 standards, with combat armor and gauss rifles. These troops are Veteran and have a leader with a Strategy skill of 17.

The bulk of the security forces will be tied down guarding the starport and the manufacturing plants, or else responding to diversionary raids by the farmers. One platoon will be stationed at the target plant, with another company available on instant readiness. the starport defenses will spare one more company once the main target of the attack is determined. A third company may be detached to block the mercs' escape route. All security forces are equipped to TL9 standards with ACRs, flak jackets and helmets. They are Green and led by leaders with Strategy skills of 12. There are few heavy weapons. The patrol air/rafts are unarmed except for their crews' weapons.

The farmers have mustered two columns of about 100 each. One forms the main strike force along with the mercenaries while the other will split up into raiding parties to do whatever damage is possible. The CAA forces are Raw, and commanded by leaders with Strategy skills of 10. They are armed with civilian rifles, with a few automatic weapons.

Resolving the Mission: This mission involves three phases. The initial attack should achieve surprise and overwhelm the defenders. Once the plant is secured, vehicles are brought in and the components loaded onto them.

The second phase sees resistance stiffen, as the response force arrives from the starport to reinforce the defenders and the guard unit makes a small but effective counterattack. This may occur as the strike force withdraws or is loading the trucks.

The third phase is a fighting withdrawal across country to the waiting starship. Security forces may pursue in trucks, air/rafts and commandeered civilian vehicles. A company of security troops may be able to cut off the strikers' retreat. Meantime the farmers' force will be disintegrating under the pressure. Each phase should be fought out separately.

Striker Ticket: Gang Suppression

Background: Tureded (see p. BTC88) is an agricultural world with no law to speak of. The starport is an important trade link on the Spinward Main, but the world itself is now classified as an Amber zone due to a rising tide of banditry and conflict. Several private companies have interests in Tureded's economy, and their business is suffering. The world relies upon a small civilian militia for defense.

Mission: Traker Bulk Shipping is offering Cr500,000 for a platoon-sized striker unit to take out one of the bandit gangs operating in the West-Central Tablelands. It is hoped that this will send a message to the others that interference in Traker interests is not a healthy idea. The gang has taken over the market town of Tendure (population 1,200) and set up a crude "kingdom" which is trying to renegotiate all the deals Traker had with the farmers who trade in the town.

The platoon is to kill or capture the bandits and liberate the town. Anyone who resists the mercenaries' reoccupation should be considered a hostile, a bandit or a sympathizer. Tureded has no weapons laws, so the bandits can be expected to possess automatic weapons and light body armor.

Game Master's Information: The bandits do not really believe that Traker will do anything except renegotiate the deals and pay a ransom for their staff. Offworld traders do not possess the will to make decisive moves, their leader claims. Traker's recent declaration that it does not recognize the new regime and will not negotiate has been disregarded.

The local citizens have been disarmed (except for a few who have joined the gang). The effort of controlling the citizens keeps the bandits alert, though they are not expecting an assault.

The bandits number about 40, armed to TL9 standards with assault rifles, light flak jackets and various small arms. Their leader has a Strategy skill of 15, and bandits themselves are Seasoned. The town is built of solid materials (concrete and stone blocks), but there are a lot of open spaces. The place can be considered a prepared position.

The defenders have a couple of machine guns emplaced near their "fortress" in what used to be the town's market complex. Some of the locals are imprisoned within the building, as is a Traker factor and his staff. An assault will be necessary. About half the bandits (including all the leaders) are billeted in the complex, while the rest are scattered among their "subjects'" homes.

In the event of an attack, the bandits will fight with courage, individual cunning and skill, but they are not a military unit and will be very disorganized.

Resolving the Mission: The bandits as an overall force should be represented as Seasoned TL9 troops with some support weapons, light body armor and assault rifles. The bandit leader has a Strategy skill of 15. The mission is in two parts: the clearance operation in the town and the assault on the market complex. Treat the bandits as two units: one in the town (prepared positions) and one in the market complex (fortified).

Alternatively, this assault makes a nightmare urban combat scenario for individual resolution, with civilians rushing for cover or picking up weapons to liberate their homes and greatly complicating the mercenaries' task.

Security Ticket

Background: Weiss (see p. BTC96) is a world with an amber travel classification owned by Spinward DevCorp, an Imperial corporation which specializes in developing backwater worlds into major trade or production centers. The planet is rather dry but otherwise quite livable.

There are irregularities in SDC's Imperial charter to the world, and the entrepreneurial Kanderson Corporation seeks to exploit them. SDC's operation is mainly centered on the development of a starport, and there has been little exploration of the undeveloped regions of the world. In one such distant region, a covert exploration team sponsored by Kanderson has discovered considerable deposits of petrochemicals close to the surface. SDC will find out about them very soon, and Kanderson intends to begin exploitation before SDC can act. A small field extraction rig and its support personnel will be landed on Weiss as a way of staking Kanderson's claim. Meanwhile the SDC charter will be challenged in the Imperial courts. SDC will certainly attempt to dislodge this toehold with its security forces, which would cause the court case to collapse and ownership to remain in the hands of SDC.

Mission: The Kanderson Corporation is offering double standard salaries plus Cr700,000 for a platoon-sized security unit to guarantee the safety of the installation and its personnel. The contract is to run for 90 days from landing on-planet. Transportation to and from Weiss is provided, as are living expenses.

The security unit can expect sabotage attempts and possibly a direct attack by SDC security personnel. SDC has about 200 security personnel on planet. Some are equipped to a military standard.

Bringing in external forces will prove that SDC's charter to the whole planet is unenforceable, and win Kanderson's case for them.

Game Master's Information: SDC will conduct a campaign of nuisance raids using the more experienced of its security staff to make fast strikes from air/rafts, snipe at personnel and equipment from cover and sabotage any equipment or installations left unattended. The aim is simply to make the position untenable for the Kanderson workers. At the same time, the non-military security staff will begin training up for a possible assault.

After about three weeks of sporadic raids (permission to attack the SDC installation will *never* be given, as this would start a trade war which Kanderson would lose), a shipment of military arms will be delivered to the SDC camp. Another couple of weeks of training will see the SDC forces able to put about 200 security personnel in the field with military weapons, plus a second-line force of volunteers with handguns, aging SMGs and no armor, who will defend the base. SDC does not know these troops are unnecessary, and will hold them back.

Finally, as the court case develops, SDC will put in an all-out assault with their retrained security force. Their aim will be to overrun and destroy the Kanderson installation.

The Kanderson base staff numbers about 60, who are armed with handguns and a few 7mm carbines for self-defense.

In the early stages of the campaign, the SDC complement has the following assets:

• One platoon (30) of Seasoned troops, with ACRs and combat environment suits.

• Two platoons (30 each) of Average troops with SMGs, flak jackets and helmets.

• Two platoons (30 each) of Green troops, with SMG, flak jackets and helmets.

The security chief has a Strategy skill of 13.

Several grav vehicles (mainly air/rafts) are available.

By the time of the assault, SDC can field:

• One platoon (30) of Seasoned troops, with ACRs and combat environment suits.

• Two platoons (30 each) of Average troops, with ACRs and combat environment suits.

• Two platoons (30 each) of Green troops, with ACRs and combat environment suits

• Two companies (100) of Raw troops, with SMGs and handguns.

The security chief will have been replaced with an ex-soldier with a Strategy skill of 16.

Satchel charges are available, and one PML (see p. UT126) and 12 missiles.

Resolving the Mission: A long period of nuisance raids, counter-sniper sweeps and defensive preparations should be played out at low level. The mercs will be constantly dealing with wounded workers and smashed equipment unless they are vigilant. Some sweeps will yield contacts that turn into sharp firefights as the SDC troopers try to draw out the mercs in small groups and wear down their strength.

Finally, an assault will be made, probably after a long period of raiding to tire the defenders. Treat the attackers as a company-sized unit with an Average skill level. The final firefight around the Kanderson extraction plant will decide whether or not SDC owns the entire planet, or just most of it.

Cadre Ticket

Background: D'Mara (see p. BTC118) is a TL6 water world, with much of the 80,000,000 population clustered in large underwater cities served by crude submarine transports. The world's constitutional monarchy is uninterested in off-world contact, which accounts for the world's low-quality starport. There is a small but growing movement that supports offworld trade, and this organization has recently begun illegally constructing a starport on a tiny island near the world's South Pole. This operation has the backing of a consortium of businesses on the planet, whose operations would benefit greatly from new markets. The port will not be a public facility, but merely a private loading dock for a few freighters.

Although the port construction is illegal, there is thought to be little threat from the government itself, which has never acted against the world's port or its operators in any way. The threat is thought to be from the general populace, some of whom are actively hostile to any offworld influence. The government may not close the new port, but neither will there be any official protection offered.

Mission: The D'Mara Offworld Consortium is offering standard salaries plus Cr150,000 per month for a platoon sized unit to train a security force from local volunteers. The security force will have to police the starport and the nautical docks where transport subs from the undersea cities come in, as well as protecting the cargoes themselves. The Offworld Consortium will pay all living expenses.

The cadre unit will have to undertake some of these guard duties at first, then pass on the duty to the local volunteers as soon as they gain enough skills. Sabotage and intimidation attempts are probable. D'Mara maintains tight controls on weapons, and when not on the port island, the security units will carry only non-lethal weapons and riot control batons (equivalent to a light club, see p. B206).

Game Master's Information: Conditions on the polar island are harsh. The sea around is frozen for about a third of the year, and the harbor waters are artificially warmed to keep them ice-free (not strictly necessary for submarines, but traffic control is easier if the final approach is made on the surface). Security forces will encounter climate problems more often than actual security alerts, one reason why the remote location was chosen. Security officers will not be issued anything more lethal than sidearms and a few SMGs or shotguns.

The contract will run for several weeks, with small teams of eager young volunteers led by the mercenaries running through security drills in the arctic conditions, traveling on cargo subs to the undersea cities and meeting hostile locals.

The mercs are welcome among the space travel supporters (though the local volunteers are somewhat inept, over-eager and a little nervous around the mercs). Elsewhere their reception varies from cool to outright hostile. There may be trouble finding suitable recreation facilities, as the island has none.

There will be a variety of incidents during the contract; petty pilfering, patrols missing in a blizzard, attempted sabotage and the occasional demonstration outside the undersea cities' warehouses. The security force must tread warily, as local courts may not recognize their authority. Excessive force must be avoided.

Resolving the Mission: There is no climactic firefight, just a series of incidents that the mercs must deal with as best they can while keeping a tight rein on the locals until they are ready to take over.

COMPANY/BATTALION MISSIONS

The Heya Campaign

The following four missions can be played separately, but form a linked mercenary campaign if run sequentially. The missions are all set at Heya/Regina.

1. Heya – Commando Ticket

Background: Heya (see p. BTC83) is a moderately populated world of 71,000,000 sentients with a good starport, but a local tech level of only 6. For several decades Heya has been plagued by insurrectionists. This has forced Heya to divert funds to counter-insurgency forces, and skimp on system defenses. Usually an Imperial cruiser squadron is stationed in the system to provide added security. Recently the squadron was temporarily removed for reasons never explained to the Heyans. Three weeks later a squadron of Vargr corsairs struck.

Heya has a habitable moon called Heya Minor, a world with substantial forest cover, a diameter of 3,000 miles and a standard oxygen-nitrogen atmosphere. It is very lightly settled because of the uncomfortably low gravity, but a number of mines and other resource extraction operations exist.

Various Imperial corporations own some of these under license (Sternmetal Horizons, Oberlindes Lines, and SuSAG are all represented). The Vargr struck here because the moon was less well defended than Heya itself. After driving off the SDBs guarding the moon, ground troops were landed and the looting of warehouses and mining camps all over the world began. The Vargr, however, got greedy and failed to retrieve their troops before the squadron of SDBs stationed around Heya got there (or perhaps they thought they could beat the defenders). The corsairs did inflict considerable damage in the ensuing battle, but were finally forced to leave the system without their troops.

The Heyan government wishes to teach the Vargr a lesson. Reconnaissance indicates that the spaceport on Heya Minor and some of the larger mines are still under the control of the Vargr forces. Orbital bombardment is out of the question because this would destroy valuable equipment and kill any humans held hostage by the Vargr. The government has elected to pursue a military campaign to retake Heya Minor, but has most of its troops tied up in counterinsurgency operations.

Mission: The campaign will open with a raid to seize and hold the spaceport to allow a holding force of Heyan militia to be landed safely. The government is offering a ticket worth MCr1, plus a MCr2 success bonus, for a spearhead force to capture the port and hold it against all comers for three days while the Heyan System Defense Force lands. The force will be transported to the forests about three hours' march from the port in SDF vessels, which should be able to slip them in undetected.

The mercenaries are asked to try to free any hostages, but (significantly) this is not mentioned in their written contract. The fact that they are not authorized to accept anything

---

REPATRIATION BOND

1. Date of Preparation	
2. Individual's Name	3. UPP
6. Occupation	
5. World	
6. Employer	

Hortalez et Cie, fiduciary agent for the *Employer*, guarantees middle passage expenses (to include medical care en route, where necessary) for the *Individual* from the *World* to any of the *Destination Worlds* in the event that the employment contract between the *Employer* and the *Individual* is defaulted or terminated under extraordinary circumstances.
Presentation of this certificate is required.

7. Destination World(s)

TAS Form 18   **Repatriation Bond**

but unconditional surrender is. The government plans to try every surviving Vargr as a criminal and does not want anything to interfere with that.

Game Master's Information: The landing will not go unnoticed. Soon after landing the raiders will encounter resistance in the form of a section of Vargr infantry armed with ACRs. This is an irregular unit with very little armor and no communications gear. They are ex-ship crew and are Green troop quality.

Any prisoners can tell the commandos that surviving humans are kept in a compound on the south edge of the spaceport. Two companies of Vargr, led by the Vargr general Dhurgeng, guard the compound. Most of the other Vargr troops are spread out at various mines and plants across the main continent, anywhere from several days' to a week's travel from the spaceport.

An attack on the spaceport will meet stiff opposition from well-trained Vargr troops in prepared positions. Dhurgeng will order the human prisoners killed at the first sign of trouble. If ousted from his position, Dhurgeng will retreat to regroup, launching a series of raids and counterattacks over the next two days until it is clear that he cannot win. He will then retire into the forest and set up camp to await reinforcements, which will arrive in two more days.

Resolving the Mission: The Vargr have two companies of Seasoned troops deployed in prepared positions. They are equipped to TL9 standards with ACRs and light body armor. The Vargr have an 81mm mortar and an HMG emplaced in the perimeter fortifications of the starport.

Saving the prisoners will involve getting to them before Dhurgeng's minions carry out his order to kill them.

2. Heya – Security Ticket

Background: The spaceport at Heya Minor, the habitable moon of Heya, has recently been recaptured from Vargr corsair forces. The Heyans were then able to land two battalions of militia supported by additional mercenary forces at the spaceport.

The Vargr general Dhurgeng and his forces are known to be camped near the spaceport to the south, while strong Vargr forces are closing in from all directions.

Mission: The mercenary force that took the spaceport has been reinforced as noted above. The ticket offered is a success-only contract to hold the spaceport against the expected Vargr counterattack. A fee of MCr1 is offered, reflecting the fact that the Vargr are desperate and likely to fight to the end in this campaign.

Game Master's Information: The Vargr counterattack will be coordinated and well-planned, with Dhurgeng's troops launching a raid to the south of the port. Once this is underway a company of Vargr will assault the west of the port. These Vargr are armed with ACRs and have a grav tank for support (equivalent to the Instellarms light grav tank; see p. 77). Depending on their success the main Vargr battalion will either join the western assault or attack the north of the camp. This battalion is equipped to TL9 and supported by a troop of light grav tanks. These will be used to spearhead the main assault.

The defenders have a company of mercenaries together with two battalions of raw recruit militia including:
- Four companies of infantry.
- One troop of four medium grav tanks (equivalent to the Instellarms medium grav tank, see p. 78).
- One battery of light artillery (e.g., M101A1 105mm, see p. HT122).

Heyan soldiers are armed with assault rifles and the infantry wear ballistic cloth jackets.

Resolving the Mission: This is a "hold or die" situation. The fighting should be very fierce with the GM allowing the battle to become a house to house Stalingrad-style action with the Vargr having a tech level advantage and the Heyan force having numeric advantage. There is plenty of scope for minor actions to affect the overall ebb and flow of the drawn-out battle.

3. Heya – Cadre Ticket

Background: The untrained Heya militia has suffered heavy losses and at present their morale is all but broken, with the recruits openly asking officers to withdraw back to Heya and let the Imperial Marines dig out the Vargr (something the Heyan government refuse for three reasons: It will take weeks before an Imperial assault force can arrive, the Imperial commander might grant the Vargr terms, and the government suspects that offworld corporations may try to get the Imperium to grant them control of Heya Minor if Heya demonstrates an inability to defend it).

Mission: The mission now offered to the mercenary company is to take control of the Heyan militia and to ready the new expeditionary force for the reconquest of Heya Minor. Triple salaries are offered to mercenaries volunteering for this duty.

Available assets are:
- Four companies of infantry, Green troop quality with Shaky morale.
- Four Instellarms medium grav tanks (see p. 78), Average troop quality with Shaky morale.
- One battery of 81mm mortars (see p. 120), Seasoned troop quality.

These local forces will be commanded by mercenary soldiers with a local officer as second in command. Other mercenaries will train the infantry and provide a core of steady troops for the local troops to rally round.

Game Master's Information: The mercenaries have their work cut out to train the scared and shaken local militia into an effective fighting force while keeping the Vargr at bay. During the training period the Vargr will constantly probe the port defenses, and even make the occasional attack in force. Training sessions may well become real firefights.

Most of these attacks will be minor affairs in platoon strength. Vargr forces should be drawn from those listed in previous missions.

The mercenary commander will also receive feelers from various Vargr sub-units wanting to give themselves up or change sides. Keeping in mind that the government have expressly forbidden granting any sort of terms to any Vargr, the mercenaries will have to decide with their own consciences whether to take the opportunity to lure these Vargr into an ambush or to get them to help with false promises and betray them afterward. Any such dealings should result in negative reputations for any mercenaries involved.

Resolving the Mission: There are countless opportunities for roleplaying in this mission, as the GM lifts scenes from favorite war movies like *Starship Troopers* or *Full Metal Jacket.* Interactions with the recruits (who may include the stereotypical gung-ho amateur, the shy recruit, the scared recruit, the guy-who's-trouble-from-the-start and the soldier-everyone-writes-off-as-hopeless) will be interspersed with firefights, which due to their minor nature are best gamed out with the normal combat rules. Some of the recruits the mercs have come to know will of course be messily killed, making for more movie-inspired scenes.

4. Heya – Striker Ticket

Background: The mercs have succeeded in turning the spaceport at Heya Minor into a fortified camp, and instilling at least a little military ability into the militia. Outside the camp the forces of Dhurgeng are firmly entrenched. Spy satellites have discovered that the Vargr are bringing up their entire force on Heya Minor, making a force of over two battalions. They have been filtering units in quietly, hoping that the build-up will go unnoticed until it is time for the final assault.

Mission: The Heyan government offers the mercs another extension to their contract. A fee of MCr1 is offered on a success-only basis, for the mercs to coordinate an assault on the Vargr positions before Dhurgeng can launch his own attack. The councils will replace any lost or damaged equipment. "Success" will be defined as the lifting of the siege around the port and the scattering of the Vargr forces there.

Game Master's Information: The Vargr forces are well equipped and dug in. They currently consist of:

• Two battalions of infantry, each with 600 Vargr equipped with ACRs and various support weapons, Average troop quality.

• One platoon of four light grav tanks (equivalent to the Instellarms light grav tank, see p. 77), Green troop quality.

• One battery of light artillery, six light guns (equivalent to M101A1, p. HT122), Average troop quality.

• One company of engineers, 120 Vargr, armed with TL7 assault rifles, Raw troop quality.

The Heyan forces can field whatever troops have survived the earlier combats. A successful defense and some solid training should by now have eliminated the morale problem. Some sub-units may have advanced from Green to Average quality.

Resolving the Mission: The Vargr are tired, and their trenches are still somewhat makeshift (hasty positions). They are not expecting to be attacked in force, and so the Heyan forces should gain a modifier for surprise if they can successfully conceal their preparations. The Heyan troops are also tired.

The GM should prepare a map of the defenses, and secretly allocate the Vargr forces. The mercs' attack can be resolved as a number of smaller engagements as the Heyan forces engage the enemy at several different points, or as a single blow against one decisive point depending upon what plan the players have come up with.

Any way it happens, the breakout will be a bloody and hard-fought battle.

If a significant number of Vargr escape, the mercenaries may be offered a fifth contract: track down and capture or kill any Vargr still at large. This could be complicated by the factors of the various Imperial corporations all wanting their particular facility guarded and being willing to bribe the merc commander to help out.

Security Ticket

Background: Junidy (see p. BTC104) is a cool world with a very thin atmosphere and a massive population, evenly split between Humans and the native race, the Llellewyloly. The native race (often referred to as Dandelions, for reasons apparent to anyone who has ever seen one) is ruled by a dictatorship that imposes oppressive laws and enforces them harshly.

After years of racial violence following the Imperial civil war, the Scout Service encouraged a new government to give equal rights to both Humans and Llellewyloly. By 1108, however, the government of Junidy was Human-dominated and began passing laws that made life harder for the Llellewyloly. The Dandelions struck back, first with terrorism and later by forming the "Junidy Liberation Army" dedicated to gaining control of the world for the Llellewyloly. The JLA works closely with Vargr corsairs and a few offworld Humans, and this has caused Junidy to be classified Amber.

Data on the Llellewyloly can be found on p. GT47.

Mission: The Human-dominated government of Junidy is offering a Cr3,500,000 success-only contract for a battalion-sized force to escort the governor-general on a three week trip to the northern (entirely Llellewyloly populated) continent and to ensure his safety during his stay in the Llellewyloly capital, Ewoyllowll. At Ewoyllowll, the governor-general will announce that Human settlement will be allowed for the first time on the northern continent, and that Llellewyloly citizens will have to be moved from the new Human homelands. The government expects trouble in the wake of this announcement.

Game Master's Information: The governor-general travels in a huge motorcade of official vehicles, with over 200 other government officials and their aides. Most of the vehicles are lightly protected against small arms fire. While grav vehicles are available, the governor-general believes that the arrival of the motorcade demonstrates his importance better than a few grav vehicles.

It will take the motorcade four days from landing at the seaport to reaching Ewoyllowll, passing through some wild and hilly country. Along the way the JLA plans to attack the motorcade with all of its available resources:

• Two companies of light infantry riding fast softskinned vehicles (mostly civilian cars) armed with light machine guns (see p. HT120), Average troop quality.

• Four companies of infantry with assault rifles, Average troop quality.

• One platoon of four tracked MBTs (see p. VE141), Average troop quality.

Resolving the Mission: The JLA forces are Average troop quality but they are very determined. They should be treated as having high morale. Their leader's knowledge of the terrain raises their leader's Strategy skill from 12 to 15. Did the mercenaries remember to bring something that can take out a tank? If not, this mission could get a little complicated.

DEEP SPACE MISSIONS

SINGLE VESSEL MISSIONS

Escort Ticket

Background: Loneseda (see p. BTC107) is a large water world under development by the Imperial colonial office. The 700 inhabitants are all members of a pre-colonization settlement readying the world for full exploitation. The system has no defenses of its own, merely a pair of utility cutters (each with a single laser) at the starport available for cargo transfer and rescue work.

A shipment of supplies on the way to the new colony was hijacked recently. The colonial office wants to avoid a repeat of this event by hiring a mercenary vessel to act as an SDB and customs vessel.

Mission: The Imperial colonial office is offering MCr5 for a single vessel to patrol the Loneseda system for three months, alternating between a defensive stance at the port and long sweeps into the outer reaches of the system to search for lurking vessels. The mercs will operate one of the armed cutters in addition to their own ship, if possible. If ships' troops are available, a few will be detailed to provide security at the starport. The colonial office will meet expenses.

Game Master's Information: This "escort" mission is more of a patrol assignment. The mercs will escort incoming and outgoing ships, board them and conduct customs searches. The duty is somewhat tedious. A few free traders and the regular supply ship are the only traffic to be expected.

After a long period of patrolling and escort duty, the mercs receive a distress call from the planet. One of the underwater research domes has suffered an accident and is being breached by water pressure. There are no rescue subs able to reach the installation in time, but the mercs could pick up personnel and reach the site quickly from orbit. With their profors experience, the mercs might even be able to carry out the rescue themselves.

There is no obligation, as this is well outside the remit of their contract, and the mercs' response depends upon whether they are heroes or just paid soldiers.

Some time later, a tramp merchant vessel, the 200-ton far trader *End of All Hope,* comes though. Her crew has some speculative cargo to trade; mainly electronics spares and entertainment chips. They stay a couple of days, then prepare to leave.

As *End of All Hope* prepares to depart, the mercs receive

a message from another vessel arriving in the system. This is a modified scout/courier operated by a marshal from the Imperial Ministry of Justice. He transmits all the appropriate ID codes and explains that the merchant's purser, Jaref Kulkikaa, is a wanted swindler. He says he has been tracking Jaref for weeks and asks the mercs to detain him.

Unknown to the marshal, the merchant captain has recently skipped with his vessel and is keeping to the backwater systems to avoid capture. He does not know that his new purser is a wanted criminal. When the mercs try to detain Jaref, the rest of the eight-strong crew of the merchant will jump to the conclusion that the mercs have found out about their status and will resist, trying to fight the mercs off and lift off.

The crewmen are armed only with shotguns and autopistols, except for two security troopers with snub pistols and laser carbines. Jaref has a gauss pistol. There are two innocent passengers aboard the merchant, which has a dual laser and a dual sandcaster turret to fight with.

The mercs' contract does require them to uphold Imperial law within their area of operations.

Resolving the Mission: The mercs need to prevent the ship from leaving, or disable her and board. They may end up with a hostage situation on their hands. Normal starship and personal combat rules should be used.

Escort Ticket

Background: Romar (see p. BTC99) is a dry, chilly, low-population world of moderate tech level. It is a source of dust-spice, which is highly prized by Aslan. An attempt to gain control of the world by Aslan ihatei was recently crushed.

Mission: The government of Romar is offering MCr2 for a mercenary starship to escort a shipment of dust-spice to Glisten. The shipment will travel via Trane rather than Horosho, to avoid entanglements with the Horosho government, which has seen fit to impose a ban on the shipment of dust-spice through its system on the grounds that dust-spice is a toxic substance. Trane is a quiet backwater, and is a jump-2 from Glisten, the same as Horosho.

The dust-spice is being transported aboard a private Far Trader, which is armed with two dual beam laser turrets. A security team is carried aboard the trader, which has made the run before. The crew is considered trustworthy.

The merchant will refuel at Trane starport, but shore leave will not be granted.

Game Master's Information: The freighter captain will consent to carrying a squad of mercenaries as additional security. Her crew has only snub pistols for self-defense. They will fight a ship-to-ship action to defend the cargo but would normally surrender if boarded. If mercenaries are carried, the merchant crew will fight alongside them.

The shipment is scheduled, and it will not take a genius to figure out the alternative route. If the shipment goes via Horosho, customs will stop and impound it. If the shipment goes via Trane, the Horoshans are prepared.

Two Horosho armed merchants (*Beowulf* class, armed with dual laser turrets) and an Aslan vessel are waiting near Trane's 100-diameter limit. The mercs cannot expect any help from local forces. The Trane system squadron (one SDB and a flight of fighters) has been bribed into non-intervention so long as any action is fought well away from the starport.

Each *Beowulf* class vessel carries a squad of boarding troops (with vacc suits and laser carbines). Members of the Aslan ship's crew could form a squad equipped with vacc suits, autopistols and accelerator rifles.

Resolving the Mission: This is a ship-to-ship action. Two vessels will engage the mercs' ship while the third tries to cripple and board the merchant. Boarding actions should be fought out with the normal combat rules. Local forces will be forced to assist the mercs if they close to within 10 diameters of the planet and request assistance. Otherwise the mercs are on their own.

Striker Ticket

Background: Echiste (see p. BTC88) is low-population world almost entirely covered in water. The small population cannot form an effective military. A small faction of workers operating the iron-mining installation on Echiste's larger moon recently declared themselves a separate corporate entity from the world's governing corporation, and entered into negotiations with Sternmetal Horizons LIC for backing.

Mission: The world corporation of Echiste wants the mine returning to its control before Sternmetal can make any kind of move. A fee of MCr2 is offered for a mercenary unit to assault and capture the installation.

The miners are known to have access to a small quantity of military small arms provided by Sternmetal or liberated from security personnel. There are 100 or so miners on the installation, of whom about half have remained loyal to the world corporation and been imprisoned in the mine complex. Rescuing these loyal workers is of vital importance, as their skills will be hard to replace.

The moon is an airless rockball, with no defenses against incoming ships. The installation is to be captured as intact as possible, but the lives of loyal personnel and ownership of whatever is left of the installation is more important than avoiding collateral damage.

Game Master's Information: Sternmetal provided more than small arms. A team of "advisors" is on hand to lead the rebel miners. These "advisors" have combat armor and gauss rifles and have a leader with a Strategy skill of 16. They also have a launcher capable of firing standard starship missiles installed in a fixed installation near the landing site.

The 50 or so rebel miners have snub pistols, accelerator rifles and a couple of laser rifles. They are Green troops (their leader's Strategy skill level is 10) but are quite determined. All personnel have vacc suits and are quite skilled in their use.

Resolving the Mission: The landing will be tricky, and the missile launcher an unpleasant surprise. A confused combat through the installation's above- and below-ground equipment will undoubtedly ensue.

Striker Ticket

Background: Catuz (see p. BTC112) is a small, tidally locked desert world of little importance. A segment of the 30,000 inhabitants are currently in armed insurrection against the Catuz Meritocracy, the legitimate government. Other than attracting official condemnation for methods used when putting down the recent riots, the Catuz government's actions have attracted little attention in the region.

That changed a few weeks ago when the rebels managed to persuade MarchLines to bring in a shipment of weaponry to a secret rendezvous that turned out to be a lot less secret than was hoped. The *March Kestrel* was seized by troops of the Meritocracy and taken to the starport. Given that she was smuggling weaponry at the time she was taken, there is little chance of getting her back through the courts. The *Kestrel's* crew have been deported and are safe, but the company wants the ship back

Mission: MarchLines is offering a MCr1 success-only ticket for a unit to land at Catuz and seize the *March Kestrel,* allowing the original crew to board her and retake control. *Kestrel* will then lift off and the mercs will withdraw.

The mercs' ship will be met in the Catuz system by the MarchLines flagship, *March Harrier.* The deported crew will transfer to the mercs' ship shortly before the assault. The starport has very minor defenses; two dual missile turrets on the ground and a pair or triple lasers at the starport, but MarchLines has arranged for these to suffer a "temporary malfunction" long enough for *Kestrel* to lift off. A platoon of Imperial Marines guards a group of observers watching for further sentients' rights violations by the government, but they will not get involved unless fired upon.

The entire armed forces of Catuz consist of two companies of TL9 infantry with a few light vehicles. A single company is stationed at the starport, with only one platoon on alert at any one time. It is expected that by the time the mercs have reached the ground, they can expect to be facing two to four unready platoons of local troops, plus a few assorted corporate security detachments. All the mercs need to do is to get *Kestrel's* crew to their ship intact and hold the defenders off for long enough to power up and take off (this will take about 30 minutes once the crew is aboard).

Game Master's Information: The situation is more or less as presented.

The world government has placed *Kestrel* in a blast pen a short distance from the main landing area. A security squad (eight personnel with vacc suits and laser rifles) is stationed aboard *Kestrel,* plus a few techs trying to disable the security lockouts and get access to the controls.

A few wheeled security cars (civilian cars armed with LMGs) are used for patrol. These weapons cannot hurt a starship, but may cause problems for the mercs.

REPATRIATION BOND

1. Date of Preparation	
2. Individual's Name	3. UPP
6. Occupation	
5. World	
6. Employer	

The Central Imperial Bank, fiduciary agent for the *Employer,* guarantees middle passage expenses (to include medical care en route, where necessary) for the *Individual* from the *World* to any of the *Destination Worlds* in the event that the employment contract between the *Employer* and the *Individual* is defaulted or terminated under extraordinary circumstances.
Presentation of this certificate is required.

7. Destination World(s)

TAS Form 18   **Repatriation Bond**

The mercs' biggest problem will be holding a perimeter for 30 minutes, and avoiding any entanglements with other vessels which may be using the port.

Resolving the Mission: Local troops are reasonably competent and more alert than usual because of the recent unrest. They are only Average, however. The bulk of the troops have assault rifles and light body armor.

Initial reaction to the attack will be surprise and dismay, then the local forces will rally and begin a counterattack. If the GM wants to give the players a hard time, have a couple of armed free traders at the port, and force both the mercs and the port authority to negotiate with them for their assistance. The mercs must tread carefully, as their contract could be considered as an act of piracy if they use excessive force.

Raid Ticket

Background: McClellan Factors and the Baraccai Technum are rival corporations operating in the rimward end of the Spinward Marches. Relations between the two vary between bitter rivalry and outright trade war. After a recent lull, McClellan has begun building up their strength for a renewal of the struggle. Rumors that MF were building a class of dedicated escort/strike vessels seemed unfounded until the destination of a trio of 600-ton "fast escort ships" being built at Grote (see p. BTC95) was traced to a dummy company fronting for McClellan Factors. Executives of the Technum are dismayed at the thought of these armed vessels cruising space under the control of their rivals, and have determined to act.

Mission: The Baraccai Technum is offering a success-only MCr9 ticket for a merc outfit to destroy the McClellan ships before delivery. At present one ship is outfitted and undergoing trials, while the other two are almost completed but not yet operational.

If at all possible, the mercenaries must avoid damage to the private dockyard that is building the vessels, and the Technum would prefer a ground assault to insure this. Grote has no armed forces to speak of, and Imperial vessels at the port will not intervene unless the port (some distance from the private yard) is endangered. The mercs will have to deal with a platoon of MF security troops in combat armor, armed with gauss rifles, plus a few flight personnel and technicians.

Game Master's Information: All is as presented, though the completed ship is able to lift and fight if necessary. She has dockyard workers aboard and many systems untested, so her performance may be erratic. The approach least likely to

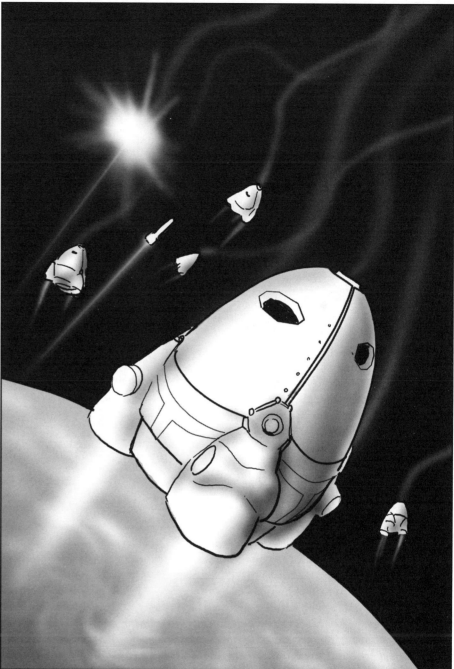

cause a backlash is to make a ground assault and take out the grounded ships with demolition charges. If the completed ship gets off the ground she can be safely engaged. Firing at ground targets from a starship is more likely to cause collateral damage which might bring Imperial forces into the conflict or cause the Grote government to launch a lawsuit against the mercs or their employers.

Cadre Ticket

Background: Zircon (see p. BTC58) is a large world with a dense oxygen-nitrogen atmosphere. The 6,000,000 inhabitants are colonists from the Federation of Arden.

The Colonial Administration of Zircon is currently forming a home government, and taking over all aspects of the world's administration, including defense. To this end, the

administration has purchased four *Dragon*-class system defense boats, a pair of 50-ton modular cutters and a squadron of twelve *Iramda*-class fighters. A small orbital station has been constructed to house them.

To demonstrate its ability to handle its own affairs, the administration has chosen to use a mercenary force rather than rely on Federation of Arden training officers.

Mission: The Zircon administration is offering a fat ticket (all munitions, fuel and life support costs covered) worth Cr250,000 per month plus standard salaries for the crew of a single mercenary vessel to train the local defense forces in search and intercept operations over a period of three months. A bonus of Cr75,000 per month is payable if the mercs can additionally offer protfors training to local shipboard troopers.

Game Master's Information: The Zircon crews are mainly Raw, though all personnel are competent in flight operations.

A few have seen service with the Federation Navy and have higher skill levels. However, these experienced personnel have been overpromoted to place them in command positions, and while the commander of the fighter squadron is a competent combat pilot, she has no command experience. None of the larger craft commanders were more than lieutenants or petty officers in Federation service. They are learning that there is a huge gulf between being a gunnery officer on a destroyer and commanding a whole vessel, however small.

The local forces, however inexperienced, are willing and able to carry out basic vessel operations. They have been assigned to customs and patrol duties, so some vessels will be unavailable for training at any given time as they learn their trade "on the job."

The training period will run for some time, with many incidents, before the crunch comes. A clique of junior officers intends to set up a military junta on Zircon. Zircon has only 12 battalions of ground troops, of which more than half have agreed to support the Junta. With help from the air defense force (operating TL9 aerospace fighters and missile systems), and with most of the non-involved ground forces remaining in barracks, the coup begins. Minor forces attempt to seize the starport.

The Zircon Administration appeals to the "Navy" for support. The administration has two battalions of ground troops plus a couple of companies of Federation troops defending the government center. They cannot hold out indefinitely, and the administration wants to relocate to the starport as a command center.

The mercs have no need to get involved, but their young trainees are about to be sucked into a civil war.

Resolving the Mission: The mercenary ship will be involved in a variety of training operations: acting as a "rabbit" in search exercises (trying to elude local ships or even ambush them with simulated weapons fire); conducting dummy ship-to-ship combats and boarding; and running endless drills and exercises. All the while the green local forces will be conducting the usual customs and defense service. Individual mercs will be assigned to keep an eye on the locals as they carry out their duties.

The GM should provide a string of incidents for the mercs to deal with:

• A fighter suffers engine failure and must be retrieved before it collides with the starport.

• Inexperienced customs troopers provoke a potential gunfight with the heavily armed crew of a shady (but just barely legal) Far Trader.

• An SDB captain cracks up under the strain and begins to behave erratically, moving to fire on an incoming passenger ship.

Finally, the coup begins. The resolution will include a mix of strategic/political play as the mercs try to decide what to do and close combat in the confines of the starport.

If the mercs decide to help the navy rescue their government, it will be necessary to fight through heavy air defenses to reach the shrinking perimeter, then fight their way out again.

AEROSPACE MISSION

SMALL UNIT

Air Defense Ticket

Background: Tarkine (see p. BTC76) is an agricultural world with a population of about 3,000,000. It is an Amber zoned client state of the Imperium, ruled from Dallia. The world has an extremely violent weather system.

Tarkine was once a member of the Agworld Combine, but was annexed by Dallia to ensure Dallia's food supply. The Dallian administration has been fair and the locals are generally happy with their lot.

It seems likely that the Agworld Combine may try to retake Tarkine now that Agworld forces have been freed from front-line duty by a lull in the tensions to Rimward.

Mission: The government of Dallia is offering standard salaries plus Cr250,000 per month for a mercenary fighter unit to protect the downport. While the starport is considered secure due to the presence of a force of Imperial Scout Service

vessels using a leased segment of the port, the downport is vulnerable to attack. The only other defenses are company of local militia and a few security personnel. A fat ticket is offered, and two months is the initial period, but an extension is very likely.

Game Master's Information: The ticket is an easy one. The mercs are an adequate deterrent and statement of Dallia's determination to hold what it has. However, within a week of arriving, a massive hurricane strikes the port region and hurtles across the coastline causing immense damage. A merchant vessel trying to beat the winds ignores warnings to sheer off and attempts to land. It is thrown across the landing area and crashes into the port buildings. Further devastation ensues, which will wreck the mercs' tracking and detection equipment and possibly their weapon systems too. The desperate port governor offers to replace all damaged equipment if the mercs, who are the most capable and disciplined personnel available, assist the local rescue volunteers and a party of scouts who are braving the hurricane's following winds to assist in damage control.

Resolving the mission: There is no combat, but panicked citizens may have to be faced down. There will always be looters.

The scout vessels will have to be brought in first. The winds are still very high and the landing nearly impossible. The mercs may have to assist. There is flooding, fires in the port, survivors to be dug out and evacuated, and another severe weather warning has just been issued . . .

The GM should place the player characters under as much pressure as possible. The mercs aren't trained for this, but they *have* been trained to keep cool and think – they are the only chance for many of the survivors.

CHAPTER SEVEN

Units and Personalities

UNITS

These units will serve as models for players and GMs who want to put together units of their own creation. Weapons are as noted in the description that accompanies each organization, except as modified by parenthetical statements in the tables. Weapons and equipment without page references are covered in the *Ironmongery* chapter (see pp. 61-80).

SQUAD-SIZED UNITS

Strouden Snipers

Unit Size: Squad.
Unit Commander: Corporal Hannah McVennie.
Unit Type: Specialist Infantry.
Tech level: 9.
Troop Quality: Veteran.

A specialist unit raised on Strouden in 1118, the Strouden Snipers form a slightly understrength squad of experts capable of acting as forward observers, scouts and, of course, snipers. Most states are capable of raising reasonable infantry forces, but sniping requires long periods of intensive, highly specialized training and this is often beyond the capabilities of local forces.

The Strouden Snipers are an example of the sort of small units of specialists most in demand around the Marches. The vast majority of mercenary units are small, highly professional outfits similar to this one.

All members have served as snipers in planetary or Imperial forces.

Organization:
   Command Section, with:
       Corporal Hannah McVennie
       1 Spotter
   Sniper Section, with:
       2 Sniper Binoms, each with:
           1 Sniper
           1 Spotter

The squad operates in pairs, one sniper armed with a sniping version of the TL8 13mm rifle (see p. GT115) with a laser sight and a stock specially customized to each individual shooter. Snipers also carry a pistol or SMG according to personal taste. The spotter in each pair (armed with an auto-rifle or SMG for close-quarters defense) has the duty of assisting the sniper by calling targets, relaying information back to local artillery, and keeping an eye out for enemy troops who may be on the prowl.

The Strouden Snipers can field three binoms, but generally only send out two at any one time (keeping the third behind the lines to rest). All personnel have combat environment suits.

Trimbell's Defenders

Unit Size: Squad.
Unit Commander: Sergeant Jef Trimbell.
Unit Type: Security.
Tech level: 9.
Troop Quality: Seasoned.

The Defenders specialize in security assignments. Their deployments have been as varied as escorting high-profile prisoners to trial (minor nobles on treason charges or famous terrorists) and guarding research installations. The unit has a history dating back to 1109, not all of which is pleasant reading. During rioting on Bevy in 1112 the Defenders were responsible for a number of civilian casualties when a mob attacked the (singularly unpopular) official they were escorting. The mob was repulsed with handguns and tear gas, but the Defenders found themselves vilified as lackeys of the oppressors. The unit has always maintained its professional integrity no matter how corrupt, oppressive or unsavory its charge may be. This has led to a reputation for reliability and respect from other mercs, but little warmth from the citizenry encountered on assignment and off.

Organization:
   Command Team, with:
       Sergeant Jef Trimbell
       1 Medic
       1 Sniper
       1 Electronics/Sensors Technician
   Guard Team, with:
       Guard Team Leader
       3 Troopers

All personnel have flak jackets and a small handgun (typically a 9mm autopistol) for low-profile bodyguard work. All personnel have personal bodyguard and driver training for a variety of vehicles. The sniper is usually deployed independently (armed with a TL8 13mm rifle as described under the Strouden Snipers, above), while the guard team (armed with pistols or SMGs as the situation dictates) plus the medic (not normally armed) protect the charge. Trimbell and the tech operate a communications monitoring and command post. SMGs, filter masks and gas grenades are available for emergency situations.

In a more conventional military deployment, the team uses combat environment suits and ACRs. The tech operates a variety of sophisticated monitoring devices from the squad command post while the guard team patrols the area.

PLATOON-SIZED UNITS

SB Rangers

Unit Size: Reinforced Platoon (Vargr).
Unit Commander: Lieutenant Colonel Steven Bond.
Unit Type: Commando/Striker.
Tech level: 9.
Troop Quality: Veteran.

The SB Rangers were formed in the Vargr Extents by Lt. Colonel Bond (see p. 126), from personnel attracted to the young leader's charisma. Seasoned in the constant border clashes in the Extents, the Rangers saw considerable action during the Riverland Campaign of the Fifth Frontier War. At one point the unit almost reached company size, but slimmed down again to keep unit quality high.

The Rangers do not have sufficient personnel to maintain a depot or training facility. New personnel are assigned to the headquarters section for an orientation period before joining one of the four line sections.

The Rangers are relatively cheap to hire, and have a reputation for honorable conduct. Their normal deployment is on mid-tech worlds where their moderate equipment level gives them an advantage over local units. With no organic transport, the Rangers rely on their employers' assets for mobility and are generally used in the commando role or to stiffen local forces (often militia).

All personnel but Bond are Vargr.

Organization:

Headquarters Section, with:
    Lieutenant Colonel Steven Bond
    1 Sergeant
    1 Medic
    2 Driver/mechanics
    1 or more new recruits
3 Rifle Sections, each with:
    1 Corporal
    4 Riflemen
    1 Support Gunner
1 Close Assault Section, with:
    1 Corporal/Section Leader
    5 LAG Gunners
1 Support Section, with:

    1 Corporal
    2 PML teams
        1 Gunner (PML, see p. UT126)
        1 Assistant PML Gunner
    1 Sniper/Observer (laser rifle)
1 MG Section, with:
    1 Corporal (assault rifle)
    1 Rifleman (assault rifle)
    2 MG teams, each with:
        1 Gunner (LMG)
        1 Loader (SMG)
1 Tank Section
    2 Instellarms light grav tanks, each with:
        1 Vehicle Commander (SMG)
        1 Driver (SMG)
        1 Gunner (SMG)

All personnel are equipped with combat environment suits. Flak jackets are worn on top in some circumstances. All personnel have a selection of hand grenades and RAM grenades available. The support gunners use 40mm auto grenade launchers (equivalent to the 40mm Mk19, see p. HT121. The close assault section is equipped with 20mm LAGs (including the section leader). In addition, personnel assigned to this section have basic demolitions training and may carry satchel or breaching charges depending upon the mission. PML gunners carry only pistols for self-defense in

addition to their PML (see p. UT126). Assistant PML gunners carry SMGs and ammunition for the PML. Bond, the tank crews and the medic commonly only carry pistols, though they have rifles available at need. The headquarters section uses an unarmed air/raft as as a mobile command post and for reconnaissance. Two riflemen crew the vehicle and perform other administrative tasks such as liaison, supply inventory etc. The LMG gunner is armed with a light machine gun (equivalent to an M60), see p. HT119) and a pistol for personal defense. The assistant LMG gunners are armed with SMGs and carry ammunition for the LMG.

Major Kilver Danaarii

Unit Size: Platoon.
Unit Commander: Major Kilver Danaarii.
Unit Type: Cadre.
Tech level: 12.
Troop Quality: Elite.

Hiring Major Danaarii entails hiring her entire staff, which amounts roughly to a platoon-sized unit. An experienced officer with extensive battle experience, Major Danaarii first placed herself up for hire in 1117, having resigned from a military intelligence posting the previous year for "personal reasons." Her staff are experienced officers and NCOs who retain their service ranks as a form of internal "pecking order" only, as the ranks themselves come from several services and are now meaningless in any case.

The unit is generally hired to provide leadership and training to small militia forces, but has a complete staff organization and can form the core of a full-sized unit raised and trained from the ground up.

The unit's personnel have a wide range of TL10-12 small arms for personal defense, but do not fight as a unit. Instead, the personnel are broken up to lead local units or to provide advice and training. Danaarii's personal contacts in the arms trade make weaponry available for her employers' purchase.

The platoon consists of three sections:

Headquarters, comprising the major and her analysis team, plus some security operatives.

Instructors, consisting of 12 NCOs and junior officers with Instruction/recruiting experience.

Command, consisting of 16 junior officers and senior NCOs with battlefield experience.

On a typical deployment, the major and her analysis team begin to advise her employers, assign some security personnel to protect important figures, and also begin to function as a "tactics school" for local officers. The Instructors immediately begin recruiting and basic training of recruits, while command staff assume command or advisory positions with local units, bringing a units' effectiveness levels up with advanced training when not on combat deployments.

The platoon is quite capable of taking over a nation's armed forces, or even of creating them if none exist. The colonel is a specialist in mobile warfare but has managed to adapt to many different TLs and styles of warfare, getting the most out of meager forces time and again.

Overall quality level is Elite, though this is often diluted by the forces the unit is hired to train or lead.

Franklin's Armored

Unit Size: Platoon.
Unit Commander: Captain Orlando D. Franklin.
Unit Type: Armored Infantry.
Tech level: 10.
Troop Quality: Seasoned.

The unit was raised in 1107 for Imperial service. The platoon served with distinction in various theaters during the war, winning a unit citation at the retaking of Knorbes where the platoon was placed in the van of light forces assigned to "bounce" the Zhodani out of their positions. Had the offensive failed, the Consulate advance base under construction at Knorbes might have posed a major threat to Imperial operations in the region.

The platoon took heavy casualties, and was reequipped at Imperial expense after the campaign. Captain Franklin was elected by the unit's personnel to command them. Franklin himself has never served in planetary or Imperial forces, but enlisted in the unit straight from college.

The platoon is well-respected unit, a small, tight outfit generally employed in rapid strikes. The tank is showing its age, and may soon be replaced.

Organization:
Headquarters Section, with:
  1 Grav Command APC (TL10), with:
    Captain Orlando D. Franklin
    1 Driver
    1 Gunner
    3 Staff
  1 Instellarms Heavy Grav Tank, with:
    1 Vehicle Commander
    1 Driver
    1 Gunner
    1 Electronics Tech
  1 Grav APC with 80mm RF Howitzer (TL10), with:
    1 Vehicle Commander
    1 Driver
    1 Gunner
  1 Air/Space Defense Vehicle (TL10), with:
    1 Vehicle Commander
    1 Driver
    1 Gunner
  3 Armored Infantry Sections, each with:
    2 Grav APCs with VRFGG (TL10), each with:
      1 Driver
      1 Gunner
      1 Rifle Squad, with:
        1 NCO/Squad Leader
        4 Riflemen
        1 Support Gunner (ASW)

Rifle troops are equipped with combat armor and ACRs. They dismount to fight, supported by the VRF gauss guns fitted to the grav APCs. The command staff have rifles and body armor available, while vehicle crews generally have a pistol, SMG or shotgun for personal defense. When air attack is not a threat, the air/space defense vehicle is often deployed in close support where its weaponry can prove quite deadly.

Carstein's Outlaws

Unit Size: Platoon.
Unit Commander: Lieutenant Ulrich Carstein.
Unit Type: Field Engineers.
Tech level: 11.
Troop Quality: Veteran.

The Outlaws are able to trace their unit's ancestry back to 798, when Marquis Serriaa saw the need for a personal force to defend her holdings and raised a combined arms battalion. The unit has gone through many changes over the years, at times reduced to a cadre of less than a dozen personnel. During the Third Frontier war the unit was twice raised to the strength of a reinforced battalion, and twice smashed to little more than a company. Finally the unit was

sent into the battle of Bloody Highway, thrown in the path of an Outworld Coalition advance on Esalin in order to gain time for a decisive counterattack. Only the battalion's detached field engineering company survived the two-day meat grinder battle.

Since this time the unit has borne the motto "Quit the Field Never" in its device. The engineers were partially disbanded after the war but saved from oblivion by Instellarms, which kept the unit as a training pool for its own field engineering units.

During the Fifth Frontier War, Duke Norris bought several units outright from Instellarms, forming a complete division of corporate mercenaries to augment his Efate campaign. The unit was rapidly converted from field engineers to assault engineers and expanded to a battalion in strength.

After the bitter Efate campaign, the remains of the battalion were officially disbanded and dismissed from Imperial service. Captain Carstein gathered a small kernel of personnel and defied the order, fleeing aboard a hired merchant ship with a weak platoon and a little salvaged gear.

The unit has since adopted the "Outlaws" name, though in 1113 the Duke granted a pardon to the unit for its "mutiny," in thanks for their stalwart and loyal service during the war.

The Outlaws are a very high-quality outfit, and fulfill three major roles. They mostly provide field engineering services; building fortifications and temporary bridges. However, the unit includes a number of personnel with extensive instruction experience, who will undertake to train and lead a force of assault engineers for their employers. Finally, the unit is often hired for explosive ordnance disposal, disarming mines, bombs and shells for a suitable fee.

Organization:
Headquarters Section, with:
  1 G-carrier, with:
    Lieutenant Ulrich Carstein
    Driver/Security Trooper
    Security Trooper
    1 Sergeant
    2 Medics
    2 Bomb disposal experts
Field Engineering Section, with:
  1 Engineering Lieutenant
  8 sappers
Assault Pioneer Section, with:
  1 Engineering Lieutenant
  5 NCO Sappers
Vehicles Section, with:
  2 G-carriers, each with:
    Driver/mechanic
    Mechanic
  1 Utility Grav Sled (TL10), with:
    Driver/mechanic
    Mechanic

Assault engineers and sappers have ACRs and combat environment suits. All other personnel are armed only with pistols or SMGs for self defense. Combat armor is worn by bomb-disposal personnel, and flak jackets are available for field wear if necessary.

COMPANY-SIZED UNITS

Death's Head Hussars

Unit Size: Company.
Unit Commander: Major Augustus Valtieri.
Unit Type: Grav Cavalry.
Tech level: 11.
Troop Quality: Veteran.

The Death's Head Hussars are fairly typical of the sort of light armored forces in demand in the Spinward Marches. Capable of conducting rapid strikes with heavy firepower, their equipment is relatively easy to maintain and this keeps the fee down to merely ruinous levels.

The Hussars are a primarily Solomani unit, raised during the Solomani Rim War and captured after the fall of Terra. The unit's personnel chose to enter service as mercenaries and be posted far from Terra rather than be imprisoned as POWs. Over the years the unit's Solomani origins have been diluted by replacement personnel, although several Solomani each year make the long journey to hire on. The Hussars carry on many of the traditions of their alleged unit ancestors, a Brunswicker cavalry unit of the pre-atomic age.

When not in field camouflage, the company's equipment, uniforms and vehicles are all a dull black with death's head badges. Most Solomani and Imperial soldiers avoid black because of the connotation of death, but the personnel of this company wear it to show their contempt for their old companion.

This morbid device has gained the company, like its Terran ancestors, the nickname of "Death-or-Glory men." The unit's personnel are proud of their reputation, a pride bordering upon arrogance which leads them to think of themselves as an unstoppable elite (which they are not, although they are very good).

The company has a number of Aslan members, who have been attracted by the reputation of the company and the fierce pride of its members.

The unit only takes short-term contracts, preferring high risk success-only tickets. Striker missions are a specialty.

Organization:
Headquarters Detachment, with:
  1 Instellarms light grav tank, with:
    Major Augustus Valtieri/Vehicle Commander/CO
    1 Driver
    1 Gunner
  3 Instellarms light grav tanks, each with:
    1 Vehicle Commander
    1 Driver
    1 Gunner
Strike Platoon, with:
  1 Instellarms light grav tank, with:
    1 Vehicle Commander/Platoon Leader
    1 Driver
    1 Gunner
  3 Instellarms light grav tanks, each with:
    1 Vehicle Commander
    1 Driver
    1 Gunner
4 Assault Platoons, each with:
  1 Grav APC with 80mm RF Howitzer (TL10) , with:
    1 Vehicle Commander
    1 Driver
    1 Gunner
  3 Infantry Sections, each with:
    1 Grav APC with VRFGG-9 (TL10), with:
      1 Driver
      1 Gunner
      1 NCO
      3 Infantrymen
Support And Maintenance Platoon
  1 Grav APC (TL10) with repair shop (TL10), with:
    1 Driver
    4 Mechanics

  1 G-carrier, with:
    1 Driver
    4 Mechanics

Infantry are equipped with gauss rifles and combat armor. Other personnel have gauss pistols for self defense. Each VRFGG APC operates in close support of its squad once they have disembarked.

Troop quality is Veteran, though the troopers consider themselves Elite.

Transplanetary Express

Unit Size: Company.
Unit Type: Transport and Logistics.
Unit Commander: Captain Kalthii Ruuniiri.
Tech level: 10.
Troop Quality: Seasoned.

The Transplanetary Express is a somewhat unusual unit, as it is not a "teeth" formation but part of the "tail" which supports military operations. This seems like a strange occupation for mercenary soldiers, but where there is a market, there is a unit.

Cash-strapped nations frequently raise far more troops than they can afford, and in order to defeat their opponents

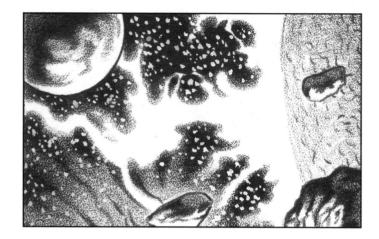

they concentrate on the front-line units – infantry, artillery, armor and air power. Then they find that they cannot support their operations because of a lack of transport assets. Perhaps the government just wants something moved that they do not have the resources for. Either way, this unit is available to fill the gap on a short-term basis.

The Express specializes in two types of mission – opposed resupply of forward units (which often entails fighting a convoy through to its destination) and conveyance of high-value items through dangerous terrain. The unit prides itself upon delivering the goods anywhere, in time and no matter what the opposition may try to do about it.

Captain Ruuniiri explains, "We are not a glorified postal service, though we deliver mail upon occasion. We are a fighting unit. Just try to stop us from delivering something and you'll see what I mean."

The greatest exploits of the Express include the Battle of Outpost 692, where the company fought through heavy Sword Worlder opposition to resupply the legendary outpost, and the famous Marastan Transit, where the unit was detailed to evacuate civilians during heavy fighting. Both actions were characterized by a series of attacks upon the convoy, which were beaten off to allow delivery of the cargo unharmed.

Organization:
Command Platoon, with:
   Headquarters Squad, with:
      1 G-carrier, with:
         Captain Kalthii Ruuniiri
         Senior NCO
         1 Driver
         4 Commo Staff
      1 Air/Space Defense Vehicle (TL10), with:
        1 Vehicle Commander
        1 Driver
        1 Gunner
      3 Fast-response Squads, each with:
        1 Grav APC with 20mm chaingun (TL10), with:
         1 Driver
         1 Gunner
         1 NCO
         5 Riflemen

3 Transport Platoons, each with:
   1 Wheeled Command ATV (see p. GT148) with 20mm chaingun, with:
      1 Platoon Leader
      1 Driver
      1 Gunner
   6 Trucks (see p. VE187), each with:
      1 Driver
      1 Relief Driver
   2 Infantry Sections, each with:
      1 Wheeled ATV (see p. GT148), with:
        1 Driver
        1 PML Gunner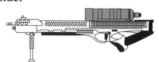
        1 NCO
        6 Riflemen
1 Escort Platoon, with:
   1 Wheeled Command ATV (see p. GT148) with 20mm chaingun, with:
      1 Platoon Leader
      1 Driver
      1 Gunner
   1 Wheeled ATV (see p. GT148) with 20mm chaingun, with:
      1 Vehicle Commander
      1 Driver
      1 Gunner
   2 Infantry Sections. each with:
      1 Wheeled ATV (see p. GT148) with 20mm chaingun, with:
        1 Vehicle Commander
        1 Driver
        1 Gunner
        1 NCO
        1 PML Gunner
        6 Riflemen

The Express generally operates on mid-tech worlds, where grav vehicles are rare. Thus the air/space defense vehicle is often employed as a scout (and its heavy firepower can be used to devastating effect in ambushes). Each transport platoon has its own escort force carried by the APCs. The command and escort formations sometimes operate as a detached force, responding to threats as needed. Fast-response units riding grav APCs may be used for commando-style raids on enemy positions.

Infantrymen are equipped with cloth body armor, helmets and assault rifles. The vehicle crews have SMGs or carbines for self defense.

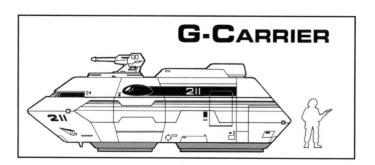

G-CARRIER

The Trantaxer Company

Unit Size: Company.
Unit Commander: Captain Harlaz Tanslaar.
Unit Type: Infantry Company (motorized).
Tech level: 6.
Unit Quality: Seasoned.

The Trantaxer Company is an example of the dispossessed units which find their way to the mercenary circuit for lack of any better options. This particular unit found itself without a home after the Trantax revolt of 1102. This was a very minor affair in which the followers of Trantax (a somewhat obscure religious cult) tried unsuccessfully to gain control of the starport on Arkadia. The world is still the site for other struggles, but the leaders of the Trantaxers were slaughtered and their surviving troops wisely left the world while they could.

The Trantaxers are not especially devoted to their religion, though some of the company observe the forms dutifully. New recruits have diluted the unit's cohesion over the years. There is a hard core of dispossessed Trantaxers, who have no home and no desire to settle. The mercenary life seems like the only option for a group of armed but homeless men and women.

The unit's low-tech origins are a major handicap, and limits their deployments to minor conflict and low paying security jobs. As a result, the Trantaxers have never managed to acquire more advanced equipment. However, their vehicles and equipment are extremely rugged and easily maintained, and this suits the company for long-term operations on underdeveloped worlds. The Trantaxers are especially good at low-intensity counterinsurgency warfare in difficult country, and man-for-man are better than many far more expensively equipped units.

Rumors persist that the unit's leaders some day hope to gather a following and sweep home to Arkadia in a holy war, to take the Holy Banner of Trantax to the people by fire and bayonet.

Organization:
Headquarters Platoon, with:
    Command Section, with:
        Captain Harlaz Tanslaar
        1 Unit Senior NCO
        4 Commo/Headquarters Staff
    1 Tracked APC with HMG (see p. VE175), with:
        1 Driver
        1 Gunner
        4 Commo/Headquarters Staff
    1 Tracked APC with EX34 chaingun (see p. HT120), with:
        1 Driver
        1 Gunner
        4 Security Personnel
    4 Jeeps (see p. VE58) with LMG (M60, see p. HT119), each with:
        1 Driver
        1 Gunner

3 Rifle Platoons, each with:
    Command Section, with:
        1 Lieutenant
        1 NCO
        1 Grenade-Launcher Gunner (see Mk19, p. HT121).
        1 Machine Gunner (MG34, see p. HT119)
        1 Loader
        1 Medic
        1 Radio Operator
    3 Rifle Sections, each with:
        1 NCO
        9 Riflemen
        1 LMG Gunner (MG34, see p. HT119).
    1 Transport Section, with:
        2 Jeeps, each with:
            1 Driver
            1 Co-driver
        8 Trucks (see p. VE187), with:
            1 Driver
            1 Co-driver
1 Weapons Platoon, with:
    Command Section:
        1 Lieutenant
        1 NCO
        2 Radio Operators
        2 Observer/Snipers (13mm rifle)
    Mortar Section, with:
        1 NCO
        1 Radio Operator
        5 81mm Mortars (see p. HT120)
            3 crew
    MG Section, with:
        1 NCO
        2 Heavy Machine Gunners (see KPV, p. HT119).
            3 Crew
    Transport Section, with:
        8 Trucks (see p. VE187), with:
            1 Driver

The Trantaxers have a training level of Seasoned. The unit is the only home many of the members will ever have. This and the common religion shared by the core members has produced a high level of morale and a feeling of "family" among the troops. The snipers are equipped with 13mm rifles, as described under the Strouden's Snipers entry on p. 102.

Free Troopers

Unit Size: Company.
Unit Commander: Piotr Kivn (no formal rank designation).
Unit Type: Light Infantry.
Tech level: about 10.
Unit Quality: Highly variable.

The Free Troopers are an oddity. The unit is a collection of oddballs, aliens and misfits, with a few lunatics thrown in for good measure. The command structure is almost nonexistent. Each month, the company votes on who the next commander is to be and reorganizes itself according to the whims of the unit as a whole. Otherwise, there is no formal structure.

Members of the company are armed with whatever small arms and support weapons they choose, and join one of the combat groups after a period as a "newbie." Within each group, partnerships and small units have naturally evolved from friendships and working relationships into small, surprisingly effective combat squads whose members seem almost able to read one another's minds.

New members are lumped together in a small group until one of the other peer groups accepts them or they form a partnership with some of the other newbies. Some decide to work alone or are too weird even for the other misfits to deal with. These loosely attach themselves to one of the groups but operate at their own discretion.

The Free Troopers are not big on orders, which cramp their style. Simply-stated tasks like "hold this street" or "capture the control tower" are where they excel. Everyone knows the objective, and finds his or her own way of helping accomplish it. Their disorganized, highly personal style of combat confounds many opposing commanders, and occasionally results in catastrophic blunders. The presence of a few complete lunatics in the unit does not help matters.

But somehow, the Free Troopers are successful more often than not, and almost always when they are left alone to do their thing. They are cheap, but only the most desperate would hire them. There seems to be some sort of hidden agenda for some of the troopers, who are selective about their employers (desperation is not the only requirement, it seems) and who spend a great deal of time discussing radical politics and philosophy.

Organization:

> Leader's Warband, with:
> > Piotr Kivn
> > 3-7 assorted personnel
> Newbie Group, with:
> > 18-25 new personnel
> Assault Troop, with:
> > 20-30 close-assault specialists
> 2 Rifle Troop, each with:
> > 25-35 rifle-armed troopers
> Heavy Weapons Troop, with:
> > 6-12 personnel armed with MGs, grenade launchers, etc.

The organization and personnel roster changes continuously, as does armament. There is some commonality – cheap and readily-available weapons are favored. Generally speaking, assault troopers use assault rifles, SMGs and shotguns as their main weapon and are festooned with grenades and backups such as pistols and blades. Heavy Weapons personnel carry grenade launchers, machine guns and similar weapons. "Rifle" troopers might actually be armed with just about anything, though assault rifles are the most common. Body armor varies from none at all to full combat armor with no attempt at commonality.

BATTALION-SIZED UNITS

Rifles, Inc.

> *Unit Size:* Battalion.
> *Unit Type:* Light Infantry.
> *Unit Commander:* Major Dyle Tarshkavik.
> *Tech level:* 9.
> *Unit Quality:* Average.

Rifles, Inc. is a mercenary unit which has outgrown its useful size. Once a highly effective company-sized unit, a string of highly lucrative successes allowed the unit to expand to its present establishment.

Rather too much was undertaken at once. Each platoon was expanded into a company in its own right, diluting the unit's quality. Funds did not permit the purchase of adequate equipment to go with this expansion, and the unit failed in its next three contracts.

Rifles, Inc. has struggled along for the past six years as a security/urban combat outfit, fields where the battalion's relatively light equipment is less of a liability. However, there is little call for such a large security unit, so the battalion has gained a reputation as a pawn in the many brushfire wars of the Marches, hired by one minor faction unable to afford better, then another. The surviving equipment is battered and poorly-paying contracts have not permitted much replacement. Constant low-intensity combat has also taken toll on morale and personnel. A long security assignment, allowing some reorganization and rest for tired personnel, would be a Godsend for this troubled unit.

Organization:
  Headquarters Company, with:
    Headquarters Platoon, with:
      Command Section, with:
        Major Dyle Tarshkavik
        Executive Officer
        2 NCOs
        4 Commo Techs
        4 Riflemen
      Medical Section, with:
        Medical Officer
        3 Medics
      Battalion Artillery, with:
        2 Grav APCs with 80mm RF Howitzer (TL10), each with:
          1 Vehicle Commander
          1 Driver
          1 Gunner
      3 Rifle Platoons, each with:
        1 Platoon Leader
        1 Assistant Platoon Leader
        1 LMG Team, with:
          1 LMG Gunner (M60, see p. HT119)
          1 Loader
        2 Rifle Sections, each with:
          1 Corporal
          1 LAG Gunner
          10 Riflemen
    3 Rifle Companies, each with:
      Command Platoon, with:
        1 Company Commander
        1 NCO
      1 Weapons Section, with:
        1 Section Leader
        1 Forward Observer
        1 Corporal
        2 Mortar Teams, each with:
          81mm mortar
          1 Gunner
          2 Loaders
      4 Rifle Platoons, each with:
        1 Platoon Leader
        1 Assistant Platoon Leader

        1 LMG Team, with:
          1 LMG Gunner (M60, see p. HT119)
          1 Loader
        2 Rifle Sections, each with:
          1 Corporal
          1 LAG Gunner
          12 Riflemen

The battalion is very lightly equipped, with no vehicles except for the grav artillery. Infantry are organized in large squads with very light body armor and cheap TL8 assault rifles. Support weapons are limited to a few rifle grenades, a squad level LAG and a few mortars and machine guns. There is no air defense, nor much in the way of anti-armor equipment other than AT rifle grenades. The command company is a little better armed, with about half the troops still retaining the combat armor and ACRs they started out with.

If the unit's luck does not change soon, desertion is going to become a major problem. This might actually be a good thing, bringing the unit back down to a manageable size.

102nd Lift Infantry Battalion

Unit Size: Battalion.
Unit Commander: Lieutenant Colonel Ian "Bulldozer" Muncy (see p. 119).
Unit Type: Lift Infantry.
Tech level: 12.
Unit Quality: Veteran.

The 102nd started life on Efate as part of the planetary armed forces. After the Fifth Frontier War, the battalion was found to be badly in need of refitting, and was withdrawn from active service. At this point the war hero Colonel Muncy took a hand. Entering a closed session with the military planning department, Muncy presented a proposal to the planners: keep the 102nd in being, let it gain experience which could then be of benefit to other units back on Efate, and let others pay for the upkeep of the unit.

The planners disliked the idea, but Muncy was able to persuade them. Unofficial sources report that he tore the starburst for extreme heroism from around his neck and attempted to feed it to the chief of the Efate Planning Department (a civilian bureaucrat who had spent the war as an evacuee on Trin).

Whatever happened, the 102nd was reequipped with gear taken from other, less fortunate, units and shipped out in 1114 after a long period of retraining. The battalion is expensive to hire, and generally operates only on short success-only contracts, though the colonel is known to approach prospective clients with a proposal of his own – offering to undertake some task that they might not have dared approach themselves, for a success-only fee.

Rumors claim that the 102nd is in fact in Imperial pay, and undertaking "dirty jobs" for the Archduke. Others claim that Instellarms has Colonel Muncy in its pocket and is using his outfit for its own ends.

The 102nd still recruits on Efate, and sometimes receives personnel transferred from other units. Some recruits do come from elsewhere than Efate, however. The battalion is listed as part of the Efate Planetary Forces as a reserve unit presently on inactive status.

Organization:

Headquarters Company, with:
  1 Command Platoon, with:
    Lieutenant Colonel Ian "Bulldozer" Muncy
    7 Headquarters/Security Staff
    2 G-carriers, each with:
      1 Driver
      1 Commo Tech
    2 Instellarms light grav tanks, each with
      1 Vehicle Commander
      1 Driver
      1 Gunner
  1 Communications Platoon, with:
    1 Driver
    2 Commo Techs
    1 EW Tech
  1 Medical Platoon, with:
    1 Surgeon
    10 Medical Staff
    1 G-carrier (surgical theater), with:
      1 Driver
    1 G-carrier
      1 Driver
  1 Field Engineering Platoon, with:
    1 Engineering Officer
    3 NCOs
    2 Field Engineering Tractor (G-carrier), each with:

1 Driver
3 Sappers
2 Field Engineering Squads, each with:
  1 G-carrier
  1 Driver
  1 NCO
  7 Sappers
1 TL6 bulldozer ("The Beast")
  (driven by one of the sappers when not in use by Muncy)
1 Support Company, with:
  1 Meson Gun Platoon, with:
    1 Meson Gun Sled, with:
      1 Vehicle Commander
      1 Driver
      1 Gunner
      1 Electronics Tech
    2 Security Squads, with:
      1 Air/Space Defense Vehicle (TL10), with:
        1 Vehicle Commander
        1 Driver
        1 Gunner
      1 G-carrier with VRFGG-9, with:
        1 Driver
        1 Gunner
      1 NCO
      6 Riflemen
      1 Support Gunner (ASW)
  1 Nuclear Damper Platoon, with:
    1 G-carrier (ND Direction), with:
      1 Driver
      1 Commo Tech
      2 ND Techs

1 *Astrin*-class APC (Damper variant), with:
  1 Driver
  2 ND Techs (Laser pistol-10)
  1 Security Squad, with:
  1 Air/Space Defense Vehicle (TL10), with:
    1 Vehicle Commander
    1 Driver
    1 Gunner
  1 G-carrier with VRFGG-9
    1 Driver
    1 Gunner
  1 NCO
  6 Riflemen

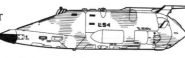

1 Aerospace Defense platoon, with:
  3 Air/Space Defense Vehicles (TL10), each with:
    1 Vehicle Commander
    1 Driver
    1 Gunner
1 Artillery Platoon, with:
  1 Platoon Leader
  4 Forward Observers
  2 Grav APCs with 80mm RF Howitzer (TL10), each with:
    1 Vehicle Commander
    1 Driver
    1 Gunner
1 Recovery & Maintenance Platoon, with:
  4 G-carriers, each with:
    1 Driver
    7 Mechanics
3 Lift Infantry Companies, each with:
  1 Tank Platoon
    1 *Intrepid*-class grav tank, with:
      1 Platoon Leader/Vehicle Commander
      1 Driver
      1 Gunner
    3 *Intrepid* class grav tanks, each with:
      1 Vehicle Commander
      1 Driver
      1 Gunner
  4 Lift Infantry Platoons, with:
    Command Squad, with:
      1 G-carrier, with:
      1 Driver
      1 Platoon Leader
      1 Assistant Platoon Leader
      5 Riflemen
      1 Fusion Gunner
    3 Infantry Squads, each with:
      1 G-carrier
      1 Driver
      1 NCO
      6 Riflemen
      1 Fusion Gunner

All infantry are equipped with battledress and gauss rifles, and are supported by squad-level fusion gunners. Security personnel have combat armor and gauss rifles.

Vehicle and support personnel carry only sidearms, but combat environment suits are worn in case of chemical weapons or similar threats. Forward observers use battledress and whatever weapon they choose.

The 102nd is a very heavily equipped formation, and is not cheap to hire, but very effective at almost any task imaginable. Striker missions are the most common, since nobody could afford a unit like this on retainer for mere security work. The 102nd has at times undertaken some cadre assignments on worlds interested in enhancing their mobile warfare – including Efate.

DEEP SPACE UNITS

Halderney's Vacc Troopers

Unit Size: Reinforced Platoon.
Unit Commander: Major Hugh Halderney.
Unit Type: Protected Forces.
Tech level: 11.
Unit Quality: Elite.

A recently-formed unit, founded in 1118, Halderney's Vacc Troopers specialize in hostile environment operations, mainly in space but undertaking the occasional exotic atmosphere operation.

The unit's role may vary from installation or shipboard security to direct assault from vacuum. Its most recent success was the retaking of the Deep Space Observation Ship *Vakliisa* from her mutinous crew. The surgical strike was conducted by "A" squad while the mutineers were still attempting to negotiate with Major Halderney, asking to exchange hostages for fuel. Loss of life was kept to a minimum in this case, but boarding actions are generally very messy affairs and the troopers' hard-boiled attitudes reflect this.

Organization:
Command Squad, with:
  Major Hugh Halderney
  1 Senior NCO
  6 Troopers
"A" Squad, with:
  1 NCO
  5 Troopers
  1 Explosives Expert
  2 Close Assault Specialists
"B" and "C" Squads, each with:
  1 NCO
  5 Troopers
  1 Explosives Expert
  2 Close Assault Specialists
Support Squad, with:
  1 NCO
  6 Technicians and Support Personnel

When undertaking security duties, troopers wear flak jackets and carry snub pistols unless on high alert. For assault, defense or rescue operations, the battledress is broken out.

The troopers choose their own personal weapon. Low-G weapons such as laser rifles and accelerator rifles are favored, and almost everyone has a snub pistol as a backup. Most close assault specialists carry snub SMGs and hand weapons.

Claymore

Unit Size: Mercenary Starship
Unit Co-commanders: Captain Mal Kytinski and Captain Kander J. Kelith
Unit Type: Deep Space Infantry.
Tech level: 11.
Unit Quality: See notes.

Claymore is a *Broadsword*-class mercenary cruiser, one of many carrying small mercenary contingents to deployments on many worlds.

Because the 800-ton *Broadsword*-class cannot carry many troops, they have to be the best personnel armed with the finest equipment. Such troops are expensive to hire, and are best suited to the striker or assault role, though the ship and her complement are occasionally hired to transport persons or items in the utmost security.

Claymore is owned by a small firm, Star Merc LIC, which operates a few other craft as well as Protected Forces contingents across the sector.

In all space operations, *Claymore* and all personnel aboard are commanded by her Captain, Mal Kytinski. On the ground, Captain Kander J. Kelith is in charge of his troops. Overall operational control is exercised by a representative of Star Merc LIC, acting as owner-aboard.

Organization:

    Ship Crew, with:
          Captain Mal Kytinski
          Medical Branch, with:
             Surgeon
             Clerk
             3 Medics (detached from infantry squads)
          Engineering Branch, with:
             Chief Engineer
             2 Deputy Engineers
             2 Drive Lackeys
          Navigation & Gunnery Branch, with:
             Navigator/Gunnery Officer
             Gunners, with:
                 2 Missile Gunners
                 2 Beam Gunners
             Cutter Crews, with:
                 1 Lead Cutter (2 crew)
                 1 Second Cutter (2 crew)
          Troop Contingent, with:
             1 Command Squad, with:
                 Captain Kander J. Kelith (Courtesy title "Major" aboard ship)

                 1 NCO
                 1 Runner
                 (Cutters if assigned to ground command)
          2 Squads, each with:
             1 Command Team, with:
                 1 Wheeled ATV, with:
                   1 Squad Leader
                   1 Driver
                 1 Medic
                 1 Fusion Gunner
             1 Fire Team, with:
                 1 Fire Team Leader
                 3 Troopers
          3rd Squad, with:
             1 Command Team, with:
                 1 Squad Leader
                 1 Demolitions Expert
                 1 Medic
                 1 Fusion Gunner
             1 Fire Team, with:
                 1 Fire Team Leader
                 3 Troopers

Operations involving space and ground personnel can be complex, but in fact the command structure operates according to a few simple rules. The owner-aboard (a representative of Star Merc LIC on a rotating basis) makes broad policy decisions and leaves implementation to the experts in their field, though he has certain absolute powers such as termination of operation and recall. In any space combat or similar emergency, the ship's captain is in absolute control and can overrule the owner aboard. The ground commander is in control of his own troops – absolutely on the ground and subordinate to the captain aboard ship. Command of cutter personnel is passed between space and ground control according to the situation.

The ship's crew have vacc suits and small arms (snub pistols and laser rifles for the most part) available to resist boarding, and additionally most crewmembers have a personal weapon of some kind.

The ground troops wear combat armor and carry gauss rifles fitted to fire 40mm RAM grenades, except for the squad support gunners who have battle dress and fusion guns. Cutter crews have combat armor available but do not usually wear it, preferring vacc suits instead.

The first and second squads deploy in wheeled AFVs, while the third is landed directly on foot. The command squad makes use of the *Claymore's* air/raft. Other weaponry is available aboard *Claymore* on a mission specific basis.

The crew of *Claymore* are Average in ground combat, Veteran in space combat. The ground combat contingent (star merc troopers) are Elite.

Spinward Guardian Services

Unit Type: Escort Starship
Unit Commander: Captain Jell Moravia

SGS, despite the rather grand title, operates only one starship, *Steelheart Defender*. *Defender* is an *Akkigish*-class 400-ton subsidized merchant. fitted with two drop capsule launchers and carrying mostly military cargoes (including extra missiles and sand canisters).

The crew of 14 (the 10 noted on p. GT146 plus 4 gunners) are armed with various small arms according to inclination, but other than guarding the ship while she is berthed, they do not fight outside their vessel.

Steelheart Defender and her crew can be hired for a single trip or a long-term contract. One of the more common assignments is as close escort to vessels carrying ground fighter mercenaries. In this case, the contract usually includes a short period acting as ortillery in support of the ground forces.

The other main sources of income are strike missions and contract patrol, where the vessel is hired to patrol a given area (which may involve one or more jumps).

When not on contract, *Defender* can be encountered in dock or making speculative bounty-hunting sweeps.

The crew are Green in ground combat, but Seasoned in ship-to-ship actions.

Aerospace Units

Star Guards LIC

Unit Size: 1 Flight and support personnel.
Unit Commander: Flight Lieutenant Ylrich Thorsanger.
Unit Type: Aerospace Interceptor.
Tech level: 12.
Unit Quality: Interceptor pilots Seasoned, all others Average.

Star Guards is an elite formation operating *Iramda*-class fighters acting as aerospace interceptors, flying from planetary surface bases to intercept and destroy incoming hostile craft. The unit was formed for the mercenary market in 1107, just before the beginning of the Fifth Frontier War. Star Guards spent the war shuttling from one threatened Imperial world to another, but never actually saw action.

After the war, a long-term contract on Zila finally led to the unit's blooding when the Vargr Dho'rr'zargh faction attempted a fast raid in two ships. The vessels were intercepted as they entered atmosphere and one was downed after foolishly attempting to fight it out in atmosphere with four heavily-armed interceptors. The other vessel withdrew and did not return.

Despite numerous alerts, no further attacks materialized, and the Zilans paid off their mercenaries after a few more months. Since then, Star Guards has served on several worlds and recently made the news with its spectacular annihilation of the New Order Freedom Alliance's entire air force (19 aircraft) on Gougestra. The combat, which lasted all of 37 seconds, attracted widespread condemnation as the NOFA is widely seen by Imperial citizens as a band of heroic freedom fighters against Sword Worlder tyranny.

Organization:
    Interceptor Flight, with:
        1 *Iramda*-class TL10 Fighter, with:
            Flight Lieutenant Ylrich Thorsanger
        3 *Iramda*-class TL10 Fighters, each with:
            1 Pilot
    Support Unit, with:
        34 technical personnel
        (locally contracted transport vehicles)
    Control & Liaison Unit, with:
        1 Ground Control Officer
        3 Staff/Liaison Personnel
        4 Speeders (grav cycle, see p. VE56), each with:
            1 Driver/Messenger
        1 Commo G-Carrier, with:
            1 Driver
            1 Commo Tech
        6 Liaison and operations staff
    Security Unit, with:
        2 Air/Space Defense Vehicles (TL10), each with:
            1 Vehicle Commander
            1 Driver
            1 Gunner
        4 Security Teams, with:
            1 G carrier with VRFGG-9, each with:
                1 NCO/Vehicle Commander
                1 Driver
                1 Gunner
                5 Troopers

Pilots and operations personnel have sidearms available. Technical personnel are sometimes required to defend the base, and have flak jackets, helmets and SMGs available, though weapons are not common issue. Security personnel answer directly to the ground control officer, wear combat environment suits and are armed with ACRs. The G-carriers in the security unit are each fitted with a VRFGG-9 (Tu) with full stabilization and a universal mount, 12,000 rounds 4mm (Tu).

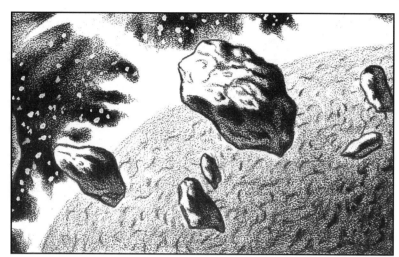

AirStrikers

Unit Size: Squadron.
Unit Commander: Squadron Leader Mik Laanksaan.
Unit Type: Mid-tech air unit (Interdiction/Strike).
Tech level: 9.
Unit Quality: Pilots Seasoned, ground personnel Average.

AirStrikers do most of their work on TL5-8 worlds, for governments which recognize the value of air power but simply cannot afford the time or money required to form a useful force. Their aircraft are almost all rugged *Port Stanley*-class VTOL fighter-bombers (equivalent to the armored vertol on p. VE62), chosen for their multirole capacity and ability to operate from poor frontier air fields – or no field at all. The squadron's media image consists mainly of holovid images of a formation of TL6 piston-engined fighters being blasted from the air by gunfire from a *Port Stanley,* which pivots slowly on its vectored thrust jets with cannon pods under each wing blazing away.

Against grav vehicles or high-tech air defenses, the Strikers' aircraft would be useless, so contracts have to be selected with care. The squadron specializes in attacking ground targets, but has the capability to conduct its own reconnaissance. Against aircraft of a lower TL, the squadron can even establish its own air superiority, though personnel are not specifically trained for air-to-air combat and the aircraft are not particularly well suited to this role. Being mercenaries and driven by necessity, the pilots just do what they must to get the job done. Despite the public image they are not, and do not claim to be, fighter jocks.

Organization:
1 Command Flight, with:
    1 *Port Stanley*-class VTOL, with:
        Squadron Leader Mik Laanksaan

    3 *Port Stanley*-class VTOL, each with:
        1 Pilot
2 Attack Flights, each with:
    4 *Port Stanley*-class VTOL, with:
        1 Pilot
1 Rescue Flight, with:
        3 utility helicopters (see p. VE120), each with:
            1 Pilot
            1 Gunner
  1 Base & Support Unit, with:
      30 technical personnel
      4 Liaison personnel
  2 Air Defense detachments, each with:
      1 Wheeled APC with 20mm gatling
        1 Driver
        Gunner
      2 AD Missile Gunners (Light SAM launchers, see p. VE203)
  1 Base Security Platoon, with:
      1 Platoon Leader
      4 Mobile Security Teams, each with:
        1 Jeep (see p. VE58) with grenade launcher (Mk19, see p. HT121)
        1 NCO/Team Leader
        1 Driver
        1 Gunner
        1 Trooper
  2 Foot Security Teams, each with:
      1 NCO/Team Leader
      1 LMG Gunner
      6 Troopers

Maintenance equipment and spare parts are carried in locally contracted transport attached to the base and support unit. Security personnel are equipped with assault rifles and flak jackets. Flight and tech personnel do not normally carry more than sidearms. Environment suits are issued to all personnel where necessary.

The squadron has an assortment of air-launched weapons available. The aircraft all mount autocannon, and can be fitted with a powerful mix of air-to-air and air-to-ground missiles, cannons or unguided rocket pods for ground attack, plus an assortment of deadfall ordnance – napalm, air-scattered mines and runway denial ordnance (see ***GURPS Vehicles*** for descriptions and rules dealing with all of these weapons). These planes are sometimes used as air-superiority fighters against lower-tech opponents.

The recce variant aircraft are fitted with a variety of sensors depending upon mission requirements, in addition to weapons.

The utility helicopters are used for recovery of downed aircraft, and (with machine guns blazing) for rescue of downed pilots.

The wheeled APC is fitted with a 20mm 6-barrel gatling (see p. VE103) in a fully rotating turret with full stabilization and a universal mount, 8,000 rounds 20mm (Tu).

Ground personnel are Average, pilots are Seasoned.

IMPERIAL MARINES

Imperial Marine Security Detachment

Unit Type: Marines
Tech level: 12
Unit Quality: Average to Seasoned

By tradition, the Imperial Army supplies security units for commercial facilities and trade posts while Marines are assigned to embassies, starports and naval vessels. Large ships and important ports will have company-sized or larger forces assigned, with attached logistics units as necessary.

For service aboard small vessels (Fleet Marines), platoons are broken down into smaller detachments led by a senior NCO or junior officer. Shipboard detachments are commanded by Naval personnel while those assigned to ports answer to the port governor or senior Naval officer present. Parent formations exist at naval bases and depots, where the technical, administrative and headquarters staff are stationed.

Organization:
    Command Team, with:
        1 Detachment Leader
        1 Medic
    2 Fire Teams, each with:
        1 Corporal/Fire Team Leader
        3 Marines

For formal duties, marines are armed with the traditional cutlass and a snub autopistol along with their dress uniforms. Normal shipboard duties are carried out in everyday uniform, supplemented by flak jackets and gauss rifles (gauss pistols for officers) as necessary. In an alert situation, they don battledress. The medic is normally unarmed.

Marines assigned to a downport or other non-space duties are equipped with battledress and gauss rifles (a gauss pistol for the detachment leader).

Imperial Marine Task Force

Unit Type: Imperial Marines
Tech level: 12
Troop Quality: Average to Veteran (Commandos are Elite)

An Imperial Marine task force is a flexible, battalion-sized organization tailored to a specific mission. A task force is built around a core of a force command headquarters (one of three in a Marine regiment). Normally attached to the headquarters are three line Marine companies (from the nine in a regiment), and a battery of meson artillery (from the five in a regiment). Other units may be attached depending upon the unit's mission (tank, engineer or commando platoons or sniper teams), but only the most common are listed here. All Imperial Marines are drop trained, and issued drop capsules if the mission warrants.

Organization:
    Force Command Headquarters, with:
        Command Post Section, with:
          1 *Astrin*-class grav APC, with:
            1 Driver
            1 Task Force Commander (gauss pistol)
            1 Task Force Executive officer (gauss pistol)
            1 Task Force Senior NCO
            2 Intelligence Analysts
          1 Computer *Astrin*-class grav APC, with:
            1 Driver
            2 Computer Techs
            2 Clerks
        1 Communications Section, with:
          1 Communications *Astrin*-class grav APC, with:
            1 Driver
            3 Commo Techs
          1 EW *Astrin*-class grav APC, with:
            1 Driver
            3 ElectronicsTechs
        1 Point Defense Section (from regimental pool), with:
          1 Air/Raft, with:
            1 Section Leader (gauss pistol)
            1 Driver
          3 Air/Space Defense Vehicles (TL10), with:
            1 Vehicle Commander (gauss pistol)
            1 Driver
            1 Gunner
        1 Nuclear Damper Section (attached from regimental pool), with:
          1 *Astrin*-class grav APC (ND Direction), with:
            1 Section Leader/vehicle commander (gauss pistol)
            1 Driver
            2 ND Techs (gauss pistol)
          2 *Astrin*-class grav APC, each with:
            1 Vehicle commander (gauss pistol)

1 Driver
2 ND Techs (gauss pistol)
4 *Astrin*-class grav APCs (Damper variant),
    each with:
    1 Vehicle Commander (gauss pistol)
    1 Driver
    2 ND Techs (gauss pistol)
1 Recon Section (attached from regimental pool),
    with:
    1 Air/Raft, with:
      1 Section Leader
      1 Driver
    5 Air/Rafts, each with:
      1 Driver
      1 Marine 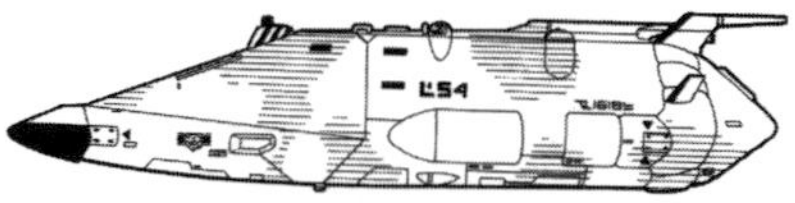
1 Medical Section (attached from regimental pool),
    with:
    1 *Astrin*-class grav APC (cargo variant, with med-
      ical equipment)
    1 Driver (not normally armed)
    1 Surgeon (not normally armed)
    3 Medics (not normally armed)
    1 *Astrin*-class grav APC (cargo variant with med-
      ical supplies), with:
    1 Driver (not normally armed)
    2 Medics (not normally armed)
    3 Medevac Air/Rafts, each with:
      1 Driver/Medic (not normally armed)
      1 Medic (not normally armed)
1 Maintenance Section (attached from regimental
    pool), with:
    1 Air/Raft
      1 Section Leader
      1 Driver
    2 *Astrin*-class grav APC (Cargo variant – recov-
      ery), with:
      1 Driver
      2 Mechanics
    2 *Astrin*-class grav APC (Cargo variant – repair
      shop), with:
      1 Driver
      3 Mechanics
    2 *Astrin*-class grav APC (Cargo variant), with:
      1 Driver
      1 Mechanic
1 Mess & Transport Section (attached from regimen-
    tal pool), with:
    1 Air/Raft
      Section Leader (chief cook) (gauss pistol)
      Driver (gauss pistol)
    4 *Astrin*-class grav APC (Cargo variant), with
      field kitchen, each with:
      1 Cook/Vehicle Commander (gauss pistol)
      1 Cook's Helper/Driver (gauss pistol)
      1 Cook's Helper (gauss pistol)
    5 *Astrin*-class grav APC (Cargo variant), with:
      1 Driver (gauss pistol)
3 Line Marine Companies, each with:
    Command Post Section, with:

1 *Astrin*-class grav APC
    1 Company Commander
    1 Company Executive Officer
    1 Company Senior NCO
    1 Driver
    1 Marine Fire Team
      1 Corporal
      3 Marines
4 Marine Platoons, each with:
    1 Platoon Command Section, with:
      1 *Astrin*-class grav APC
        1 Platoon Leader
        1 Assistant Platoon Leader
        1 Driver
        1 Gunner
    5 Marine Squads, each with:
      1 *Astrin*-class grav APC
        1 Squad Leader
        1 Driver
        1 Gunner
        2 Marine Fire Teams, each with:
          1 Corporal
          3 Marines
1 Meson Gun Battery, with:
    1 Battery Headquarters Section, with:
      1 *Astrin*-class grav APC
        1 Battery Commander
        1 Battery Executive Officer
        1 Battery Senior NCO
        1 Driver
      1 FDC *Astrin*-class grav APC
        1 Driver
        3 Commo techs
      3 FO Air/Rafts, each with:
        1 Driver
        1 Forward Observer
      1 *Astrin*-class grav APC (Cargo variant – fuel),
        with:
        1 Driver
        1 Fuel Handler 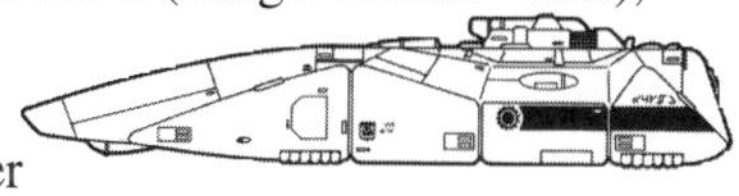
    4 Firing Sections, each with:
      1 Meson Gun Sled, with:
        1 Vehicle Commander
        1 Driver
        1 Gunner
        1 Electronics Tech
    1 Battery Security Section, with:
      1 Air/Raft, with:
        1 Section leader
        1 Driver
      2 Marine Squads, each with:
        1 *Astrin*-class grav APC (TL12)
          1 Squad Leader
          1 Driver
          1 Gunner
          2 Marine Fire Teams, each with:
            1 Corporal/Fire Team Leader
            3 Marines

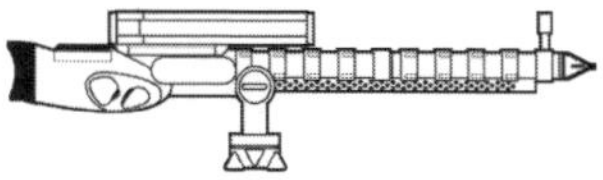

Commando Company (from regimental pool)
Command Post Section, with:
  1 Company Commander (gauss pistol)
  1 Company Executive Officer (gauss pistol)
  2 Commo Techs
  1 Clerk
5 Marine Commando Platoons, each with:
  1 Platoon Leader
  1 Assistant Platoon Leader
  1 Medic (not normally armed)
  5 Marine Commando Squads, each with:
    1 Squad Leader
    2 Marine Commando Fire Teams, each with:
      1 Corporal/Fire Team Leader
      3 Marines

Marine Grav Tank Platoon (from regimental pool)
1 Command *Intrepid*-class grav tank, with:
  1 Vehicle Commander/Platoon Leader
  1 Driver
  1 Gunner
3 *Intrepid*-class grav tanks, each with:
  1 Vehicle Commander
  1 Driver
  1 Gunner

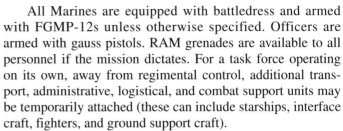

All Marines are equipped with battledress and armed with FGMP-12s unless otherwise specified. Officers are armed with gauss pistols. RAM grenades are available to all personnel if the mission dictates. For a task force operating on its own, away from regimental control, additional transport, administrative, logistical, and combat support units may be temporarily attached (these can include starships, interface craft, fighters, and ground support craft).

All commandos are equipped with commando battle dress and armed with FGMP-12s, unless otherwise noted. RAM grenades or other weapons are issued as necessary for a particular mission. The company senior NCO doubles as platoon leader for the first platoon. In combat, the company clerk doubles as headquarters security.

One or more tank platoons are sometimes attached to a task force, usually replacing a platoon of infantry in one or more line companies. Marine tank crewmen are equipped with combat environment suits. Each tank carries a gauss pistol and two gauss rifles (along with a supply of RAM grenades) for use by the crew in the event they have to fight on foot.

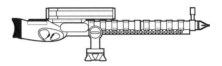

PERSONALITIES

"RIFLEMAN" KERN VALSAII

ST: 11, **DX:** 12, **IQ:** 11, **HT:** 12

Advantages: Combat Reflexes, Reputation +1 (other mercenaries 9 or less), Contacts (Mercenary).

Disadvantages: Sense of Duty (to comrades), Obsession (become fighter pilot), Incompetence (Leadership, Administration).

Quirks: Looking for a home, lives out of duffel bag, dislikes security missions.

Skills: Guns (Rifle)-17*, Guns (Light Auto)-16*, Guns (Grenade Launcher)-15*, Knife-12, Electronics Operation (Commo)-12, Forward Observer-12, Pilot (Grav)-13, Pilot (Small Craft)-12, Pilot (single engine prop)-11, Pilot (Helicopter)-11, Pilot (Aerospace Fighter)-13, Tactics-12, Holdout-11, Stealth-12.

*Includes bonus for IQ.

Quotes: "Looking for a co-pilot?"

Kern was born in 1095 on Ivendo/Lanth. His early memories include an orbital bombardment by Sword Worlder ships during the Fifth Frontier War, and this event has shaped his future. As a young man he entered the planetary COACC forces, hoping to become a pilot and defend his home from attack. Despite a certain aptitude for piloting, he failed at the final hurdle. All pilots are officers, and Kern has no officer ability. He was washed out of the pilot program and assigned to security as a common trooper.

The work was dull, guarding aerospace installations and patrolling the exclusion areas around them. After a term of this, Kern mustered out. A series of security jobs followed, aboard merchant ships and at starports, until Kern was fairly sure that his fate was to forever stand around outside fences.

More out of despair than anything else, Kern joined the ill-fated Aldersen Expedition, operating in the Outrim for McClellan Factors. His company was soundly trounced by forces serving the Baraccai Technum, who promptly recruited the best of the surrendered Aldersen troops and sent the rest packing.

Kern worked for the Technum for a year, serving in various units. Offered promotion, he has declined on several occasions. In early 1118, Kern left Technum service and began to drift from unit to unit. He is eagerly hired wherever he shows himself, as his reputation as a cool head and an excellent rifleman precedes him. He never stays long, though. A contract or two, and Kern will give notice and leave with his rifle, moving on. Most recently, he has served for six months with Reynolds' Raiders, earning several bonus payments for excellence. He has not been persuaded to stay, though.

Most of his colleagues understand that Kern is a restless spirit, searching for something. This is not uncommon in mercenaries, and does not bother anyone unduly. He is somewhat aloof and does not really bond with his comrades, but does his duty by them. He is calm and reliable under fire, and while nobody considers him to be a friend they know that they can count on him. He is perhaps the ultimate professional soldier – obeying orders and fighting with a cold precision that makes him a deadly foe. Despite this, Kern does not seem to be very interested in what he is doing. Mercenary work is just his day job. Nobody has gotten close enough to find out what Kern really wants from his life.

Kern is a solidly-built man of middling height. He is 25 years old, with dark brown hair and a mustache. He speaks little, but there is something intense about him, as if he was thinking about something else, something important.

Kern carries a 4mm gauss rifle with a 40mm RAM grenade launcher attachment. His only backup weapon is a large combat knife. He possesses a suit of combat armor and a personal comm set with a scrambler for forward observer duty. He carries few personal items, and seems to live out of an overnight bag most of the time.

Kern's great obsession is to be a pilot. At the end of every ticket he takes piloting lessons or clocks time as a copilot aboard anything that flies in the air or travels in space. When he has sufficient experience he hopes to gain a pilot's papers and join an aerospace interceptor unit. This will take time, he knows, as you have to be very, very good to be given an Interceptor. But it is what he wants. Everything else is just a means to an end.

Lieutenant Colonel "Bulldozer" Muncy (102nd Lift Infantry battalion)

ST: 13, **DX:** 11, **IQ:** 12, **HT:** 12.

Advantages: Combat Reflexes, Ally Group (102nd Lift Infantry, 15 or less), Charisma +2, Reputation +2 (combat arms), Military Rank 6, Status 1.

Disadvantages: Intolerance (bureaucrats), Reputation -2 (bureaucrats and military administrators).

Quirks: Collects weaponry, collects construction equipment, uses bulldozer as therapy, distrusts psionics, thinks that most people in civilian governments are crazy.

Skills: Intimidation-13, Guns (Light Auto)-14*, Guns (Rifle)-12*, Guns (Pistol)-12*, Brawling-12, Strategy-14, Tactics-15, Leadership-15, Pilot (Grav)-11, Driving (Tracked Construction)-12, Armory (Small Arms)-12, Stealth-11.

*Includes bonus for IQ.

Quotes:

"Bulldozers are admirable machines. Simple, noisy and unstoppable, rather like my chosen recruits. You don't like something? Tear it to bits with the tracks or crush it to flinders with the blade. Most therapeutic. Life is better with a bulldozer."

"You must be ready to fight at any time, and keep fighting until there is nobody else standing up. If your opponent is bigger or tougher than you, sneak up and hit him with a fencepost while he's asleep. You do that if he's weaker, too. If you have a favorite weapon, use it. If you haven't got it, get it. Don't bring a knife to a gun fight, bring a tank. Never, never fight fair. Nobody else will."

One of the many heroes of the Fifth Frontier War, Muncy was elevated to command of an entire sector of the Efate planetary defenses by the unusual promotion route of a hit by Zhodani ortillery. A successful strike took out the command staff of the corps defending the vital Stanley Down starport, leaving the force in utter disarray as the Zhodani assault forces poured in to capture their chosen bridgehead. The surprise attack was so successful that the first the colonel knew about it was when he found himself face to face with a team of psionic commandos in his own command bunker. Bitter hand-to-hand combat ensued as Muncy rallied the headquarters clerks and quartermasters to repel the assault and then pushed out to link up with the dazed and leaderless Imperial forces. More senior officers had survived the assault, but the colonel reasoned that they weren't doing anything useful, so he ignored their orders to retreat, regroup, surrender or change positions and instead formulated his own plan: kick the invaders right off the planet.

From small beginnings – an aerospace gunnery company and a squad of combat engineers, plus the headquarters staff – Colonel Muncy was able to rally a sizable force to hold a small corner of Stanley Down, gaining time for other units to collect their wits and begin fighting back.

Booting the Zhodani back into space proved impossible, so the colonel decided on a new strategy. His forces would make the place so unpleasant for the invaders that they would be glad to leave. Cut off from outside assistance for six months until the breakthrough of Operation Cudgel, the defenders grimly held on, ensuring that the Zhodani could not land transports at the port without taking heavy damage. This denial of port facilities proved to be the key to the defense of Efate, as the attackers were never able to land their heavy equipment and had to use makeshift bases or return to orbit after each operation.

Once reinforced, the colonel was able to take the offensive and retake the port. For his actions the Imperium's highest military honor was bestowed, the starburst for extreme heroism. However, he offended so many senior officers – threatening some with unutterable violence if they interfered with his operation – that no promotion was offered and a knighthood nomination was firmly squelched.

The grim determination to defend Stanley Down until there was absolutely nothing left of it is typical of the colonel's approach to warfare. In his capacity as commander of the 102nd Lift Infantry (see p. 110) he has been able to put his ideas into practice. Muncy believes that every member of the unit is a fighting soldier, and should be armed to the teeth at all times.

The colonel is a tall man of solid build, aged about 35. He could easily be mistaken for a platoon machine gunner when in unmarked combat armor. His manner with civilians, especially bureaucrats, is abrasive and occasionally threatening. Proven combat soldiers or those he respects see a different side of the colonel. He possesses a wry sense of humor and projects a sense of disbelief at the insanity of the people who actually run planets. This attitude of, "They're all mad out there. Stick with me and I'll look after you," helps foster a strong feeling of belonging in the personnel of his unit, and tales of the colonel's latest assault on some local bureaucrat (mostly verbal but occasionally physical) cause gales of laughter among the troops, who see him as their champion and shield against pen-pushers. Deeper down, his men know that their colonel cares about their welfare and won't allow little things like requisition forms and red tape to stand in the way of getting food and ammunition when they need it.

The colonel has two hobbies: firearms (his weapon of choice is an FGMP-11, but his collection of tools of destruction is immense) and low-tech earth moving equipment. Muncy collects bulldozers. His favorite, "The Beast," travels with the battalion for the colonel's relaxation. Questioned about this odd fascination, Muncy replies with the quotation noted above.

The colonel's direct methods are known across the sector. He actually favors the surprise attack and prefers to maneuver to gain advantage, but many enemies have been taken in by his image as a brainless thug.

Colonel Muncy is commanding officer of the 102nd Lift Infantry battalion of the Efate planetary forces. The 102nd is at present slightly overstrength and serving as a mercenary unit, with the planetary government's grudging approval.

GROUV'VOUG

ST: 10, **DX:** 13, **IQ:** 10, **HT:** 11.

Advantages: Combat Reflexes, Ally (Psycho Prof), common sense

Disadvantages: Amnesia.

Quirks: Gets personal with claws and teeth, Pack rat.

Skills: Guns (Shotgun)-15*, Brawling-15, Pilot (Grav)-12†, Mechanic (Starship)-12†, Gunner (Beam)-12†, Merchant-10†, Tactics-10, Stealth-14.

*Includes bonus for IQ.

†Grouv'voug does not remember that he knows these skills.

Quotes: "Watch what you say about my friend!"

JILE KORRIGII, "THE PSYCHO PROF"

ST: 10, **DX:** 12, **IQ:** 14, **HT:** 10.

Advantages: Combat Reflexes, Ally (Grouv'voug), Charisma +1

Disadvantages: Overconfidence, Impulsive, Odious Personal Habit (Marxist Rhetoric), Delusion (I am fighting "The Struggle").

Quirks: Dislikes nobility, prints own pamphlets, constantly studying when not in the field, wears hammer and sickle crest on beret.

Skills: Guns (SMG)-16*, Guns (Pistol)-14*, Thrown Weapon (Grenade)-12, Knife-12, Garrote-12, Brawling-12,

Driving (Wheeled)-12, Tactics-13, Stealth-12, History-14, Politics-14, Bard-15, Economics-14,

*Includes bonus for IQ.

Quotes: "A true government derives its mandate from the masses, not from some outdated, oppressive nobility . . ."

This unlikely pair are members of the Free Troopers (see pp.108-109). Both are oddballs in their own society, but in the wacky world of the Free Troopers they are accepted for what they are.

Whatever that may be.

Grouv'voug was the only survivor of a Vargr merchant crew hired as naval auxiliaries for the Imperium in the Fifth Frontier War. The ship was shot to pieces over Garda-Vilis by an unknown assailant. Lost, alone, suffering from delusions and amnesia induced by a violent blow to the head, he was picked up by a squad of the Free Troopers, who were fighting on Garda-Vilis at the time. The troopers found Grouv'voug's ravings amusing and adopted him as a sort of mascot, nursing him slowly back to health. Grouv'voug formed a special attachment for "Professor" Jile Korrigii, a would-be intellectual serving in the Troopers. With only a patchy set of memories, Grouv'voug knew no other home than the Troopers. His place was at the side of his friend and mentor Korrigii, of whom he had become fiercely protective.

The pair quickly became an effective team, with Grouv'voug serving as the voice of caution to Korrigii's recklessness. For several years they have campaigned together, and seem invulnerable when together. Both have been wounded when operating alone.

Grouv'voug is large for a Vargr. He is fond of dyeing his long, shaggy, nondescript sandy-brown fur in clashing colors when off ticket, and in appropriate camouflage in the field. He disdains the use of body armor, and is armed with an auto shotgun. For close combat he prefers to get in with claws and teeth. Grouv'voug's combat kit is festooned with things that "might be handy" – grenades, bits of wire or string, screwdrivers, a can of spray oil. He invariably carries everything that anyone has mentioned they "could

have done with" in the past few days, and dumps the lot as soon as it starts to get in the way. Fellow troopers say that if you can't track these two by the corpses, you can follow the trail of junk.

Jile Korrigii, the "Psycho Prof," holds a political science degree, and holds forth on political issues at any opportunity. Along with a few other members of the Troopers, he has formed a debating circle, which wrangles over political, social and philosophical issues, with occasional digressions into the realms of art or basketball. The prof has studied and been enthralled by certain ancient Terran political systems, and spouts communist or socialist dogma continually. He speaks of "The Struggle" and seems to have a particular dislike for the Imperial nobility. This has caused him to be arrested several times as a suspected Ine Givar agitator, but each time he is released as a (relatively) harmless nut.

Somewhere in Korrigii's deranged mind, he believes that he is carrying on "The Struggle," fighting to free the workers from tyranny. A few of the Troopers have been impressed by his fervor and have begun to hold political rallies (mostly for the fun of hearing the prof rant). On a couple of particularly depressed worlds, locals have attended these rallies, and gone home talking earnestly among themselves.

Korrigii is a close-combat specialist, a complete psychopath. He is, however, very effective in his chosen role, and with his friend Grouv'voug forms a dangerous two-sentient killing team.

Korrigii is a tall, very thin man of about 40. When not in combat he wears black coveralls and a beret bearing the insignia of an agricultural implement. In the field, he adds a flak jacket and a helmet, plus weapons harness carrying an SMG and two autopistols (all 9mm), several grenades and knives, a garrote and a small satchel holding political pamphlets he has produced over the years. If encountered off the field, Korrigii is likely to be at a university, reading the political science library (and making loud comments about the writers to all who will listen) or trying to set up a political rally.

Korrigii is effective, but he is certainly not normal.

Devlin Mercé

ST: 12, **DX:** 13, **IQ:** 11, **HT:** 11.

Advantages: Combat Reflexes, Ally (Sebastian Arvaughn 6 or less), Charisma +1, Reputation +1 (Mercenaries), Contacts (Mercenaries).

Disadvantages: Code of Honor (only essential jobs, always keep word).

Quirks: Accepts handshake contracts, Likes challenging work.

Skills: Guns (Rifle)-18*, Beam Weapon (Rifle)-16*, Pilot (Grav)-12, Tactics-12, Stealth-15, Savoir-Faire-12, Survival (Forest)-12, Traps-13, Demolitions-13, Merchant-12, Streetwise-13.

*Includes bonus for IQ.

Quotes: "Why do you want them dead?"

"It is better of one man to perish, than a nation to dwindle in unbelief."

"Six hundred ACRs . . . no problem."

Sebastian Arvaughn

ST: 10, **DX:** 12, **IQ:** 12, **HT:** 11

Advantages: Combat Reflexes.

Disadvantages: Odious Personal Habit (Constantly runs sensor equipment).

Quirks: "There is no such thing as privacy."

Skills: Guns (Light Auto)-15*, Pilot (Grav)-12, Tactics-12, Stealth-13, Survival (Forest)-12, Streetwise-13, Electronics Operation (Sensors)-14, Lip Reading-12.

*Includes bonus for IQ.

Quotes: "The third one from the left has a body pistol in a shoulder holster."

Devlin Mercé is sometimes referred to as "The Problem Solver." He is a sniper/hit man, who also acts as an agent for the procurement of arms. He is a consummate professional and extremely well trained. Having been raised on a backward "off the beaten path" world, where his woodcraft and hunting skills were a survival necessity, he naturally excelled in these areas. His talents were spotted soon after he enlisted in the Imperial Army. Devlin attended sniper training and went on to serve 12 years in the Imperial Army before resigning due to pressure to move "up or out." Since this time he has operated as a freelance, doing what he does best.

Devlin is extremely expensive, with high up-front costs and accompanying "additional expenses for travel and etc." People pay, because they know that he will succeed.

When he is called in for a hit, a particular situation has gone to the point that the client feels cannot be resolved by any means other than violence. He will pursue a target relentlessly and with tenacity until the hit is made, or the client is satisfied.

Devlin will not take a job for a client's personal gain, vengeance, or any other "non-essential" reason. The "Problem Solver" pursues tasks that have an urgency for the "greater good," at least by his perceptions.

Devlin is a tall, lanky man of attractive looks. He keeps his brown hair cut short and tight, and his piercing hazel eyes display a keen intelligence. His most prominent physical attributes are his charming smile and mannerisms. Devlin is a friendly and amiable individual. He is completely comfortable within his chosen occupation and even sees himself as providing a needed service for society in order to "keep the peace by helping to release the pressure valve ever so slowly to prevent a big blow-up." His engaging personality has contributed greatly toward gathering contacts and outside services for needed skills that he does not have.

In addition to his personality, he has another characteristic that has earned him his high-quality reputation: Devlin is a man of his word. When he finally makes a commitment, his clients know that it *will* get done. He allows himself no exceptions. He has never failed a client and he has never fallen from his word. He lives by a strict warrior's honor code of keeping one's promises. It is not uncommon for Devlin to accept a contract by a handshake only. No one questions his integrity and no one would ever cheat him out of his contract terms. Two clients have done this and have paid for that thievery with their lives.

On several occasions, the "Problem Solver" has worked with a military service friend of his, Sebastian Arvaughn. Sebastian is a technical wizard and an accomplished field craftsman as well. While in the Imperial Army, Sebastian worked for several years with Devlin as his spotter. Sebastian, like Devlin, resigned when confronted by the "up or out" policy and has pursued a vocation as a free lance security consultant/high tech "snooper." He has a similar philosophical outlook to Devlin's, but a more reserved personality. Over the years the two have struck up a strong friendship and positive working rapport. When the two professionals combine their skills, they become a deadly team. Both work throughout the central to spinward edge of the Spinward Marches.

SERGEANT ALEX PETTER

ST: 10, **DX:** 11, **IQ:** 12, **HT:** 10.

Advantages: Combat Reflexes, Military Rank 1.

Disadvantages: Missing Digit.

Quirks: Drinks when depressed, Intolerant of Imperial army, Intolerant of civilians, Always has lots of spare parts.

Skills: Gunner (Beam)-14*, Pilot (Grav)-12, Tactics-13, Electronics Operation (Sensors)-13, Armory (Beam)-12, Administration-14, Merchant-12, Accounting-12.

*Includes bonus for IQ.

Quotes:"It would be better to buy a shipping container of spares for the tanks than a spare air-raft."

Petter entered the Imperial Army in 1108, during the Fifth Frontier War. Prior to this he had been on a training contract as an accountant to a private firm. His first experience of military life came as something of a shock, especially as the new recruits were at that time undergoing accelerated training to replace battle casualties in front-line units.

Immediately upon completing basic training, Petter was assigned to the combat zone as a casualty replacement, and found himself hurtling into combat aboard a light grav tank only four months after receiving his draft papers. For the next couple of years, Petter was shuttled between combat zones, seeing occasional action. While his service was competent, he won no special distinctions during this period, and left the service at the end of hostilities despite the offer of inducements to "go career" which were being offered at the time.

Back in civilian life, Petter found it hard to fit in. Unable to find a firm willing to pick up his unfinished training contract, he found himself in a limbo encountered by many veterans of the Fifth Frontier War. His career had been interrupted, and while the Imperial Army had been keen enough to recruit him, no real provisions were made for reintegration afterward.

Petter became depressed and began to drink heavily, which led to a number of encounters with law-enforcement officers. His prospects were at rock bottom when ReConstruct LIC offered him a job. ReConstruct was a civilian organization dedicated to repairing the damage done by the war, both to individuals and to the worlds of the Spinward Marches. The firm operated a number of rebuilding projects on several worlds, employing people like Petter whose skills outweighed their qualifications. The firm was genuine enough, and its function as a clearing house for mercenaries was only secondary.

After a short period working as an assistant administrator on a reconstruction site, Petter was approached by mercenary recruiters. His job with ReConstruct was in no danger, they said, but if he would ever consider joining a mercenary armor unit then they knew of a couple of bunks open with Trelgil's Tankers . . .

Not long afterward, Petter found himself in uniform again.

Alex Petter is a small, but stocky man of 32 years. He has some burn scarring on his left shoulder and a finger missing from his left hand, the souvenirs of a round that almost destroyed his tank. His demeanor is quietly professional, with a strong interest in logistics. His light grav tank platoon always has a good supply of spares available, even if others in the unit are short. Although not an officer, he is second-in-command of his platoon and holds responsibility for much of the supply and administration work in the company and within his own platoon.

Petter is often asked to accompany the company officers as they negotiate for spares and supplies. His insight into the corporate world, coupled with his natural talent for administration, makes him indispensable to his unit.

In combat, Petter is prudent and cautious where other tankers are aggressive. Nobody who has seen him fight calls him a coward, but his is the sort of conduct that preserves tanks intact rather than scoring stunning victories. To a mercenary unit, this is a good thing. Although Petter is unlikely to win medals, he does win battles.

Petter has a strong resentment for the Imperial Army, and for the civilian population that turned its back on him and other veterans when they tried to come home. Unless his buttons are pushed, Petter is calm and reserved, polite but not especially friendly. If pushed on the subject, he could be induced to admit that he likes the mercenary life, and can't imagine doing anything else.

FLIGHT OFFICER TANYA EDRI (LUDDINGI'S FLYERS: FIGHTER SQUADRON)

ST: 9, **DX:** 13, **IQ:** 11, **HT:** 12 .

Advantages: Combat Reflexes, 3-D Spatial Sense, Military Ranks 3, Reputation +1 (Mercenaries).

Disadvantages: Obsession (be the best pilot).

Quirks: Only parties away from her unit.

Skills: Gunner (Beam)-16*, Gunner (Missile)-16*, Pilot (Aerospace Fighter)-16+, Pilot (Grav)-13†, Tactics-12, Electronics Operation (Sensors)-13, Armory (Beam)-11, Mechanic (Fighter)-12, Carousing-14.

*Includes bonus for IQ.

†Includes bonus for 3-D Spatial Sense.

Quotes: "Is that a smudge on the canopy?"

"Almost got you that time, Major!"

Edri wanted to be a fighter pilot since she was a little girl. As soon as she was old enough, she signed up for her homeworld COACC flight school, and graduated with honors. The service accepted her gladly, provided her with advanced flight training and finally pronounced her fit to fly.

Then came the day when pilots are handed their assignments. Everyone wanted to go to orbital interception or air superiority, despite the long lectures on how interesting and exciting being a bomber or logistics plane driver can be. Edri knew she'd get a single-seater. While other cadets fretted, she was quietly confident. She knew they'd be smart enough to assign her where she would do best.

They sent her to transport and logistics.

Edri protested, but to no avail. So she handed back her wings and left the service, disgusted and heartbroken. She got no further than the nearest bar. A young couple approached her, shared a few drinks and chatted, then handed her a business card. "You still want a single-seater?" the man asked. Edri, shocked, said yes.

"We've seen your record," said the woman. "It's good enough to get you a shot. Come to this address at noon tomorrow. Come prepared to fly."

Edri kept her appointment. The couple drove her to a nearby airfield. Among the civilian planes was a two-seat trainer. Edri and the young man climbed in. The woman left.

The young man asked Edri to perform a few basic maneuvers. In the middle of one routine a second fighter attacked the unarmed trainer. For several minutes Edri maneuvered frantically, trying to stay alive long enough for her repeated distress calls to bring local COACC fighters. Nobody came. Finally the second fighter got a clear cannon shot, but instead of shredding metal Edri heard the young woman's voice say in her ears, "OK, you're good enough. Anyone who can survive against me for a few minutes can beat almost anyone else. You want in?"

"Yes . . . who . . .?" stammered Edri.

In reply her backseater, silent throughout the engagement, said softly, "That's my wife, Major Yllen Liddingi . . . Luddingi's Flyers. Land us and we'll talk contracts."

Edri has served six years with the Flyers, and gained a reputation as a fearsome dogfighter. She is extremely skilled, but has yet to achieve her goal of beating the CO in a practice fight.

When not actually flying, Edri tends to hang around the base, fussing over the maintenance work being done on her plane. She is obsessive about getting the absolute best from the aircraft, and has hand-picked a team of expert mechanics, who she terrorizes constantly in case they should ever become lax in their efforts.

Tanya Edri is a petite woman of slender build, with blonde hair cut quite short. She is obsessively tidy about the base, and possesses only a few personal effects. With this fussy and reserved demeanor she could be mistaken for an administrator or even the unit's lawyer. She does not ever get visibly angry, but will pursue a quarrel with ruthless, cold determination, much as she would a dogfight. She loves aircraft and flying, though actually downing another plane is just part of the job.

She never carries a sidearm in the cockpit, and there are rumors that her ejector seat is deliberately disabled. If she is ever defeated, she believes she would rather die instantly than survive and know that she was beaten. Besides, if defeat means certain death, she has a little more incentive to do her utmost.

Off duty, Edri does not keep to the company of pilots. She can be found in the rougher bars, carousing with ground pounders and spacehands. Conversation often turns to combat, as she tries to gain new insights by listening to spacecraft pilots and grav tank crews. Most of the time she is just "letting off steam," as she gets pretty intense around the airbase. Her fellow pilots don't know where she goes after hours, and would be shocked to see the reserved and fussy officer turning into a wild party animal.

Private-Recruit James Laughan

ST: 12, **DX:** 10, **IQ:** 9, **HT:** 11

Advantages: None.

Disadvantages: Obsession (Become a mercenary), Delusion (Thinks he is a trained soldier), Gullible.

Quirks: Easily offended, Will take any position offered.

Skills: Guns (Rifle)-12, Driving (Wheeled)-10, Tactics-3 (Default).

Quotes: "Got a ticket, huh? You should take me, I'm a real good shot."

"It's not fair, I'm just as good as any of those *old* guys."

Laughan is a would-be merc, a recruit typical of the many who arrive in recruiting offices full of hope and enthusiasm and the certain knowledge that they have what it takes to survive in an environment where second-best means you quit breathing.

Barely 18 years of age, Laughan has completed his basic education and wasted no time in spending his graduation-gift credits on a "Combat and Survival" course offered by a private firm. There are many such courses, which deliver basic firearms or bodyguard training and some fieldcraft and tactics. Some are high-quality orientation courses that emulate a military boot camp and advanced combat training – and actually give the graduates a realistic chance at employment in their chosen field.

Laughan has attended a course of the opposite sort. For a large fee, he has been granted the opportunity to run around in the wilderness with a rifle for a few weeks, firing off a great deal of ammunition but learning very little of any use, and nothing that will make him more employable in the trade he so desperately wants to enter. Anyone showing promise on such a course tends to be headhunted by recruiting agents and offered training with a real mercenary unit. What's left are the amateurs, the mentally ill, the soldier-boys and the ones who just like to do this for fun.

Recruiters can spot the likes of Laughan a mile off. Quality units will usually turn them away, though a few are promising enough to be worth retraining – though erasing all the dangerously wrong ideas now firmly drilled into them is a problem.

Since people like Laughan can at least demonstrate that they know which end of a rifle is which, they are sometimes hired by low-quality units desper-ate for recruits, where they behave like cannon fodder until they learn from experience – or die.

Laughan is a tall and solidly built young man, of somewhat below average intellect. He is gullible and rather too full of himself to get along well with seasoned soldiers. When somebody puts one over on him – and veterans would find Laughan too easy pickings to pass up – he tends to take it hard and hold a grudge. His overinflated ego and dubious tactical training make him a dangerous incompetent, though his basic skills in pointing a rifle are sound.

He could someday become a good soldier, but first he will have to forget everything he "learned" on his orientation course. He is becoming increasingly desperate to find a bunk with a unit, any unit.

He would take any job offered without a moment's thought, and is very likely to be killed the first time he sees action. Many a prospective employer doesn't find this necessarily a bad trait in recruits of Laughan's caliber – what scares them is the chance that their incompetence will endanger the lives of their more proficient squad mates.

LIEUTENANT COLONEL STEVEN BOND, SB RANGERS

ST: 11, **DX:** 12, **IQ:** 13, **HT:** 11.

Advantages: Combat Reflexes, Military Rank 5, Charisma +2, Daredevil, Ally Group (SB Raiders).

Disadvantages: Overweight, Sense of Duty to Troops.

Quirks: Always tries to impress his troops; has "gone native"; pretends to be berserk in combat.

Skills: Gunner (Beam)-15*, Beam Weapon (Rifle)-16*, Pilot (Grav)-12, Tactics-14, Electronics Operation (Sensors)-13, Armory (Beam)-12, Administration-14, Tactics-13, Leadership-15.

*Includes bonus for IQ.

Quotes: "That was a very funny Vargr impression. I'd show you mine, but it would involve ripping your throat out with my teeth."

Steven Bond hails from the spinward portion of the Vargr Thoengling Empire. During the early phases of the 19th Thoengling/Yoetygg border war his homeworld was attacked by forces from the Union of Yoetygg, setting the career of this military legend in motion.

The local forces of the Empire did not have a very charismatic leader, and quickly fell back or joined the Union forces, until the fighting reached the outskirts of the human enclave where Bond, then aged all of 15 years old, turned out with a mixed group of humans and Vargr to defend their homes. Bloody hand-to hand fighting ensued as each building was stormed or defended to the last.

It was during this battle that Bond found himself cut off among a handful of Thoengling Vargr who were on the verge of running as a squad of Union troops stormed their position. In a moment of visionary clarity, Bond saw that if the Vargr fled they would leave him to die. Having lived all his life among them, he knew how to rally his wavering comrades. Enraged at the slaughter of his friends and neighbors, Bond charged the Union troopers, firing at them with the ACR he had taken from a nearby corpse. The Union Vargr panicked and fell back, and in that instant Bond's charisma was determined. Nearby Thoengling Vargr followed this lucky madman back into the fray and threw the Union forces back.

Bond's berserk fit lasted long after the battle had ceased, and in the weeks that followed he led a ragtag band of followers on daring raids against the Union forces. The cost was high but each raid gained him more glory and greater charisma, so there were always three new Vargr to replace every fallen one. By the time of the Union surrender Bond was leading an oversized platoon, and had gained a rough-and-ready knowledge of the soldier's trade.

After the war, Bond was a hero. His charisma was such that although he never led more than a platoon of troops he was awarded the rank of lieutenant colonel as an honorary title.

Bond led his troops in the many brushfire wars fought in the twelve years before the Fifth Frontier War. The outbreak of Imperial-Zhodani hostilities also saw a new Thoengling emperor ascendant, and in a shrewd move intended to prevent risk to his charisma, Bond led his force into Imperial service as mercenaries.

Bond's force was involved in the campaign conducted by Sector Admiral Vadid Ligl against the Zhodani worlds of the Riverland Wall. The Riverland campaign was a failure, but Bond managed to establish a reputation as a reliable and competent commander. Following the war his force remained in Imperial space as mercenaries, making a good living out of a series of commando tickets.

Colonel Bond is a heavy-set man who looks younger than his 39 years. His long black hair is dyed to hide any gray and generally pulled back in a long pony tail. His dress sense betrays his long association with Vargr, with bright orange being a favorite for off-duty wear.

Bond possesses an analytical mindset and is very careful never to lose charisma to anyone but a major Vargr leader. He is fond and respectful of his Vargr troopers, and likes Vargr company in general. He is often described as having "gone native" by Imperial officers. Bond has another slant on the same statement: "Vargr follow a leader because he can lead. Not because his granddad once polished an Admiral's boots."

The colonel is greatly fond of Vargr dishes and can often be found trying out a new delicacy. Whenever his services are required, potential patrons send out agents to search the local Vargr curry houses for this strange but highly respected mercenary leader.

Bond commands a platoon of Vargr with two grav tanks as support vehicles. His nominal base of operations is Jesedipere/Aramis (Spinward Marches 3001).

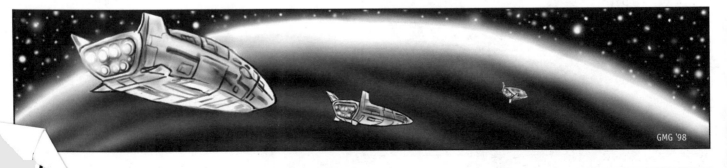

GMG '98